F. O. Matthiessen

F. O. MATTHIESSEN, 1926
This portrait by Russell Cheney was probably conceived when
Matthiessen and Cheney spent part of the summer of 1925
together in Paris and elsewhere in Europe. (Courtesy of the
portrait's owner, Paul M. Sweezy)

Frederick C. Stern

F. O. Matthiessen

Christian Socialist as Critic

The University of North Carolina Press   Chapel Hill

© 1981 The University of North Carolina Press

Manufactured in the United States of America

Library of Congress Cataloging in Publication Data

Stern, Frederick C
  F. O. Matthiessen, Christian Socialist as
critic.

  Bibliography: p.
  Includes index.
  1. Matthiessen, Francis Otto, 1902–1950.
2. Critics—United States—Biography.　I. Title.
II. Title: Christian Socialist as critic.
PS29.M35S8　810'.9 [B]　80-29013
ISBN 0-8078-1478-4

To my mother,

to the memory of my father,

and, of course,

to Naomi, Carrie, David, Paul, and Jeremy

Contents

Prefatory Note

THIS book about one of the greatest literary critics in the history of the United States is a token of my admiration for its subject. The inclusion in my opening chapter, rather than in a preface, of a brief record of my personal experience with Matthiessen's work during the last years of his life is part of the evidence for my admiration, for it seems to me that the effect his work had on my own life is exemplary of the effect it had on the lives of others like me. For those of us who thought of ourselves as radicals in the late forties and very early fifties, and as radicals who cared a great deal about literature but could find very few critics among our elders whose work we found inspiring, Matthiessen was the model we thought we could follow. In that role he surely made a contribution to the study of literature in the United States, though it is a role one can best document through the personal anecdote.

That my admiration is not uncritical demonstrates one of the lessons that I learned from his work. Matthiessen surely loved Whitman, but he was willing to write, in *American Renaissance*, that Whitman "reverted to the hackneyed cadences and imagery of his first newspaper verse in producing 'O Captain! my Captain!'" (p. 618), or that the poet "could address God, with ecstatic and monumental tastelessness, as 'thou reservoir'" (p. 530). Although I charge Matthiessen with no such "monumental" lapses, and especially no such lapses in taste, it would be a disservice to his memory not to be, in the fullest sense of that term as he used it, critical of his work—that is, to appreciate it, to understand it, and to place it, but also to note its limitations and flaws. That is my endeavor in this volume. Others have recently begun again the work of examining Matthiessen's commentary concerning our literature. It is my hope that the sum of all our work will help to stimulate the needed recovery of a fuller understanding of Matthiessen's contribution to the criticism of the culture of the United States.

Such a recovery is especially needed at present because the study and appreciation of literature is undergoing, as I write this, rather severe trials, and especially trials which come from the left. The approaches taken by structuralists, deconstructionists, and other recently developed critical schools provide serious and important challenges to the kind of literary study and the assumptions underlying it at which Matthiessen excelled. I do not believe that the outcome of the challenge will be, as some seem to fear, the destruction of literature or of literary study, nor do I think that is the intention of the challengers. Rather, I think that their contributions to our understanding of arts and letters will lead, in classical Hegelian and Marxist fashion, to a new unity of ideas, which will preserve, perhaps in unexpected forms, the importance of literature and its contemplation. A renewed study of Matthiessen's work, then, in addition to having value simply for its own sake, can provide one among several elements that will come together to form one of the terms of the opposites, which will, in time, help to form a new unity, on a higher level, as the Hegelian paradigm suggests. The forming of such a new unity will not be unlike that Matthiessen himself was able to achieve in synthesizing, at least to some extent, the apparent opposites of his moment, textual and sociological approaches to literature. Furthermore, the quality of Matthiessen's mind can stand as an example of the kinds of minds that will be needed, and which, in the course of things, will emerge to effect such a new unity.

I did not have the privilege of knowing the man whom his friends called "Matty," though I might have done so when I was an undergraduate. I have spoken with some of his friends, and read what he has written, but I certainly do not pretend that I know the man, in the way his friends did, or in the way that his eventual biographer will know him. Thus my judgments as to the quality of his mind are based on my study of his ideas, especially his ideas as a critic. The mind and the feelings I have come to know by this means have rendered for me, as I would like to think this volume renders, a man whose mind and spirit were profoundly affected by his thinking as a political and religious person and by his caring—painfully, passionately, totally—about literature and art and about their preservation, especially in a world that he believed was threatened with near-total dehumanization. Influenced by the hunger of Americans in the thirties, by worldwide agony under fascism in the thirties and forties, and by the great threat of world destruction in the last decade of his life, Matthiessen struggled with all the means at his command, including his study of literature, to preserve and cherish art and the human beings who alone can create it. It is my hope that another way in which my effort to recover Matthiessen will be useful is in precisely the way he was useful to me more than thirty years ago—that it will help not only to recover the man's ideas but also the passionate quality of his concern for human life and for the product of human life that he knew best—works of literature. If there is to be hope for a more humane life for us and for our children, that hope must rest first of all on the actions of those men and women who are prepared to devote their energies to making a better world—as Matthiessen did, to caring about the world and its people—as Matthiessen did, and to caring about art—as Matthiessen did.

For those who value literature as one of the finest products of human beings, for those who believe that the clash of critical ideas leads to new and richer ideas, and for those who believe that a concern about good literature and a concern about "the good society" are symbiotic, Matthiessen can stand as model and as example. It is my fondest hope that this book will help to make that model, that example, more available than it has been.

Acknowledgments

A N Y work that is more than a decade in the writing must owe a great deal to a very large number of persons. Since this work was first undertaken while I was a superannuated graduate student at Purdue University, it will have been thirteen years or so from conception to publication. The acknowledgments made here, then, are bound to be inadequate and to miss some persons to whom much is owed. What is more, some persons to whom I feel much gratitude is due are no longer alive to receive my thanks and that is a source of great regret for me and of some feelings of guilt for the length of time it has taken to see this work into print. The thanks I list here, then, come with a request for forgiveness from those whom I may overlook and from those whom I can no longer effectively thank, and with heartfelt gratitude to those who can receive it. If I do not separate here the quick from the dead, that is only a sign of my equal gratitude to them all.

I wish to thank Chester E. Eisinger, of the Department of English at Purdue University, from whom I have learned much and whose friendly criticism, unfailing insight, and unflagging energy helped not only with my doctoral dissertation, which was an earlier version of this work, but with my eventual entry into the profession he values so highly and serves so well. Others at the same institution to whom I am grateful include A. Darrel Abel, William Braswell, and J. Raymond Himelick, who did much more than to provide detailed comments for the earliest version of this essay, and to Maurice Beebe, Ray Browne, Angelo DeVitis, Barnet Kottler, Robert Lowe, and Henry Salerno, all of whom were important to me.

To members of the faculty at the University of Chicago, where I resumed academic studies after many years of other pursuits, I owe a great debt as well. Among those I wish to mention especially are Catherine Ham, Arthur Heiserman, Gwin Kolb, Norman

Maclean, James Miller, Jr., Richard Stern, Robert Streeter, Stuart Tave, Edward Wasiolek, and Napier Wilt.

Many persons who knew the subject of this work, or who know a great deal about him, have been willing to share with generosity their insights and information. Without their assistance, this work could not have been completed. I am especially grateful to C. Lombardi Barber, Archibald Byrne, Eugene Current-García, Rufus W. Mathewson, Henry G. Reifsnyder, and Jaroslav Schejbal. There have also been several anonymous readers of my work in manuscript, whose comments have been very valuable in making final revisions, whose personal acquaintance with Matthiessen is clear from those comments. Protocol prevents me from thanking them by name, even when I suspect I know it, but I want them to be aware of my gratitude. I want especially to mention also two men who have themselves written about Matthiessen, who have been extremely generous in many ways with their support in what I think of as our joint effort to "place" Matthiessen rightly. I refer here to Giles B. Gunn and George Abbott White.

I wish also to thank many of my colleagues in the Department of English at the University of Illinois at Chicago Circle who have been generous with advice and, when it was most needed, with encouragement. I mention none by name, lest I slight some, but those whom I most mean will most know it. A grant from the Research Board at "Circle" enabled me to work in the Matthiessen papers housed at Harvard's Houghton Library, and aided in the publication of this book. A sabbatical leave permitted me to complete the manuscript. For all, I am grateful.

The staffs of several libraries have been courteous and helpful. I wish to thank those often unsung contributors at the University of Illinois at Chicago Circle Library, at the Regenstein Library of the University of Chicago, at the Newberry Library in Chicago, at the Purdue University Library, at the Houghton Library at Harvard University, at the New York Public Library, and at the Beinecke Manuscript Library at Yale University.

Several scholarly works have been most instrumental in making my task possible. Chief among these is the Matthiessen memorial issue of the distinguished, independent, and entirely exemplary

Marxist journal, *Monthly Review,* edited by Paul M. Sweezy and Harry Magdoff. At the time of the memorial issue's publication it was jointly edited by Sweezy and the late Leo Huberman. Sweezy to this day carries on the important work Matthiessen helped him to begin, with the kind of integrity Matthiessen had come to expect of Sweezy. Among much else that is invaluable in that volume is C. L. Barber's bibliography of work by Matthiessen, which, with a later supplement by Barber, is virtually complete. Another such work of great value is John Rackliffe's collection of Matthiessen's essays.

The editors of The University of North Carolina Press have been most helpful to me. My thanks to former editor Malcolm L. Call, to Gwen Duffey, and to Sandra Eisdorfer can stand for them all.

I do not want to leave unacknowledged the work of the subject of this book, F. O. Matthiessen. His *American Renaissance* and others of his works have been constant inspirations to me in my own developing concerns with literature and other arts while I was professionally employed in other pursuits for many years after I first read his work. Matthiessen's life, moreover, has been one of the examples that has continued to spur my ongoing commitment to something Matthiessen understood so well, Bertolt Brecht's injunction to us to "Change the world! It needs it!"

Finally I give thanks to those who neither need nor ask my gratitude but without whom few things in my life, including this book, would have been possible. I mean, of course, my wife, Naomi, and my children, Carrie, David, Paul, and Jeremy.

F. O. Matthiessen

1 ❦ The Man and His Work

THAT Francis Otto Matthiessen (1902–1950) made a substantial contribution to American literary criticism during the relatively short period of his productive life is no longer an issue in doubt. As Richard Ruland writes: "In 1904 the first volume of Paul Elmer More's *Shelburne Essays* announced his intention to help create a truly American criticism, while the publication in 1938 of *Understanding Poetry*, the Brooks and Warren textbook which soon came to dominate the teaching of literature, made the eventual triumph of formalist criticism certain. In 1941, however, while New Criticism was still gaining momentum, F. O. Matthiessen's *American Renaissance* signaled the very assimilation of the new techniques to earlier aims which has characterized the most fruitful work of our own day."[1]

The nature of Matthiessen's contribution, however, is varied and complex. He made a contribution first of all as the writer of a remarkable number of significant books and articles. He made a contribution as well as the teacher of a surprisingly large number of important critics and teachers in a wide diversity of fields. He made a lasting impression on his friends and colleagues during the relatively short forty-eight years of his life. He was, furthermore, an example to those who knew him only by reputation and by his writing.

It was Matthiessen as example that led me personally to years of involvement in his works. When I was an undergraduate student at New York University from 1946 to 1949 my interests were political and cultural as well as scientific. I read *American Renaissance* during those years and found in that volume, for the first time, a combination of critical endeavors that excited me. Here was a work that dealt most carefully with the texts under discussion but one that also displayed a deep concern for the social and cultural milieu from which the writers of these texts sprang. Moreover, *American Renaissance* was a book of controlled passion. Through every page of scholarly words there gleamed

3

the deeply personal involvement of its author with the materials of his study. For every figure and work discussed one sensed Matthiessen's "partisanship," a partisanship, however, that did not lead to distortion of texts to suit an a priori conclusion but a partisanship that provided a place on which to stand, a ground from which to reach toward conclusions validated by the most careful scholarship. Here was a literary text that seemed deeply concerned with a literature for a democratic culture but one that was not a piece of propaganda, in the most pejorative sense of that term.

My readings in other literary texts by writers who also shared my radical, left-wing concerns had provided no other such experience. When the passions seemed right to me, the literary discussions seemed forced in ways I did not then understand and the deck stacked toward conclusions that might please my politics but which were not literarily or intellectually convincing. When the literary scholarship seemed sound and persuasive, the conclusions were often politically conservative or even apolitical, both of which deeply troubled my youthful disaffection from the then-developing cold war America of the mid and late forties.

What I recall taking with me from *American Renaissance* at that first reading was less a knowledge of the five literary figures of the 1850s it discussed than a general feeling, an awareness of what seemed so sound, so right as literary commentary, and yet so passionately concerned with regard to the nation's democratic possibilities. That awareness lasted through nearly two decades of other, primarily nonliterary pursuits. When I returned to the study of literature, the awareness reasserted itself with full force. Further reading and study reaffirmed, in more mature contemplation, my early memory of Matthiessen's work and produced before my mind's eye a now-dead figure who was as fascinating as his writing, whose glow radiated outward to his time and to those who knew him.

The man behind these contributions is no more a simple figure than are the writers whose work was his subject matter. Though it is by no means my intention to write a biography of Matthiessen here, it would violate his own methodology not at least to "sketch in" the critic who so carefully presented something of the lives of Whitman, Melville, Hawthorne, Thoreau, and Emerson in *American Renaissance*.[2]

Matthiessen was born on 19 February 1902 in Pasadena, California, the son of Frederic William, Jr., and Lucy Orne Matthiessen. He was the youngest of four children. His brothers were Frederic William III and Dwight George. His sister was Lucy Orne, who married Harold B. Neubrand and lived much of her adult life near Tarrytown, New York. Dwight married, and, though apparently hardworking, suffered financial difficulties during the depression, especially after an illness. Correspondence indicates that Francis Otto stayed in touch with Dwight and Lucy, and more indirectly with his oldest brother's often-deserted wife, and that his financial assistance to them and his nieces was generous and graciously given.

Matthiessen's parents separated when their youngest child was only five years old, a separation that was clearly Frederic's doing and that seems to have devastated Lucy Orne, the wife, and her youngest son. His parents were divorced when Matthiessen was thirteen. Commenting about news he had received of some of his father's escapades, Matthiessen says in a letter written in 1925, "I long ago accustomed myself to an empty space where my father should have been. But it reminds me of what mother suffered for so long."[3] There was some modicum of reconciliation between son and father, and they saw each other several times in 1947. Matthiessen had the deepest affection for his mother who died while he was a student at Oxford.

Frederic William Matthiesson, Jr., Francis Otto's father, inherited considerable wealth from his father, Frederic William Matthiessen, Sr., the founder of the Western Clock Company, later the Westclox Company. The younger man seems to have squandered his wealth in classical, wastrel second-generation-wealth fashion, and did not even, apparently, assist Francis Otto's brothers when they or their families were in real need and requested help. At his death there were some small legacies left, but the bulk of his wealth had been dissipated.

Most of Matthiessen's childhood after his parents' separation was spent in or near La Salle, Illinois, where a grandfather lived, an experience that he was to recall and that influenced him as a grown man. In 1914 he began his secondary school education at the Hackley School, in Tarrytown, New York, a small preparatory school of little prestige. The institution, he wrote later, "had prepared well for the college entrance examinations but had taught you nothing else."[4]

After a short stint in the Canadian Air Force, just as World War I was ending, Matthiessen entered Yale in the fall of 1919. He has written interestingly about his Yale experience and especially about the influence upon him of a professor of English, Robert D. French. What stands out about his Yale experience, in addition to the excellent education he received, was that it developed in him an attachment and loyalty that was to last all his life and that represented perhaps the least democratic aspect of his attachments. It is remarkable to think that among the items Matthiessen removed from his pockets before jumping to his death from a window of Boston's Manger Hotel, some thirty-one years after he entered Yale, was his Skull and Bones key.

Matthiessen seems to have become aware of his homosexuality quite early in life and, after undergoing the struggles to be expected from such a discovery, came finally to accept his orientation as well as could be expected under the social conditions and views of sexuality of the period. In a letter to Russell Cheney, with whom Matthiessen shared intimately more than twenty years of his life, he writes of early discussions of his homosexuality with such friends as Yale classmates Dick Tighe and Russell Wheeler Davenport, with whom he shared his growing conviction that he "might very likely be altogether homosexual."[5] The role that his homosexuality played in developing Matthiessen's sympathy for the "outsider" is incalculable, of course, but such a role is certainly probable. The increased discussion of the experiences of homosexuals in our society, engendered by the "gay liberation" movement in recent years, has surely raised our awareness of the difficulties homosexuals experience. These difficulties, similar to the difficulties experienced by other groups not in the mainstream of our culture by virtue of race, poverty, or culture, can make the homosexual particularly sensitive to what it means to be the "other." Certainly this sense of "otherness" must have been more sharply a factor during Matthiessen's youthful years than it is now. Although Matthiessen's radicalism, then, certainly derived more from intellectual than from visceral sources, it was perhaps his homosexuality that provided the experiential base on which this son of a wealthy father, this Yale and Harvard man, could draw to provide him with some of the emotional sources for his wide-ranging sympathy, understanding, and support of those who lacked privilege, power, and position.

It was at Yale that Matthiessen's heterodox political opinions began to be formed. His contact with Robert French played some part in this development, but he has testified also to the importance of his friendship with Jerry Voorhis, who was later to become an outstanding member of Congress and who was one of the earliest victims of Richard Nixon's mendacity. Under these influences, Matthiessen soon became a supporter of Socialist party leader Eugene V. Debs and he became actively involved in the Yale Liberal Club. At the same time his religious convictions were in no way diminished by his leftward-moving politics, and they were, if anything, strengthened by his growing sense of Christian fellowship. Thus his concomitant positions as vice-president of the Yale Liberal Club, vice-president of the university religious society (which was Yale's Y.M.C.A. called Dwight Hall), and chairman of the Bible Study Committee gave early signs of the disparate sources that would shape his ideas, which would remain constant throughout his life. Paul M. Sweezy's biographical sketch is quite accurate: "Practically all of Matthiessen's later interests and activities are foreshadowed in his record at Yale."[6]

Matthiessen went on to Oxford on a Rhodes Scholarship, which he was awarded after graduating from Yale in 1923. It was on the crossing to England that he first met Cheney. His thesis at Oxford on Oliver Goldsmith is a work Matthiessen never published. He received his Bachelor of Letters from Oxford in 1925. As important for Matthiessen as his actual study at Oxford was the first contact with Europe that the experience provided, a contact that was to be repeatedly renewed and that provided important distance for his understanding and exploration of the United States.

Upon his return from Oxford, Matthiessen began graduate study at Harvard, where he received a Master of Arts in 1926 and a doctorate in 1927. His thesis, concerning translations by important Elizabethan figures, was published in somewhat revised form as his second book, *Translation: An Elizabethan Art*. Matthiessen had the opportunity to study with outstanding figures in literary criticism and scholarship at Yale and Harvard, and he was deeply impressed by such figures as Chauncey B. Tinker, John Livingston Lowes, George Lyman Kittredge, and Irving Babbitt, figures with whom he did not always agree. Their impact, and especially Babbitt's, was to help Matthiessen shape his own critical views.

After two years as an instructor at Yale Matthiessen returned to Harvard, where he was to spend the rest of his academic career. As a member of the English department he became deeply involved in the tutorial system. He was the head tutor at Eliot House for two years, a resident tutor until the 1938–39 academic year, and a tutor for the remainder of his life. He was the chairman of the Board of Tutors in History and Literature, an aspect of the tutorial system that had attracted him to Harvard in the first place. As a result of that experience he and several associates developed the program in American Civilization.

Folklorist Richard M. Dorson, one of the graduates of the program and a distinguished representative of the talented minds it was to produce, has pointed out that the impetus for the program came from the several reevaluations of the American past published in the late 1920s and the early 1930s. He has described the program's inception thus: "The close association of American literature and American history professors on the Harvard faculty lead to their appointment to an interdepartmental Committee on Higher Degrees in American Civilization which began accepting candidates in the fall of 1937. These professors were all actively engaged in broad investigations of American subjects." Dorson describes some of the major figures in the program as he experienced them:

> This is how I recall them. Matthiessen was short, balding, a disjointed lecturer who interrupted a thought in midflight to pursue a tangent thread, but inspired a devoted coterie. His close friend [Perry] Miller, who dwarfed him in size, delivered a flow of ideas at an incandescent pace that left his students

gasping. [Howard Mumford] Jones, also tall and confident, maintained a midwestern informality of manner; I have the picture of him in class doing a circular dance step on the podium to illustrate the jigging tune of the Arkansaw Traveler. [Bernard] DeVoto had the squat build of a prize-fighter, fitting the pugnacity of his prose style, but in his lecture appearances he seemed ill at ease and in need of reinforcement from friends in the audience. [Ralph Barton] Perry projected an image of the philosopher he was, soft-spoken, earnest, questing, a slight modest man pursuing truth but a firebrand in defense of democracy. Each injected himself into a great book about America during these years.[7]

Dorson's description is of the figures he recalls personally, but other names must be mentioned as well to convey the scope and worth of the program. Most important of these, at least in a study of F. O. Matthiessen, is Kenneth P. Murdock, the committee's first chairman and a major figure in the study of American literature. Murdock was probably Matthiessen's closest friend among his Harvard colleagues, and it was the Murdocks whom Matthiessen visited the night before his suicide. Murdock and Matthiessen were collaborators in *The Notebooks of Henry James*. Also of importance were two distinguished historians, Samuel Eliot Morison and Arthur Schlesinger, Sr., who helped develop the program's interdisciplinary thrust and gave its historical component additional force.

Any effort to attempt a complete listing of the figures of importance in American thought who emerged from this program, especially of those who were particularly close to Matthiessen, runs the grave danger of injuring by omission. Suffice it to say that I have met a surprising number of persons who knew him, who were in some way close to him as students, and who were deeply impressed by him. Most of these "graduates" of the Matthiessen experience can, of course, be found in various branches of history and literature. They include teachers and scholars in American Studies and other components of English and American literature, and, as in Dorson's case, in folklore. Matthiessen's students became attorneys, writers, editors, political activists, and academic deans—in brief, they have enriched the broad spectrum of humanistic professions and pursuits, and many who emerged from the curriculum of the Committee on Higher Degrees in American Civilization have become especially eminent.

The feelings of these students for their former professor, who was also often their friend, are frequently warm and even adulatory. Discussing Matthiessen with many of them was a moving experience. Tears would barely be held back by some, more than two decades after the event, especially when they talked about his suicide. One of his students, Eugene Current-García, one of the founders and until 1978 the editor of *Southern Humanities Review* at Auburn University, has written to me, as recently as 1979, that Matthiessen's suicide "devastated" him.

Current-García has also supplied me with one of many samples of Matthiessen's evident concern about his students, an example that explains much. In a letter sent to him from Kittery on 9 August 1944, as Current-García was "still slogging away on the dissertation (while teaching a full 18-hour load of freshman comp) and wondering whether it would ever amount to anything," Matthiessen offers helpful suggestions about possible jobs, advice, and encouragement. Matthiessen writes while he had a term off and explains: "I have been paying a visit to my father in California before settling down to the proofs of my book about Henry James." He goes on, indicating the catholicity of his interests: "The trip was also a fine holiday after three years of steady teaching and ranged from a lunch given by Harry Bridges and his union's leaders at the best restaurant in San Francisco to a properly convivial evening with Barry Fitzgerald [the actor, whom Matthiessen admired greatly]." He encourages Current-García: "You are dead right in your conviction that now is the time to finish your thesis with the minimum of delays so the question really is: how best and where?" The last paragraph of the letter provides a characteristic comment about Matthiessen's favorite cat, Pretzel, and concludes: "Be sure to let me know if I can be of use on any further details, since although I won't be back in Cambridge to stay until November 1st, I can easily be in touch with everything there. My very best regards to Alva [Current-García's wife]. As always, Matty."[8]

Matthiessen was not universally beloved. I have met former students of his who were of two minds about him, or who disliked him, or, as is often the case, find it now, in the light of the esteem in which the dead scholar is held, difficult to admit their dislike. But the dislike was clearly there. In an essay entitled "Teaching: F. O. Matthiessen," historian Kenneth S. Lynn, a student of Matthiessen's in the mid-1940s and a participant with him at the inaugural session of the Salzburg Seminar in American Studies, in the main supports the portrait of Matthiessen as a brilliant and inspiring teacher, but also writes: "The multiple ambiguities in his beliefs made a number of thoughtful students suspicious of him. In fact, there were some who hated Matthiessen, as did quite a few of his colleages on the Harvard faculty."[9] That is no doubt true, as it is also true as I have discovered that some students disliked him because they felt that they were not invited often enough to his home at Louisburg Square or his cottage at Kittery, or because Matthiessen did not attend to them as much as he did to those he thought more promising or found more consanguine. I have been told that there was snobbery on Matthiessen's part toward those who came from less elite backgrounds than he did, and I have even had suggestions of a hidden and unconscious anti-Semitism on his part. All these feelings may be based on fact or on the peculiarities of individual students. Suffice it to say that such feelings existed and are not simply to be ignored in any effort to understand Matthiessen's role as teacher.

More important, however, than any possible negative readings of Matthiessen's relations with some of his students is the brilliance, the dedication, the passion, and the intellectual stimulation that seemed to flow from him to most of those whom he taught. In no case have I met a student or heard of one who has forgotten him or who was not impressed by him. A surprising number of former students still have their notes from one or another of his courses, in many cases after more than a quarter of a century, notes that reveal remarkably rich, well-organized, and thoughtful lectures.[10] In his discussion of Matthiessen's teaching in the Matthiessen issue of *Monthly Review*, Leo Marx, one of the most distinguished of the graduates who studied with him, writes:

He was a great teacher because he unstintingly taught out of himself. In the classroom, in tutorial conferences, and in politics he steeled himself to speak from as deep in his heart as he knew how to reach. Ideas and literature were never things apart, they were always felt experience. If he was able to avoid the obvious dangers of so personal a method it was through the rigorous use of a cool and incisive mind. And yet he never allowed his students to ignore for a minute the severe limitations of the human intellect. He had read too deeply in Hawthorne and Melville to forget the inevitable doom of the solitary thinker. Though himself wholeheartedly committed to the life of the mind, he had an unusually vivid and unrelenting awareness of the desolation that awaits an intellect unsustained by affection, a life not bound to other lives. This he need not have taught those who knew him well. It was his own tragedy. [*FOM*, p. 43]

During his years at Harvard Matthiessen was deeply involved in and sustained by the permanent and loving relationship he had established with Russell Cheney. Twenty years older than Matthiessen, Cheney was a painter, the scion of a wealthy Connecticut family, and a Yale graduate, class of 1904. Cheney's life was filled with the effort to paint, with unceasing bouts with lung problems of various sorts, and with a virulent alcoholism. He was the most important person in Matthiessen's life, from the time they met on the *Paris*, Matthiessen making the crossing to begin his work at Oxford, Cheney bound for painting in Europe. They were lovers, a deeply devoted couple whose relationship, even when difficult and tempestuous, was mutually and profoundly supportive.

The two men rented a cottage at Kittery Point, Maine, in the summer of 1927, and shortly thereafter purchased an old fisherman's house in that community. Cheney made this home his year-round headquarters, although he was often in Europe or in the Southwest where he went for his health and to paint. At times he went to various institutions in order to "dry out." The Kittery Point house was to be the locus of the two men's activities in many ways. For Matthiessen, it was a place to bring friends, often graduate students who had become friends, and to work in an atmosphere less demanding than the one at Eliot House. It was a place of beauty, grace, and ease. In 1938, when Matthiessen gave up the resident tutorship at Eliot House, the men rented an apartment at 87 Pinckney Street in Boston. The apartment overlooked the glorious but fading splendor of Louisburg Square, an appropriate setting for the man who was writing about the United States of the mid-1850s. Both in Kittery Point and at the apartment social gatherings and especially holiday festivities were the rule, with Cheney the excellent cook and Matthiessen the ebullient host. Perhaps the greatest blow Matthiessen suffered in his adult life was Cheney's death from a thrombosis in 1945.

In 1938, while in the middle of writing *American Renaissance*, Matthiessen underwent a bout of depression so severe that he admitted himself to McLean Hospital, where he stayed from 26 December 1938 to 13 January 1939 and began a course of psychiatric treatment. His depression was in part evidenced by terrible doubts about his abilities as a critic, doubts about producing the book he wanted to write. He was also filled with a fear of Russell Cheney's death, a death that had been foreshadowed in part by a recent drinking bout of Cheney's. Given the age difference between the men, Matthiessen's fear was not irrational. Louis Hyde has provided a most moving record of Matthiessen's own descriptions of his state of mind while at McLean and of his recovery from the terrible depth of suicidal depression that he suffered.[11] Matthiessen's death wish was usually associated, apparently, with fantasies of jumping from a window, and it was in that manner that he ended his life some twelve years later.

One of the remarkable aspects of this episode of depression is that despite the most profound personal crisis, Matthiessen was able to complete *American Renaissance*, the book that is at the center of his critical reputation. That *American Renaissance* is essentially a hopeful book is even more remarkable. It is entirely speculative, of course, but I cannot help but feel that at least in part the richness of Matthiessen's insights into the troubled mind of a Melville was aided by his own state of mind. He recovered his equilibrium eventually, "bastioned," as he writes in his record of the experience, "into a will to live by the mounting devotion of those to whom I am devoted."[12]

Despite oppressive feelings of loneliness, Matthiessen's life was filled with rich and vital friendships. Old Yale classmates, outstanding members of the Harvard faculty, political figures in Boston and elsewhere, a few members of Cheney's family, the children, the wives, the former wives and widows of friends, all these and more were part of Matthiessen's circle. It is such friend-ships he had in mind, in addition to his relationship with Cheney, when he wrote of "those to whom I am devoted." The many entries in the section "Statements by Friends and Associates" in the Matthiessen issue of *Monthly Review* are only an indication of the number of men and women Matthiessen could count among his friends, though it would appear that, in the end, even so powerful a circle was insufficient to help him to choose life.

On the other hand, it appears that Matthiessen was often caus-tic and sharp, an unpleasant adversary, and not always a gentle companion. The difficulties of his life and the pressures under which he functioned seem at times to have made him irascible. With friends, with those he loved or respected or both, apologies came as easily as flashes of anger. Although he had a limited capacity for relaxation, he was able to enjoy things intensely—the theater, hearing music, listening to or watching Boston Red Sox games, playing tennis, and contemplating the sea and landscape at Kittery Point. He was, in every sense, a devoted friend and an often joyous, though never simple, companion. May Sarton's 1955 roman à clef, *Faithful Are the Wounds*,[13] is heartily disliked by most of Matthiessen's friends and admirers, because they feel that its protagonist, who is largely modeled after Matthiessen, is a seriously distorted portrait of the original. They are no doubt quite right, for a variety of reasons. Nevertheless, and despite the many faults of the novel as a rendering of the man, Sarton may well have caught in her fictional protrait aspects of the real person that are not easily revealed directly in other media, especially the combination of irascibility and generosity, flashing anger and meaningful apology, moodiness and warm caring, which one can find, as it were, between the lines of letters, anecdotes, and other memorabilia.

Matthiessen was, it is clear, a man of great complexity and of great power. The complexity of his personality provoked complex responses from friends and companions, and his power left deep impressions on the lives of all those who knew him. Part of his important role in the development of criticism in American letters, I suspect, is due to the power of the person behind the ideas as much as to the ideas themselves, if such an obviously artificial separation can be made. Had he been a less arresting person, his ideas might well have been less influential. Anyone who has followed Matthiessen's career is aware that he left few who knew him untouched. His was a personality no one forgot. As teacher or as friend, as adversary or as supporter, as radical political figure or as Christian, as critic or as political writer, the mind and the personality of F. O. Matthiessen imprinted itself on those who had contact with him with indelible permanence.

No sketch of Matthiessen could be complete without some discussion of his intense and active political life. A left-wing radical, though never a Marxist, Matthiessen participated in some of the most important political struggles of the quarter-century that ended with his death. He was involved during the thirties with many labor causes, and he helped to form and then served several times as president of the Harvard Teachers' Union. He came to the defense of labor leaders and workers under attack, most notably in the case of a group of New Mexican miners, which led to a *New Republic* article by him; in successful efforts to stop the deportation of Harry Bridges, president of the longshoremen's union on the West Coast; and in opposition to the Smith Act indictments of a group of Minnesota Teamsters Union and Socialist Workers party leaders, chief among whom was Vincent R. Dunne.

Matthiessen was active in the Massachusetts Civil Liberties Union. He also served on the board of the Samuel Adams School for Social Studies in Boston, where he taught courses from time to time. I have been told by a former student of his that he also arranged for Harvard graduate students in various fields to teach or to give lectures at the school—sometimes even though such students were not nearly as far to the left as Matthiessen or as the school. My own memory of the Samuel Adams School's sister institution in New York, the Jefferson School, brings to mind a vitality of endeavor and interest—even though sometimes of a foolishly doctrinaire quality and rather stern Communist party domination—which had much to recommend it and which must have appealed to Matthiessen.

Matthiessen was also deeply involved with the student politics of Harvard University. He supported such groups as the Harvard Student Union during the thirties. Leo Marx has given us the flavor of that period. He writes:

> Those were tense and exciting days: rival torchlight processions clashed in the Yard at night; any strike in Harvard Square enlisted a corps of student pickets; the Brattle Street ladies came with earphones and sealskin capes to see Leonard Bernstein's superb production of *The Cradle Will Rock*; Leadbelly sang on behalf of the Spanish Loyalists; and Matty spoke to hundreds of students at the annual Peace Strike. One of the few faculty members wholeheartedly sympathetic to the Student Union, he generously gave time, money and advice. [*FOM*, p. 41]

One of the most important issues which concerned Matthiessen during this period was the well-known Walsh-Sweezy case, in which there was reason to believe that the two young radical Harvard professors were not given tenure because of their politics.

The National Citizens Action Committee took a good deal of Matthiessen's efforts as it emerged during the 1944 elections. When it developed, along with other forces, into the Progressive party, which ran Vice-President Henry Wallace for president and Senator Glenn Taylor for vice-president in the 1948 elections, Matthiessen was very active in the campaign. As a member of Students for Wallace when the Progressive party convention took place, I can remember how impressed I was that the famed Harvard professor had given a forceful, though somewhat too long, seconding speech for Wallace's nomination. The overwhelming defeat Wallace suffered at the polls in that election, as Harry Truman emerged narrowly victorious and as many Progressive party members admitted having themselves voted for "the lesser of two evils," must have been a severe blow to the hopes for a more open and forward-looking America that Matthiessen shared with most of those who worked in support of Wallace's fore-doomed effort.

Although Matthiessen was no Marxist, he was a student of Marx. I have been told, by a student of Matthiessen's, that Matthiessen was part of an informal Marxist discussion group led by philosophy professor David W. Prall, the author of several works on aesthetics and Matthiessen's co-worker in the founding of the Harvard Teachers' Union and in the protest engendered by the Walsh-Sweezy case. Matthiessen had made clear in his writings, however, that he found Marxism limited, and especially found it so as a Christian. In that sense, Matthiessen was part of an important non-Communist and non-Marxist streak in American radicalism that has often been inspired by such concepts as "the social gospel."

He was a lifelong communicant in the Episcopal church. His religious convictions do not appear as manifestly in his works as do his political convictions, with some exceptions of course, but I agree with Giles B. Gunn's perceptive comments about Matthiessen's religious views: "I do not say that Matthiessen, any more than Eliot, always derived his critical norms from Christian theology, or that he ever regarded the spiritual factor in literature as paramount. I merely suggest that virtually everything Matthiessen ever thought or wrote acquired its sanctions from concerns that to him were essentially religious, and, further, that those concerns defined the range of experience in terms of which he considered any questions."[14]

The feelings and ideas in Matthiessen's political and religious views had within them great potential for contradiction. In that regard, however, Matthiessen was by no means alone. Had he lived longer, he would have been aware of many more Christians who developed radical social views than had been the case in his lifetime. One can imagine him in important conversations with the Fathers Berrigan and their radical Catholic allies, with Dr. Martin Luther King, Jr., with the other members of the black clergy who made of social action the primary evidence of their adherence to the Gospel, and with other such figures who emerged during the turbulent sixties.

A good deal of Matthiessen's life seems to have been spent in the search for community, a search that grew directly out of the needs of his personality but one that was rooted in his Christianity as well as in his desire for a more social—that is, a socialist—society. He made repeated efforts, from his Yale student days on, to come into solid contact with working people, whom he considered politically crucial and whom he romanticized in the manner of the 1920s and 1930s radicalism that had helped to shape his mind. He rarely succeeded. Canvassing for Wallace in Boston or meeting workingmen and working women in Czechoslovakia was a great joy to him, but he remained a Harvard professor, with all the class distance implied by that title. His efforts to cross such boundaries were probably futile for reasons having only a little to do with his personality and much to do with the social situation in which he lived. The futility was especially meaningful to him, however, as it exposed over and again some of the fundamental contradictions not only in his life but in the life of any socialist intellectual in the Western world and in the United States in particular.

Matthiessen often attributed the difficulty he perceived in this connection to the lack of a political party to which a socialist intellectual could be committed. He was roundly criticized and considered naive when he wrote, in *From the Heart of Europe*, that if he were French, he would have to join the Communist party of Duclos and Thorez. In large part, what that statement was responding to was his feeling that within the French Communist party, or, for that matter, within the British Labour party, which he said he would join if he were English, there was the possibility for genuine unity and interaction between radical intellectuals and radical workers.

It is this search for a party, for unity, for a mass-based socialism that a Christian could join, I believe, which explains in greatest depth, whether it justifies or not, Matthiessen's frequent adherence to socialist causes and political movements associated with the American Communist party's orbit. His own political ideology was never doctrinaire, and he was not a member of the Communist party. If nothing else, his willingness to support such "Trotskyites" as the Socialist Workers party's Vincent R. Dunne in the Smith Act case against him, which the Communist party, to its shame and eventual peril, either ignored or found justified, is evidence of Matthiessen's independence, as is his "angeling" of the independent Marxist journal *Monthly Review*. In regard to the latter of these instances, I can remember personally the vitriol of the attack on Paul Sweezy and Leo Huberman, the editors of *Monthly Review*, which Communist party intellectuals unleashed at the time of the journal's founding.

And yet Matthiessen was attacked as a Stalinist, especially during the hottest days of the cold war period. An interesting case in point is a letter to him from Irving Howe, dated 17 August 1948, and sent from Princeton, New Jersey, on the occasion of a speech of Matthiessen's, which he had sent to Howe, and which was to be considered in a "larger study of political belief among American intellectuals" and in a "squib on [his] political views, as expressed in the book [*From the Heart of Europe*] and elsewhere" for *Partisan Review*. Howe writes:

I don't know if you're acquainted with my views or the things I've written, but I think I should say that my piece will be very harsh and polemical, though I hope fair. For it seems to me that by associating yourself with the Wallace movement, and those behind it, you have done great harm both to your socialist motivations and to the intellectual community of which you are part. I think that you thereby help delay the reckoning with the main problem—Stalinism—that faces any new socialist movement. It seems to me nothing short of tragic that you, who are one of the few literary intellectuals left still aware of the need to be concerned with politics, should fail to take the inescapable minimum stand for a democratic socialist: total rejection of the Stalin dictatorship, its satellites and its supporters. To fail to do that is to muddy the necessary struggle against capitalist society.

However, my purpose in this note is not to preach. To me it is a cause for genuine regret that you have associated yourself with the Wallace movement, and I say this as one who is as opposed to the status quo at least as much as you. I hope

that you will in the near future do what you have failed to do
in your book: engage in a fundamental consideration of the
relationship between socialism and the Stalin dictatorship.[15]

Such charges came from all sides, especially after the publication of *From the Heart of Europe*, and must have added to Matthiessen's growing sense of isolation. For Matthiessen and for
others on the left in those early cold war years, Howe's "main
problem" was not the one that they perceived. It is not my intent
here to rehash once again the acrid quarrels among American
socialists that have been—and, indeed, are now—characteristic
of the American left, and perhaps of the left all over the world.
But I think it is important, in order to understand Matthiessen, to
understand his motivations for supporting the Progressive party
and other such endeavors that also had the support and even the
sponsorship of the American Communist party. I suspect that the
most important source of Matthiessen's support came from his
already-mentioned search for a party and a political community
with ties to significant numbers of the "masses." The various
other sections of the socialist left in existence during the early
post-World War II era seemed to have no mass appeal at all. The
Progressive party did appear to be, to its adherents and even to
many of its detractors, a possible large and important third party
for those of liberal and radical bent—a party that proposed to try
to create "sixty million jobs," a party that made peace with the
Soviet Union a cornerstone of its foreign policy, and a party that
would end the two-headed reign of donkey and elephant. After
all, it was a party that had in its leadership a distinguished former
vice-president and cabinet member, a United States senator (from
Idaho no less), and it had filled Yankee Stadium in the summer
of 1948.

The appeal of the Progressive party and of much else that the
American Communist party supported, especially from the end
of World War II to the close of the decade, was that it appeared to
be the only game in town. The liberals were busy proving that
they were not reds, and the other radical factions were tiny to the
point of invisibility. If, then, you were an intellectual looking for

community, for contact with working people in a mass party, and for a policy that aimed at peace and full employment, there was nowhere else to turn. The main issue was not socialism and therefore was not a self-cleansing by the left of its Stalinist connections, it appeared, but it was the building of a mass movement on the left. The accelerating cold war, rising McCarthyism, the execution of the Rosenbergs, the American commitment to new versions of "normalcy," as the Eisenhower administration followed Truman's last term in office, all these, following upon the Progressive party's failure to make significant inroads into American political life, ended such dreams within the next several years—and of course, Matthiessen died before the debacle on the left became all too obvious. Perhaps Matthiessen's increasing isolation from former political allies and friends, an isolation experienced by most who remained in any way committed to radical activism during this period, convinced him before he died that any notion of achieving a mass radical party was much further in the future than he had thought and that one of the key problems for such a party would be precisely its relationship to American communism and to the Soviet Union. Vincent R. Dunne reports that in January 1949 Matthiessen told him, after attending a meeting of the Socialist Workers party, "I envy you, Dunne. You have a political party. Probably that's what I need. I'm a socialist too" (*FOM*, p. 104).

One other matter can explain Matthiessen's support for the Progressive party and his unwillingness to break with groups that had connections with American communism. It was what he described as his acceptance of the Russian Revolution. He wrote in *From the Heart of Europe*:

What gives the central drive to my desire to find a political position to correspond to my philosophy is that, unlike most Christian Socialists, I accept the Russian Revolution as the most progressive event of our century, the necessary successor to the French Revolution and the American Revolution and to England's seventeenth-century Civil War. The discipline of history seems valuable only if it can enable you to perceive and to hold fast to such broad analogies, even to the extent of recognizing that the iron age of disillusionment which descended upon so many European intellectuals after the excesses of Robespierre was no less somber and hard than our own. Let us grant that it was unfortunate that our revolution had to take place in Russia, a country backward in economic and political development, with a brutal tradition of Czarist oppression and of secret police which could hardly fail to leave some disfiguring mark on its immediate successors. But we do not have the luxury of choice in the place and conditions for a revolution. Revolutions happen because conditions have become so insupportable that the people are driven to right them by whatever violent means. But they also happen only when the people and their leaders possess a sufficiently defined goal which they hope to achieve, and the vitality and courage to drive towards it.

In the early nineteenth century plenty of turncoat liberals rejoined the reactionaries in deploring that the French Revolution had ever happened. But writers like Hazlitt and Michelet held fast to the fact that unless one accepted the Revolution, that is to say, the reasons why it had become necessary and the goals it had aimed at, one could not begin to understand the meaning of modern history. For the core of that meaning lay in a fundamental change in conception: from man as subject to man as citizen. The comparable acceptance required by twentieth-century history is to recognize that, owing to the vast developments in industrialization, political revolution now can and must be completed by an economic revolution. It must be so completed because we have now learned that otherwise the immense concentration of wealth in a few hands makes for a renewed form of tyranny. This is the truth we grasped through the theory and practice of Lenin. It would be the worst folly to lose sight of it, no matter what aberrations from or distortions of it have occurred in the special circumstances of current Russia. And the Russians, whatever their failures in practice so far, however short they may have fallen of some of Lenin's aims through the grim pressures of dictator-

ship, have not been deflected from the right of all to share
in the common wealth.[16]

It is little wonder that such an opinion brought him attacks from
cold warriors and their liberal colleagues. It is a little less obvious
why other socialists would overlook Matthiessen's concerns about
Stalinism, as expressed in his comment about "failures in practice" in the Soviet state. How aware he was of these failures is
frequently demonstrated, and especially so in *From the Heart of
Europe*. Reporting on a discussion concerning "the official suppression of the poetry of Akhmatova" by the Soviet government,
Matthiessen goes on to muse, in his own voice:

> The Soviet state takes the position, which states have tended
> to do throughout history, that thought can be dangerous.
> Indeed, thinkers and artists often mean it to be as dangerous
> as possible. They try to do everything they can to break
> through all expected reactions, to disturb, to shock, to compel
> people to keep life fresh by not allowing it to stay hardened
> to any conventional molds. At this point the cleavage between
> official life and real life becomes absolute, whether in the
> Athens of Socrates or the Jerusalem of Christ. . . .
> No one questions her [Akhmatova's] skill or integrity as an
> artist, simply her possible effect on some of her readers. What
> is "true" or "false" in poetry is often hard, even meaning-
> less, to establish. But suppose what she says about life is not
> true, what then? Could not a state that believes in the widest
> possible diffusion of education among its citizens trust them to
> discover such a fact for themselves, as they compare their
> reading with their experience? Isn't one of the chief functions
> of education to prepare people to be able to do that continually
> in their daily lives?
> But no one claims that what Akhmatova says is not true—
> true, that is, to her own experience, to what a sensitive nature
> has felt in certain moments of loneliness and suffering during
> the long agony of war. The question is whether such feelings
> are good or bad for other citizens now. And there we are in
> the realm where legislation is most futile, and can even do

great harm. Lives will always have their crises of agony, as the inheritors of the language of Dostoevsky and Chekhov and Gorki can well know.

There is all the difference between the inevitable tragedy attendant upon the fact that every man who is born must die, and the avoidable special tragedies attendant upon the capitalistic system. But even if we believe that life in a socialist state will necessarily be happier for more people, we are faced with one further fact. Human reality as it is felt by people living it is always concrete, not abstact; complex, not simplified; richly various, not standardized or uniform. You will not make people more cheerful, you will not make them better workers for the next five-year plan by preventing them from reading Akhmatova. Those among them concerned with poetry will feel that they are thereby being deprived of something. That is itself bad for morale.[17]

This is not the language nor the thinking of a Soviet apologist. Rather it is the language of a member of the American Civil Liberties Union, an American socialist deeply imbued with civil libertarian concerns.

An understanding of the feeling-tone of the period in relation to international affairs is required to understand Matthiessen's allegiance to the Progressive party, of the dismay of those who criticized him for it. It must be remembered that *From the Heart of Europe* was written, though not published, before the occurrence of events in Czechoslovakia, which led to the complete control of that government by Gottwald's Communist party, or to the death of Matthiessen's acquaintance, foreign minister Jan Masaryk. It was written before the fateful attack, in the spring of 1948, on Tito's Yugoslavia by Stalin and the Cominform. It was written, therefore, before the horror of the many "Titoist" purge trials that followed and that led to the execution of some of Europe's leading Communists, including leaders of the Czechoslovak Communist party, among them the impressive Rudolf Slansky. These trials and other such developments as the "doctor's plot" in Russia raised once again the specter of Russian anti-Semitism under the Soviet regime and would have been a further difficulty for Matthiessen had he lived through the reign of terror that characterized the last years of Stalin's rule. The Progressive party came into being, then, while it was still possible for many American radicals to believe that the Soviet state, powerful as it had never been before and though still far from democratic, was moving in the right direction and needed only peace in order to develop into a socialist society for which socialists in Europe and the United States and elsewhere need not apologize. Before the November election in 1948, that hope began to fade because some of the events I have mentioned began to take place in eastern Europe.

On the other hand, President Harry Truman had announced on 12 March 1947 that the United States was prepared to "support any nation resisting Communism, and that in his [Truman's] view it was the duty of 'nearly every nation' to resist. This was the Truman Doctrine, America's answer to Stalin's advocacy of 'Communism in one country.'"[18] That public sign of the cold war, which was, and in some sense still is, the dominant fact in international affairs, gave socialists and progressives great and real cause for alarm as to the peaceful intentions of the United States. Truman's and Dean Acheson's policy seemed to betoken a new era of American imperialist adventures abroad and an effort to decrease, by any means short of full-scale war, Russian influence in the rest of the world. Such radicals as Matthiessen, then, who "accepted the Russian Revolution," found themselves once again in the position in which their counterparts had been placed shortly after the revolution, that is, as defenders of a regime about which they had questions, but as thinkers who felt that they had to choose one side or the other.

Other socialists and radicals, however, who had long opposed Stalinism in Russia and in the Communist parties of the western world, held a different view. They felt that Stalin's rule had so perverted socialism in Russia that it was indefensible and that the main problem was not defense of the revolution but "reckoning with Stalinism." In light of the experiences of Trotsky and of others purged by Stalin, they felt Stalin's peace protestations entirely untrustworthy and thought that the most important step in any effort to advance socialism's cause in the West was to make a clean break with the Soviet model. They saw the Progressive party as inimical to such a step, because of its "peace" program and its failure to separate itself from the American Communist party.

That Matthiessen supported the Progressive party side of this disagreement among socialists is consistent with his general stance. Although he had been clearly willing to incur the wrath of some Communist party members by his support of such "Trotskyites" as Vincent Dunne, and although he was soon to support the unaffiliated Marxists of *Monthly Review*, he believed that the Progressive party and other causes also supported by American Communists were the only viable way to secure world peace. Aware of the "grim pressures of dictatorship" in the Soviet Union, he did not consider that a break with Stalinism was the first priority, but rather that the establishment of peace and the "defense of the revolution" were primary. His evocation of Hazlitt's and Michelet's defense of the French Revolution, even after Robespierre's reign began, indicates his position clearly. That Matthiessen's position was not by any means his alone is borne out by as judicious an observer as Howard K. Smith, who wrote in 1949 that the Truman Doctrine "sounded like an ultimatum to the rest of Europe to be with us or to be counted against us."[19] Thus the conclusion reached by Matthiessen and many others that peace had to be supported and that the best hope for peace was the Wallace-Taylor candidacy is certainly understandable.

Matthiessen's discussion of Dreiser's act in joining the Communist party in 1945 states with clarity many of the reasons that made Matthiessen an adherent of the Progressive party three years later:

He was deeply stirred also by the way in which European writers and artists—Picasso and Sean O'Casey among them—were affirming their adherence to international solidarity by the symbolic act of joining the Communist Party. . . . In judging his act we must remember the temper of the period in which it was made. His major concern was the prevention of further wars, which he was convinced would destroy civilization. He had slowly learned the lesson that there could be no humane life in the United States until the inequities should be removed that had thwarted or destroyed so many of the characters in his fiction. He now believed that the next step was to do everything he could to break down the destructive barriers of nationalism, and to work for equity among all the peoples of the world. Otherwise there would be no world in which to live.[20]

Although Matthiessen was roundly attacked and considered fool-ishly naive for attributing such causes to Dreiser's action, he was speaking, I believe, from the deepest sources of his own beliefs in doing so and understanding Dreiser's act from sources in his own recent experience.

Matthiessen and others who supported Wallace in 1948 were mistaken about the possibilities and realities of Soviet life in the period after World War II. They were listening to their own wishes rather than to evidence and reason in too sanguine hopes for Soviet democracy and were gullible in their unwillingness to be-lieve the tragic facts that became indisputable after Khrushchev's famous report to the 1956 Twentieth Congress of the Communist party of the Soviet Union. On the other hand, I do not believe they were wrong in the alarm they felt at the developments in American foreign policy that were betokened by the Truman Doctrine. These developments foreshadowed the debacle that we have more recently experienced in Vietnam. Matthiessen was right when he saw in American foreign policy a serious danger to world peace, and it is possible that he was right when he believed that democracy in Russia could only develop if there were real peace.

It is clear that a man holding such views, searching seriously for a community of democratic socialists where he could be com-fortable, seeing great danger to peace in American foreign policy, and committed to the defense of the socialist revolution he per-ceived as the next necessary stage in human history would be allied with causes that others found reprehensible. In hindsight, it is easy to question Matthiessen's wisdom in this regard. The sincerity of his beliefs, however, and their consistency with the principles that informed his life is beyond question.

In the summer of 1947 Matthiessen traveled to Europe to become the leading voice at the first Salzburg Seminar in American Civilization at the sumptuous Schloss Leopoldskron. His contact with European students there was of great importance to him, and his impact upon those students is amply exemplified by a number of the tributes to him in *F. O. Matthiessen: A Collective Portrait*. From Salzburg he traveled to Prague to teach there and eventually returned to the United States to write his *From the Heart of Europe*. The work, uncharacteristic for Matthiessen, is a kind of travel book in which he examined his views about the United States from the vantage point of his European experience. The book's expression of hope for Czechoslovak democracy became ironic, because the volume appeared after the Czech government had been totally taken over by Gottwald's Communist party in a legal coup. Jan Masaryk, who had agreed to stay on as foreign minister, died a few days after this governmental change, possibly a suicide, and Matthiessen had written most admiringly of Masaryk. Although he had seen galley proofs of *From the Heart of Europe*, Matthiessen chose not to change what he had said, writing to Louis Hyde that "in our savagely changing world it's not likely to please anybody!,"[21] a prophecy that turned out to be quite accurate. His depression was already a palpable presence. Despite honors that continued to come his way, it seems that depression deepened continuously. To the depression there were now added calumny, press attacks, disdain, a subpoena from the House Committee on Un-American Activities, and the loss of old friends and colleagues. Above all, of course, there was the void left by the death in 1945 of Cheney.

I would not presume to say why Matthiessen committed suicide. It is illuminating to know that he had considered such a course earlier in his life, and it helps us to understand the act to know of his growing feelings of desperation about the state of political affairs, which meant so much to him. Essentially, however, I suspect that Louis Hyde, who knew Matthiessen so well, is on target when he writes:

> Missing among his supporters in 1950 was the painter Russell Cheney, with whom he had maintained an extraordinary friendship for over twenty years until Cheney's death

in 1945. A few months before Matthiessen died he wrote to me about "the problems of living alone for one who has known love and companionship. There is no real solution that I can expect for that kind of incompletion, and . . . one of the passages that keeps recurring to me is the one from Donne on how a united love 'defects of loneliness controls'" (August 13, 1949). His last letter to me, which I found on his apartment desk the day he died, continued ". . . I can't seem to find my way out of this desperate depression. I'd try to stick it out, if I didn't think it would recur. . . . I have fought it until I'm worn out. I can no longer bear the loneliness with which I am faced" (March 31, 1950).[22]

His loneliness and the fear of future loneliness as he realized he would not develop another relationship with a lover like the one he had had with Cheney, and his terrible, uncontrollable depression, foreshadowed by the bout with the disease in 1938 were surely the major forces impelling Matthiessen toward the window of the Manger Hotel from which he jumped during the night of 31 March 1950.

But certainly other factors help to explain Matthiessen's suicide. I do not share Barrows Dunham's view that "when Professor Matthiessen died, the cold war made its first martyr among scholars" (*FOM*, p. 102). That is too didactic and simple and stark, and written out of the passions of the cold war era, in which Dunham himself suffered a good deal. Rather, I think Matthiessen might have chosen to live had there been for him greater hope for a community of political and intellectual associates bound together in social action. Most socialists and other political radicals felt a mounting despair during those years of incipient McCarthyism and the abandonment by all too many liberals of any serious defense of the rights of left-wingers; during those years when the American labor movement, always something other than a proletarian movement in the European sense, bent its greatest energies toward purging the "reds" and supporting the Marshall Plan rather than organizing the unorganized; during that particular year, 1950, which was to see in the outbreak of the war in Korea one of the logical consequences of the

Truman Doctrine and the growing East-West conflict; and during those years in which Stalinist repression became increasingly clear to socialists willing and able to see it. Those were years in which a person searching for a community of shared socialist and Christian concerns needed the greatest personal support and fortitude to keep from the bottle, from an ignominious abandonment of all previous social concerns, or from the window ledge. Matthiessen chose to end his life, but others of his contemporaries I have known who shared his ideas at some point gave up lifelong commitments to socialism for goals far less honorable during that period. Matthiessen jumped because he suffered from depression and from a terrible personal loss so severe that, coupled with the despair all radicals felt during those years, it became impossible for him to see hope beyond the window frame. His suicide note bears out such a reading of his act:

> I have taken this room in order to do what I have to do. My will is to be found on my desk in my apartment at 87 Pinckney St., Boston. Here are the keys. Please notify Harvard University—where I have been a professor.
>
> I am exhausted. I have been subject to so many severe depressions during the past few years that I can no longer believe that I can continue to be of use to my profession and my friends. I hope that my friends will be able to believe that I still love them in spite of this desperate act.
>
> F. O. Matthiessen
(over)
>
> I should like to be buried beside my mother in the cemetery at Springfield, Mass. My sister, Mrs. Harold Neubrand, 490 Bellwood Avenue, N. Tarrytown, New York, will know about this.
>
> *but not until morning*
> Please notify / Kenneth B. Murdock, 53 Chestnut St., Boston and Jonathan Ogden Bulkley, 295 Madison Avenue & E. 79th Street, New York City, who will notify my other Yale friends. Also Mrs. Farwell Knapp,
> *but not until morning*

136 Myrtle Street, Boston, or Mrs. Ruth Putnam at the same
address. I would like them to go to my apartment and to see
that the letters on the desk are mailed.

How much the state of the world has to do with my state of
mind I do not know. But as a Christian and a socialist believing
in international peace, I find myself terribly oppressed by
the present tensions. [FOM, pp. 91–92]

One cannot help but be moved by that last paragraph, by the
concern for others expressed in the inserted warnings not to
waken friends with such chilling news until morning, or by the
concern that his friends will believe in his love for them. That he
had been with the Murdocks the same evening and had expressed
his love for them quite directly, that Helen Knapp, Cheney's
favorite niece, a dear friend of Matthiessen's, and the widow of
his Yale classmate Farwell Knapp, and Ruth Putnam, former wife
of another Yale classmate and a great friend of his, should be
asked to do him a last errand—these add to the poignancy of the
note.

Such a brief sketch of Matthiessen's life can only touch the
surface of the complex personality he was and can only adum-
brate the wealth of material that his eventual biographer will find
fascinating. I have offered it here by way of introduction to a
discussion of his critical work, because it seems to me that in
Matthiessen's case, more than in most, the criticism grew—in a
word he thought so important—"organically" out of the man's
life, out of his very being. It was the Christian, the socialist, the
Yale and Harvard man, the troubled homosexual, the feisty intellectual putting body and soul into politics or criticism or teaching,
the teacher and the lover of literature and art and music, who
wrote those works that so passionately and yet so deeply search
into the core of our literary tradition.

It was also the personality, which contained so many contradictory impulses and which combined such contradictions with
intellectual powers of great acuity, that was able to link the several modes of critical thought influential during Matthiessen's
years of active work. It was that ability, perhaps, which was his
greatest contribution—beyond the specifics of the analysis of

individual writers and individual texts—the ability to combine literary theories that seemed so totally at odds with one another that it appeared they could not be brought together into a whole. Matthiessen, however, combined in his very person the influences of various critical schools and could understand by experience as well as by thought the philosophical bases from which such critical principles derived. Central to the divergences he managed to recombine was the disagreement among critics over the "form-content" issue, that is, over the relative importance of what the writers had to say and the way in which it was said.

If this important aspect of Matthiessen's contribution to our literature is to be understood, it is necessary to provide a brief sketch of the critical situation in which Matthiessen found himself. Any such sketch of one of the most complex and fecund periods in the history of English and American criticism cannot be presented here as a general critical history but must be limited to the context of one particular critic. That very limitation must inevitably lead to some important omissions and perhaps even to some unwitting distortion. Nevertheless, the effort is necessary, it seems, if Matthiessen is in some sense to be "placed," if his contribution to the spectrum of critical thought is to be understood. The sketchy discussion of some critical forces active during the years of Matthiessen's working life that follows, then, is in no way intended to be complete. Rather, the selection of persons, groups, and movements mentioned is based on their relevance to Matthiessen's own developing critical craft, that is, on their direct effect on Matthiessen or on the critical atmosphere in which he worked. Of greatest interest, from that point of view, are those critics most engaged in the debate over the form-content issue, although it must be remembered that such a debate is carried on, not in isolation but in the context of all forces at play within the particular discipline and within the world of intellectual endeavor in general.

The positions of Marxists, Parringtonians, and neohumanists on the one hand, and New Critics or Fugitives on the other, was such that the emphasis that each of these schools of thought placed on its literary theories had to lead to an unusually great dissociation between form and content. This dissociation, always a major problem for the critic since Aristotle, became a focus of critical dispute in the last century or two, as our older metaphysics broke up and changed. Form and content become increasingly dissociated when men and women are no longer sure of their God, their place in the universe, the nature of goodness, and hence the function of art. W. H. Auden puts the matter positively when he says: "We are all consciously or unconsciously seeking some form of catholic unity to correct the moral, artistic, and political chaos that has resulted from an over-development of protestant diversity (using these terms in their widest sense)."[23]

For Americans, the lack of a long critical tradition exacerbates the problem, as Matthiessen himself has pointed out. "We have lacked," he says in his introduction to *The Oxford Book of American Verse*, "until very lately a formed critical tradition in anything like the European sense."[24] It is the last phrase in this sentence—"in anything like the European sense"—that is crucial. For though the United States has had a tradition, it was not one that derived from or was related to the central experience of American critics or artists. Critical thinkers from Emerson to Tyler to Sherman and More have attempted to create such a critical tradition, one that is related to American experience. Matthiessen's solution to the form-content problem is one of his major contributions to the development of that tradition. The solution he assays as critic, furthermore, is a derivative of his efforts to live his life.

John Dewey gives us a useful summary of the issues in the form-content problem:

The great question concerning substance and form is: Does matter come first ready-made, and search for a discovery of form in which to embody it come afterwards? Or is the whole creative effort of the artist an endeavor to form material so that it will be in actuality the authentic substance of a work of art? The question goes far and deep. The answer given it determines the issue of many other controverted points in esthetic criticism. Is there one esthetic value to sense materials and another to a form that renders them expressive? Are all subjects fit for esthetic treatment or only a few which are set aside for that end by their intrinsically superior character? Is "beauty" another name for form descending from without, as a transcendent essence, upon material, or is it a name for the esthetic quality that appears whenever *material is formed* in a way that renders it adequately expressive? Is form, in its esthetic sense, something that uniquely marks as esthetic from the beginning a certain realm of objects, or is it the abstract name for what emerges whenever an experience attains complete development?[25]

The questions Dewey outlines for us take peculiar forms at different periods in literary history and in different localities, and they vary also when the art form in question is literature rather than painting or music. When sides are taken (and they always are), the partisans are often intransigent. "These antitheses of subject, matter, substance on the one side, form, treatment, handling on the other, are . . . a field of battle; and the battle is waged for no trivial cause," writes A. C. Bradley.[26]

Some of the particular causes around which the battle was waged during the years of Matthiessen's work, roughly the two decades from 1930 to 1950, can be exemplified by critics and groups representing various literary viewpoints. Although I would by no means want to suggest that the antitheses cited by Bradley are the only concerns these groups had, the form-content issue was a concern for each of them.

The first of these to be mentioned, if for no other reason than that it was composed of the oldest generation of scholars of concern here, can be encapsulated by the term "humanism." Exemplified by Irving Babbitt, Paul Elmer More, and the pre-World War I Stuart Pratt Sherman (whose position had changed by the 1920s), this group represented one influential school. Especially influential for Matthiessen were Irving Babbitt, against whose ideas Matthiessen had learned to hone his own while a graduate student at Harvard, and Sherman, about whom he wrote with feeling and insight.[27]

Marxist literary thought, in any form, has not been able to generate, until recently, many representatives of distinction. That is especially true in the United States and is even more true if one tries to connect such representatives with organized political movements. Worthy of mention, however, in the 1920s and the early 1930s are Max Eastman and others associated with *The Masses*. Eventually V. F. Calverton, Granville Hicks, Michael Gold, and Sidney Finkelstein in the United States, and Christopher Caudwell in England, became prominent. All had differing degrees of interest and ability and all were associated directly with Communist party ideology. Matthiessen was especially taken with Caudwell, as will be seen in the last chapter of this book.

Less directly affiliated with any political organization, and often of greater interest in the later 1930s and in the 1940s were a number of other critics influenced by Marxism, or by similar sociologically based and hence content-oriented ideologies, all with notions at least related to Marxism. Chief among these critics, most independent, and in many ways most influential and important, was Edmund Wilson who was, at least at one stage of his remarkably varied and interesting career, influenced by Marxism. Wilson was a direct and acknowledged influence on Matthiessen.[28] Noteworthy in his own way and exemplary of several efforts to combine Marx and Freud, was Harry Slochower, who was certainly not as well known or as influential as Wilson, but whose work, especially in his *Three Ways of Modern Man* (1937), had a particular currency. Kenneth Burke added to the Marx-Freud mixture the study of myth and of Jungian psychology, but, possessed of a particularly original cast of mind, he was also concerned about and interested in "the rhetorical aspects of language and . . . the structural aspects of a literary work."[29] Still another group of socially concerned writers with socialist orientations were those associated with the journal *Partisan Review*, although as many issues separated the members of that group as united them. Alfred Kazin has provided a description of this group from his own experience:

> There were brilliant WASPS and Yale men in the *Partisan Review*
> orbit, Dwight Macdonald and Fred Dupee, for whom radical
> activity had been an extension of their personal restlessness
> in the twenties, their excited discovery of another America
> during the Depression. There were scholarly anti-Fascist exiles,
> Nicola Chiaromonte and Paolo Milano; Irish Catholics, William

Barrett, James T. Farrell. Mary McCarthy from Seattle was
the star of the magazine. Elizabeth Hardwick from Kentucky
wrote extraordinarily sensitive stories and essays. But for
the many brilliant Jews around what Edmund Wilson called
"Partisansky Review"—[Lionel] Trilling and [Saul] Bellow,
Philip Rahv, William Phillips, Delmore Schwartz, Meyer
Schapiro, Harold Rosenberg, Paul Goodman, Irving Howe,
Daniel Bell, Sidney Hook, Lionel Abel, Isaac Rosenfeld,
Clement Greenberg, Leslie Fiedler—the "movement" had
become another theology to be sloughed off like Judaism.[30]

Many of the chief critical voices of this group appear in Kazin's
list. These critics were indeed disaffected from any "movement,"
although they were all in some sense socially concerned, and in
that sense at least, if not in many other ways, content-oriented.
They were also united by their profound anti-Stalinism.

Another group of critics who shared many views with one
another, despite significant differences, can be seen as followers
of Parrington rather than of Marx. Although they were socially
aware, their awareness was less political than cultural, and therefore they were more likely to be concerned with the experience of
the United States than with the world as a whole. Included in this
group were several of Matthiessen's colleagues on the Committee on American Civilization at Harvard, among them Howard
Mumford Jones, Bernard DeVoto, and, in a somewhat different
sense, Kenneth P. Murdock and Perry Miller. Not to be left out,
especially because of his wide-ranging influence, is Lewis Mumford. Although some of Van Wyck Brooks's earliest work pre-
cedes Parrington's major book, Leslie Fiedler has written that
"between 1936 and 1952, however, Brooks completed a Parringtonian series of books . . . finally called . . . *Makers and Finders: A
History of the Writer in America, 1800–1915*."[31] "Parringtonian"
seems to me apt, despite the chronological sequence of the two
writers' work. One must keep in mind, however, in regard to
Brooks, the unfortunate sentimentality that suffused his later
works and about which Matthiessen was to write in increasingly
sharp critical terms.

The chief group concerned with the other side of the form-content dispute was the New Critics. This group, as varied as any other I have mentioned so far, was without doubt the most influential during the last decade or so of Matthiessen's life. Chief among its members are surely T. E. Hulme, I. A. Richards, and T. S. Eliot, whose influence was felt quite directly by everyone concerned with literature during the period and certainly by Matthiessen. Among the many brilliant writers who followed the essentially form-oriented tradition developed by Richards and Eliot were Richards's dazzlingly brilliant student William Empson (who at one point in his career, and to a limited extent, was also influenced by Marxism), John Crowe Ransom, and such erstwhile Southern Agrarians as Allen Tate, Cleanth Brooks, Robert Penn Warren, and many others still of importance. Ezra Pound occupied a special place in this group, both because of the profound influence his personal role had on the poetry of so many, including Eliot, and because his critical opinions were often influential with others as much by dint of his powerful personality as by his critical writings. Although they each occupied sharply differing positions in other ways, Yvor Winters and F. R. Leavis were certainly of importance and were both deeply influenced by Eliot and his followers.

Other unique contributors to the literary theory of the period were Eliseo Vivas, Arthur O. Lovejoy, René Wellek, Austin Warren (who should, perhaps, be grouped more closely with the New Critics), R. P. Blackmur, the "Chicago School," including especially Ronald S. Crane, and a group of literary historians and biographers which would include such names as Newton Arvin and Raymond Weaver.

A glance at the foregoing paragraphs will make clear how many issues divided these various critical schools from one another and from others I have not even mentioned. Among these divisive issues are the sources of literature, the function of criticism, the role of the artist in society, the relationship between artist and audience, the relationship of American literature to the European tradition, the value of democracy and the role of the frontier, the nature or even the very existence of an American tradition, and the relationship between form and content.

Of major importance to Matthiessen and to many of his contemporaries was the dynamic tension between the schools of criticism that emphasized form as the crucial concern in literature and those that emphasized content. Virtually every school disavowed such Kantian dichotomies,[32] but the arguments of various groups and individuals make it clear that they were among the several points around which disagreements turned.

V. L. Parrington, in his now-famous explanation of purpose in the Introduction to volume 1 of *Main Currents in American Thought*, stated his side of the argument in such a way as to make the issue clear:

> I have undertaken to give some account of the genesis and development in American letters of certain germinal ideas that have come to be reckoned traditionally American—how they came into being here, how they were opposed, and what influence they have exerted in determining the form and scope of our characteristic ideals and institutions. In pursuing such a task, I have chosen to follow the broad path of our political, economic and social development, rather than the narrower belletristic; and the main divisions of the study have been fixed by forces that are anterior to literary schools and movements, creating the body of ideas from which literary culture eventually springs.[33]

With such a view, but from very different social and historical premises, stand the neohumanists, the Marxists, and the school that, in part following Parrington directly, is best exemplified by the work of the earlier Van Wyck Brooks. These strange bedfellows differed heatedly on many matters: the value of the tradition stemming from Rousseau; the importance of the democratic ideal; the Humanists' essentially antidemocratic bias; the Marxists' search for an expanded concept of democracy that included its economic aspect; the celebration of the democratic experience found in Brooks. But they all agreed that the primary questions to be directed at a work of art had to do with what it said, with its ideology, and not with its formal structures.

In the opposing camp we find the group of critics whose primary interest lies in the structures and forms of literature. A passage from John Crowe Ransom, surely one of the seminal figures in American criticism, can exemplify their position clearly. After a clever, true, and slightly tongue-in-cheek distinction between Marxist and humanist critics, between Norman Foerster on the one side and the 1941 versions of Edmund Wilson and W. H. Auden on the other, Ransom writes:

> The thing I wish to argue is not the comparative merits of the different moralities by which poetry is judged, but their inadequacy to the reading of the poet's intention. The moralistic critics wish to isolate and discuss the "ideology" or theme or paraphrase of the poem and not the poem itself. But even to the practitioners themselves, if they are sophisticated, comes sometimes the apprehension that this is moral rather than literary criticism. . . . I have not seen the papers of my colleagues in this discussion . . . but it is reported to me that both Mr. Wilson and Mr. Foerster concede in explicit words that criticism has both the moral and the esthetic branches; Mr. Wilson may call them "social" and esthetic branches. And they would hold the critical profession responsible for both branches. Under these circumstances the critics cease to be mere moralists and become dualists; that is better. My feeling about such a position would be that the moral criticism we shall have with us always, and have had always, and that it is easy—comparatively speaking—and that what is hard, and needed, and indeed more and more urgent after all the failures of poetic understanding, is a better esthetic criticism. This is the branch that is all but invariably neglected by the wise but morally zealous critics; they tend to forget their dual responsibility. I think I should go so far as to think that, in strictness, the business of the literary critic is exclusively with an esthetic criticism. The business of the moralist will naturally, and properly, be with something else.[34]

Thus the issues in the form-content controversy are clearly stated. It is my view that F. O. Matthiessen made a successful effort to synthesize these opposite views. He approached literature in a way such as to eliminate Ransom's dualism and to substitute for it a critical theory and even more so a practice that comes close to bridging the gap between "moral" and "esthetic" criticism.

The form-content matter was certainly not the only one in dispute in American letters during the period under discussion here. The changes in critical thought in the first three decades of the twentieth century and the changes that played a leading role in shaping the concerns of Matthiessen and his contemporaries were far more widespread. John H. Raleigh, in an essay significantly entitled "Revolt and Revaluation in Criticism: 1900–1930," has described some of these changes:

> But not only the subject matter of criticism underwent a significant change during the period. Attitudes and assumptions altered radically as well. First, there was a new sense of spaciousness and amplitude, which came out in a variety of ways. Taboo subjects, such as sex, were brought out into the open. Old values were called into question and new ones were enormously enlarged in various ways; there was first a horizontal extension, particularly into psychology, sociology, philosophical esthetics, and the other arts, and a further extension culturally by the taking into account of foreign critical theory. . . .
>
> If there was an extension in width in American criticism at this time, there was also an extension in depth, backward into time, and the massive door that the nineteenth century had opened on the fathomless abysses to the rear was now swung wide open. More's sweep was majestical—Oriental thought, Greek thought, western philosophical and theological speculation, all this backed by a solid knowledge of western history in general. . . .
>
> The Marxist critics, such as Calverton, helped to establish, even for non-Marxists, this sense of the enormity of the past and of the urgency with which one must travel back up the stream to ultimate sources. . . . Moreover, the Marxist analysis of history had some of the appeal of the literary epic—sweep, drama, and inexorability. . . .
>
> One of the major significances of this turning back to the

sources was the resurgence of an interest that had always enchanted Western man, that is, Oriental thought and art. . . .

But even more urgent and explicit was the desire to come to terms with Europe and the European heritage. . . .

For it was as if the physiognomy of American criticism which hitherto had been, at its best, forward looking and prophetic, had now, at its best, become backward looking and critical.[35]

It is not surprising, after such a description of the three decades preceding Matthiessen's largest body of work, to find C. Hugh Holman depicting the 1930s and 1940s as follows: "I suspect that Philip Wheelwright is correct when he calls the 'three elements of contemporary criticism—the anthropological, the psychological, and the semantic,' but certainly the sociological and the historical need to be added if we are attempting a record rather than an evaluation."[36]

For an overview of the critical ideas and movements that shaped the entire half-century of Matthiessen's life span, that is, both the years of his apprenticeship and the years of his most active work, we may turn to the table of contents of William Van O'Connor's *An Age of Criticism, 1900–1950*. The list begins with "The Genteel Tradition," and then goes on with "Sophistication and Impressionism," "Realism and the Aegis of Science," "Organic and Expressive Form," "The New Awareness of America," "The New Humanism," "Social and Activist Criticism," "Psychoanalysis and Myth," and ends with "Analytical Criticism."[37]

Such a grouping indicates only the trends that shaped the critics of Matthiessen's period. For Matthiessen, to use Holman's terms, the "semantic" on the one hand, and the "sociological and historical" on the other, were the most important categories, although he was certainly aware of and successfully used the "anthropological" and, less successfully, the "psychological." But he was not, except on rare occasions, or parenthetically, a formulator of critical theory. He is not the one who wrote the theoretical manifestos correcting or opposing or supporting the Fugitives or Marxists. The bulk of his work is what we may call "practical" criticism, that is, the examination of specific works of literature in order to explicate, place, and judge them.

Even if we ignore his unpublished master's thesis on Oliver Goldsmith and his doctoral dissertation on Elizabethan translators, his works covered a wide range in time and subject matter. Matthiessen's interests in American literature cover more than a century, ranging from his work on Poe, one of the first major figures in the history of American letters, to criticism of his contemporaries, like Stevens, Tate, and William Carlos Williams. His interest in form includes the novel, poetry, and the essay. (Although he loved the theater, I have found no significant drama criticism by him.) He is able to respond with cogency and respect to critics as different from one another as Hicks, Rosenfeld, and Ransom. He is concerned with the highly respected and the obscure, with Melville and with the now-forgotten poet Marshall Schacht, and to all of these figures and genres he brought his close acquaintance with the European tradition, as revealed especially in his work on the symbolists Malraux, Yeats, and the early Sartre.

Matthiessen's work constitutes a search for a usable American past—and present—and Matthiessen was surely part of a great movement in this regard. I have already cited Richard M. Dorson's description of this movement at Harvard. Leslie Fiedler has written that "as late as fifteen years ago [that is, in 1943], the graduate student who devoted himself primarily to American literature instead of, say, Renaissance drama or Medieval epic was looked on as not quite 'serious.' Since 1928, however, the battle has been really won; and it becomes clear now that the continuing resistance of the thirties and the forties was only a rear-guard action."[38]

But even a rear-guard battle must have combatants, and in Matthiessen's active years the battle must have seemed quite sharp. Matthiessen's role in the combat was a significant one. He insisted, over and over again, that when American letters were treated with the respect for form demanded by the New Criticism, with the historical insight demanded by Marxists and Parringtonians, and with an abiding sense of what makes for great art at any time, there was a usable American past and a useful American present. That the intensity of his search for a usable past was fueled by his politics and theology seems quite clear.

What Matthiessen meant by the usable past was not quite what others meant by it, perhaps, for he escaped at almost all points the vulgarizations of the later Brooks and the even crasser vulgarizations of a V. F. Calverton. But like them he insisted on a tie between history and politics and art. Furthermore, unlike most of the critics mentioned so far, he insisted both on literary and on philosophical grounds that the most significant yardstick for the judgment of great literature derived from an awareness of the tragic. Literature, Matthiessen was to insist, must reflect the tragic nature of man's condition. Thus he created a postlapsarian, essentially Christian yardstick, one that derived from his most profound philosophical and theological convictions. The way in which he fused all these strands, which seem to some irreconcilable, into a strong critical knot will be the subject matter of this study.

There were aspects of the literary situation that Matthiessen either did not see at all or saw only dimly. He seems to have developed only a very limited understanding of the contributions made by Freud, Freudians, and other psychoanalytically oriented critics, although at times he used their techniques. He seems to have had, along with most of his white contemporaries, little awareness of the renaissance of black writing, especially poetry, that began with the Harlem Renaissance led by Langston Hughes, Countee Cullen, Jean Toomer, Arna Bontemps, and others, although he does cite Hughes as contributing "left-wing blues."[39] He seems to have shown only limited awareness of the significant, though often confusing, work that was being done in aesthetics by philosophers like Susanne K. Langer, Arnold Isenberg, and many others, or of the work in semantics by Korzybski and his followers. He seemed to have no awareness—and few other Americans did either—of new currents in European Marxist thought. But there is not much use in complaining, as Matthiessen said of Henry James, about what a man did not do. While it must be noted, it does not much affect what he did do, and that is what must be understood and weighed.

What Matthiessen did do, I submit, was enough to warrant for him a permanent place as a major critic of American literature. Though Fiedler may speak rather disparagingly of "such hybrid forms as Matthiessen's socially oriented formalism,"[40] the contribution Matthiessen made seems to me to be precisely the result of his willingness, perhaps even his need, to weld together seemingly different, even opposing, elements. One can view Matthiessen's work as "hybrid" or as an approach that united disparate elements into a new bond. That such a bond was called for, at the height of Matthiessen's career, by the sharp polarization in American critical thought seems to be self-evident.

As I have already pointed out, Matthiessen made very clear that he was not a Marxist, because he found a serious lack in the psychology of Marxists who did not believe, as he did, in "the doctrine of original sin, in the sense that man is fallible and limited, no matter what his social system, and is capable of finding completion only through humility before the love of God."[41] But his methodology as a critic, though not in any pure sense Marxist (whatever that may mean, in an era when that term has become so protean), comes closer to the distinguished efforts of some of the Marxist critics of Europe than does the work of just about any other major American critic of Matthiessen's time.

Such a claim for Matthiessen's work is a commentary concerning the inadequacy of most American Marxist literary criticism written prior to Matthiessen's death. The 1920s and 1930s and even the 1940s produced in the United States only a small amount of Marxist criticism that can be read today with continuing profit and pleasure, and often the best works produced by critics who considered themselves for a time Marxists were "one-shot" propositions by writers who moved into and out of a Marxist "phase" with remarkable rapidity. Marxists of all disciplines, whatever their skills, too often spent an inordinate amount of energy on what were essentially internecine struggles between the various socialist factions, a phenomenon Matthiessen noted in *From the Heart of Europe* and which continues to plague American radicalism to this day.

In the absence of any major Marxist criticism in this country, then, Matthiessen stands out as one who used aspects of Marxist thought to good advantage. His insistence that the work of art is a product of its times and that it reflects the social conditions in which it is created was surely influenced by his study of Marx and by his acquaintance with the Marxist thinkers among his radical friends. That such views of the relations between art and society can be found in others of Matthiessen's contemporaries, including some of the major figures mentioned in Dorson's description of the Harvard American Civilization program, is no accident. Although such a concept is always difficult to prove, it suggests that the ideas of the 1920s and 1930s, which gave us a Parrington, also gave us those who followed him, and that all of these figures felt some Marxist influences, which they readily acknowledged. Matthiessen, however, seems to me to have used his acquaintance with Marxism more thoroughly than any of the others mentioned, and he seems to have been most willing to acknowledge its influence on him.

The best way to understand Matthiessen's contribution is through a careful examination of his major critical works. Chief among these of course is *American Renaissance*. But his *Sarah Orne Jewett*, the first of his published books, is instructive in that it shows us the intellectual distance his mind was to travel to reach his later and more profound books. His works concerning T. S. Eliot and Henry James, written respectively before and after *American Renaissance*, give us fine examples of the essential parameters of Matthiessen's methodology. His posthumously published *Theodore Dreiser* put to its most severe test Matthiessen's abilities as a critic who valued both form and content. His entire body of work is illuminated by his occasional pieces and especially by his most extended theoretical work, the Hopwood Lecture at the University of Michigan entitled "The Responsibilities of the Critic," delivered just a year before his suicide.

2 ❧ Maine Lady in a Garden

HE genesis of some of Matthiessen's thought was already apparent in the early work of the young, twenty-seven-year-old scholar when he published his first book in 1929. *Sarah Orne Jewett* is not a great work of criticism. Although it demonstrates Matthiessen's perceptiveness, his awareness of landscape and setting, his sensitivity to literature as the created product of the artist's imagination, and his consciousness of the interaction between environment and artist, it lacks the profound insight and critical acumen that we will find in later work. Nevertheless, it remains, fifty years after its publication, one of the standard works and one of only a few full-length works concerning Jewett.[1]

It is worthy of attention in this study of Matthiessen's critical development because it demonstrates in its concerns what will make him an important critic and in its failures what he will have to gain to achieve that stature. Its concerns are at least threefold: the American past, which so strongly informed Jewett's work; the role that the Maine landscape and the Maine population played in transforming Jewett from a "mere" local colorist into a consummately skilled miniaturist; and the growing perception of the importance of form as the crucial ingredient in judging Jewett, from the good work of *Deephaven* to her little masterpiece, *The Country of the Pointed Firs and Other Stories*.

The pictures with which Matthiessen chose to illustrate his work are a sign of his awareness of the role of setting and of the force of the past in Miss Jewett's work. The ambience of the past is effectively suggested by the book's three illustrations, paintings by Russell Cheney, respectively of the Jewett house at South Berwick, of its hall, and of its front door. One is impressed, as Matthiessen obviously was, by the sound New England architecture, the solidity and breadth of the staircase shown in the painting of the hall. The widow's walk, which surrounds the roof of the Haggens House first built in 1774 and which was purchased in 1820 by Miss Jewett's grandfather, a successful ship's captain and merchant,[2] is the most evocative item. The house, Matthiessen was aware, had to do with the New England that had once been but that had now been replaced by widespread industrialism and the spirit resulting from it, which made Sarah Jewett's stories the chronicles of an anachronism. "'There are electric cars in Exeter now, but they can't make the least difference to me,'" Matthiessen quotes Jewett as writing to Sara Norton near the turn of the century, and then adds, "No difference to her, for her memories were secure. But New England wasn't."[3]

Matthiessen's awareness of the importance of the social milieu in which the writer works is even more apparent in his description of the world in which Jewett grew up:

> Berwick was no longer an inland port, a busy artery between Santo Domingo and London. It was an up-country station on a branch railway line, grappled by bonds of steel and wire to Lawrence and Lynn.
>
> Throughout New England the invigorating air that Emerson and Thoreau had breathed was clogged with smoke. A mile away from Sarah's house the textile mills at Salmon Falls were employing larger and larger numbers, and rows of drab rickety houses were growing like mushrooms overnight. The native village folk were slowly crowded out by Irish immigrants. Their hearts were not destined to know the bold resolve and high achievement of Sarah's grandfather. They were not to glean strange knowledge of the world from the lips of friends who had been to Archangel and Marseilles, but to learn their rumors fourth-hand from a dingy local paper. They clung grimly to their stony farms and mouldering fishing shacks and worked out their uneventful lives cheered only by the bright memory of the past. A woman was counted lucky if she could find a husband in the dwindling countryside, and her son was also lucky if he could find a job in the mill along with the foreigners, and didn't have to shoulder a lean pack, and take the cars for the West. Sarah Jewett was growing up in a period of decline. The village's proud feeling of self-sufficiency was gone forever.[4]

Such a perception of the relationship between social fact and the writer's art must have been a little unusual for many American readers in 1929, although "sociological criticism" was, indeed, "in the air." In a 1929 review of two works by Norman Foerster, Matthiessen himself gives us the credo that was, in part at least, the obvious impulse behind *Sarah Orne Jewett* and similar works by other critics at the same time:

Its [literature's] new historian must take into account every side of American culture: the effect of our religion and education in forming it (although anything like a complete study of either of these forces has still to be written), the increasing ease of communication and travel, movies and cartoons, the Ford, and the radio, the significance of the fact that the village reads Whittier and Longfellow, and the city Whitman and James. In brief, he must follow the impressive lead of historians like Turner, Andrews, Adams, and Beard, who have given us a new vision of the forces dominant in our political and social past. But he must not lose himself in his background, or forget that he is dealing primarily with literature.[5]

How startling such new, sociologically based insights still were can best be seen from Howard Mumford Jones's testimony in regard to Parrington's *Main Currents*. Jones wrote: "But who can forget the tingling sense of discovery with which we first read these lucid pages, followed this confident marshalling of masses of stubborn material into position? . . . Readers in 1927 felt the same quality of excitement, I imagine, as Jeffrey experienced when in 1825 young Macaulay sent his dazzling essay on Milton to the *Edinburgh Review*. . . . We were free of Anglophilism, of colonialism, of apology at last. . . . Here was a usable past, adult, reasonable, coherent."[6] Matthiessen's views about Jewett, to the limited extent that he followed in Parrington's footsteps without really yet having been much influenced by Parrington's so recent work, share in that sense of the new and the exciting.

Matthiessen's perceptions of the sociopolitical background to Jewett's fiction were useful, and the approach he developed in his analysis is still adhered to by more recent commentators about her work. That, however, he did not yet fully know how to *use* these perceptions and that they were still limited perceptions, I shall show further on.

He was also acutely conscious of another component of the social insights that underlie Jewett's work, the component that does make her part of the regionalism that was so important in late nineteenth-century American writing, that is, her use of the character, language, and mores of the local populace. At a time when Beard's *The Rise of American Civilization* was only two years old, when the writing of social history other than the history of important persons was still quite a recent innovation, Matthiessen saw the importance of the minutiae of an earlier New England life in Jewett's work. He wrote: "As long as she [Jewett] stayed within the limits of Dunnet township she flourished abundantly. And if the trailing arbutus is the symbol of her form, Almiry Todd stands stalwartly as the essence of its content."[7] And again, in reference to the acknowledged Jewett masterpiece, *The Country of the Pointed Firs*, "The events of the book are almost too simple to recount, for they are the ordinary life in a Maine coast settlement of the last century, and through catching their essence Sarah Jewett has preserved for America a segment of its past."[8]

Such a concept is less extensive but also more developed than the functions of the literary historian that Matthiessen called for in his review of Foerster's books. It suggests that the artist as well as the historian may be a significant chronicler, an important preserver of the past. Matthiessen thus assigns to the artist as part of his or her task the function of a historian. He was to use that concept as one important criterion in estimating the value of writers he considered later in his career.

In a somewhat different sense, the artist as chronicler was dealt with by Matthiessen in a work written earlier though published later than *Jewett*. In his Harvard doctoral dissertation, *Translation: An Elizabethan Art*, Matthiessen's concluding comment is that "the great miracles of North's *Plutarch* and the Bible can be explained only by the fortunate circumstances of the Elizabethan age. Knowledge was fresh, language could be bent to one's will, thoughts swarmed so eagerly that they could not be separated from emotions. The language was more fully alive than it has ever been, which means that the people were also."[9] While the hallmark of Matthiessen's mentors, John Livingston Lowes and George L. Kittredge, may be seen in such a statement, there is also an indication here of the "spirit of the times" idea that fore-shadows the most cogent argumentation of *American Renaissance* in the 1940s and of *Theodore Dreiser* in the 1950s.

In *Sarah Orne Jewett* Matthiessen also manifests his concern with form and style, both as crucial criteria in judging the merit of an artist's work and as organic parts of the artist's response to the total environment. The metaphor of the trailing arbutus—the flower known for its odor but also for its retiring woodlands habit of trailing over rockcliffs and abandoned New England rock walls—is an indication of Matthiessen's sensitivity to style and form. In the concluding chapter of *Sarah Orne Jewett* we read:

> Style means that the author has fused his material and his technique with the distinctive quality of his personality. No art lasts without this fusion. If the material is important and the technique crude, the work will continue to have historical value, such as even the clumsiest Dreiser novels will have in throwing light upon their time, but they are not works of art. If the technique is skillful but the personality hollow, the product will fade like that of the poetasters of every generation. Without style Sarah Jewett's material would be too slight to attract a second glance. With it she has created—not a world, but a township in the state of Maine.
>
> This is what chiefly separates her from Miss Wilkins. . . . Style has not been such a common phenomenon in America that its possessor can ever be ignored. Sarah Jewett realized its full importance.[10]

The critic who wrote this in 1929 was surely ready for—indeed was a part of—the "revolution," as William Van O'Connor calls it, which was most effectively and widely promulgated in the United States by Brooks and Warren's *Understanding Poetry* in 1938, but which had already been well launched abroad earlier by T. S. Eliot, I. A. Richards, T. E. Hulme, and others.[11] Here was a critic, then, who combined sociological analysis with stylistic analysis in order to understand and elucidate literature. Both critical approaches were still relatively new when he wrote *Sarah*

Orne Jewett, and he was to be instrumental in giving both of them stature.

But what is *not* in Matthiessen's first published book, or what is only partially there, is perhaps more interesting than what *is* there. One aspect of what is missing is discussed by Bernard Bowron:

> *Sarah Orne Jewett* is, it seems to me, "sentimental." But it is certainly not unconcerned with ideas. Matthiessen was experimenting here with method: how does one "use" the usable past? But the problem of method presupposes a problem of value: what does one use it *for*? When he wrote *Sarah Orne Jewett*, Matthiessen was not quite sure. . . . She [Miss Jewett] had the sense, herself, of belonging to the past: she felt it to be superior to the present, from whose grasp she instinctively withdrew. These views and this attitude (for four chapters) Matthiessen seems rather wholeheartedly to approve. . . . Later, it would be industrialism's pressure toward standardization that would appall Matthiessen. Here, it is simply offensive to the private sensibility; and Sarah Orne Jewett's own nostalgic feelings for that purer, pre-industrial New England air is what makes her work a "usable past."[12]

Bowron goes on to cite the "electric cars in Exeter now" quotation and connects it with repeated mentions of the private garden that Miss Jewett loved so at her grandmother's house in order to indict Matthiessen for a serious lapse. "In context, it is clear that Matthiessen's mind, at this stage of his career, chimed with Miss Jewett's. Sensibility was a heritage of the past that could not survive the smoke and social leveling of factory society. The remedy was to withdraw, to build fences, to cultivate one's own private garden."[13]

Bowron's point is well taken. The fact is that Matthiessen seems to swallow almost whole Miss Jewett's bittersweet vision of an earlier time without challenge, question, or any but the most kindly value judgment, at least for most of his book. Although, as Bowron points out, he acknowledges the limited nature of Jewett's achievement in the fifth and last chapter of *Sarah Orne Jewett*, although he recognizes the Anglophile, snobbish, reactionary nature of many of the major literary influences of her life, still Matthiessen never subjected Jewett's vision to the kind of tough-minded, searching examination of values to which he was to subject Emerson, for instance, later in his career.

But the reason Bowron gives for Matthiessen's failure is limited and partial:

> I do not find it strange that Matthiessen should be guilty of such evasion himself in this particular book. Here he was yielding to his subject, and especially to the easy charm of her milieu; he was writing a back-to-the-womb lullaby to himself and his readers, not challenging them to exploration and judgment. And so he had as little wish to probe Miss Jewett's art as he had to see the peace of her grandmother's garden disturbed by the toot of a passing train. Both literary analysis and electric cars were an ungenteel invasion of privacy. . . . Four chapters of *Sarah Orne Jewett* pointed backwards toward Van Wyck Brooks. The fifth points forward toward Louis Sullivan, to *American Renaissance*, and to *Henry James: The Major Phase*.[14]

There can be no doubt that Matthiessen was personally involved in Jewett's life and in the setting she depicted so well. His book is dedicated to his mother, Lucy Orne Matthiessen, a distant relation of the Maine writer. Matthiessen's sister, the sibling to whom one suspects he was closest, bore the same first and middle names. Perhaps more important, in June 1927 Matthiessen and Cheney rented "The Ditty Box," a cottage at Kittery Point, Maine. Shortly thereafter they purchased a seaside cottage in the same community, a home that was to be the center of their lives together until Cheney's death.[15] Thus Matthiessen was writing *Sarah Orne Jewett* as he was in the process of establishing on a permanent and stable basis what was to be the most important personal relationship of his adult life, and he was doing so from a locale related to the subject of his book. Although Kittery was not "Dunnet Township," it was similar enough, and that several of Howells's letters to Jewett were written from Kittery established a further connection. Furthermore, Matthiessen has told us that it was Cheney who suggested Jewett as a subject for his book,[16] and it is Cheney's paintings that illustrate the volume, in the only collaborative literary effort the two men were to make. Such aspects of the particular moment in Matthiessen's life when he wrote *Sarah Orne Jewett* could, and in this case I believe did, lead quite easily to thoughtless acceptance of the sentimentality in Jewett's work.

Another, more far-reaching possible cause for this flaw in Matthiessen's book combines aspects of his personal life and his critical technique. His personal life rendered him incapable of using fully some tools of critical analysis which were available to him. He was never to use psychological analysis as effectively as he might have, and perhaps he failed to do so particularly in *Sarah Orne Jewett* because he was personally too involved in his subject. This failure is the cause of a major problem in this book, which thus becomes a "back-to-the-womb-lullaby," so that the lack is more obtrusive than it was ever to be again.

One is struck by Matthiessen's refusal in writing what is, after all, a literary biography, to examine closely Jewett's failure to marry or to have contemplated, apparently, any sexual attachment at all, serious or slight. We have certainly had enough critical speculation about Emily Dickinson's supposed lover to make the question an obvious one. Its importance lies not in any effort to psychoanalyze Jewett on the basis of history, rumor, or artistic productivity, but rather to explain an aspect of Jewett's work that, at least in part, Matthiessen himself perceived. "A faint odor of rose leaves emerges," he says of her work. "You are reminded of her inability to portray passion in her books. She always paints the gentler emotions: blinding hates and jealousies, the fever of lust and thirst of avarice never throb there. Even her few lovers are invariably wooden and silly."[17] But Matthiessen never followed this lead into Jewett's personal life. He never did extensively accept the primarily Freudian critical methodology that came into vogue from 1919 on, with figures such as Waldo Frank, D. H. Lawrence, and Ludwig Lewisohn.[18] Although he attempted, at least in some of his work, to use the new knowledge provided by the application to literature of psychoanalytic techniques, that was never his forte—and in *Sarah Orne Jewett* he hardly attempted it. For the sexual aspect of Jewett's personal

life, especially as it is reflected in the fiction, he offers no explanation, although he points scantily to the very strong bond with
her father and to the grandmother (really a step-grandmother)
whom she knew and feared. He makes only the barest mention
of her mother.

But it is a fact that neither Sarah nor Mary Jewett, her sister,
ever married. The third girl in Dr. Jewett's household, Caroline,
to whom "A Native of Winby" is dedicated, is never mentioned
by Matthiessen at all. Matthiessen presents evidence of the complexity and intensity of Jewett's attachment to her father, an attachment that continued long beyond Dr. Jewett's death in 1878
when Sarah was twenty-nine years old. One example of such
evidence, which as careful a scholar as Matthiessen must have
known about, is the collection of Jewett's verse, privately published by her sister in 1916, seven years after Sarah's death.[19]
This collection of rather slight verse—Jewett never thought of
herself as a poet—contains in its scant thirty-three pages a number of surprisingly passion-filled poems about her father, surprising especially in light of the apparently otherwise held view
that "life is on the whole a sequence of pleasantly muted inter-
changes,"[20] which suffuses the rest of her writing.

That a well-read sophisticate of the 1920s like Matthiessen
could have failed at least to raise questions about the source of
that "faint odor of rose leaves" in the personal life of his subject
cannot be explained sufficiently by Matthiessen's family, or by
his locale at the time of writing the work, or by the particular
moment in the state of his own developing private life. Another
possibility, one that I think probably unprovable but at least possible, suggests itself. Matthiessen's obvious concern with "sexual
perversion,"[21] engendered by his own homosexuality, may have
made it too touchy for him, especially at the age of twenty-seven
or twenty-eight, to examine Jewett's life in this area in any detail
or even to discuss to any extent the absence of evidence of sexual
life on her part.

In all fairness, it must be said that Matthiessen is by no means
alone in failing to follow in any depth Jewett's life in this regard.
Richard Cary writes that "in childhood she prized the companionship of elderly men; in adulthood her intimate friendships were

predominantly feminine. Many of these were of course based on social and temperamental congeniality, and their artlessly passionate quality may be judged from the correspondence which signalized and nurtured them. . . . Although Miss Jewett remained unmarried all her life, and seems not to have had a single serious affaire de coeur, she established and sustained affable relationships with scores of men."[22] Margaret Farrand Thorp is ready to settle for the following:

> She was convinced very early that she would never marry. She had all through her life many excellent male friends of all ages but there is no record of even the faintest shadow of a love affair. This state of mind was easily explained by the pre-Freudian nineteenth century. Miss Jewett's Country Doctor says of his ward while she is still quite young: "I see plainly that Nan is not the sort of girl who will be likely to marry. When a man or woman has that sort of self-dependence and unnatural self-reliance, it shows itself very early. I believe that it is a mistake for such a woman to marry . . . and if I make sure by and by, the law of her nature is that she must live alone, I shall help her to keep it instead of break it, by providing something else than the business of housekeeping and what is called a woman's natural work, for her activity and capacity to spend itself upon."[23]

It is beyond the scope of my discussion of Matthiessen to attempt to provide other readings for the lack of passion in Jewett's writings, but surely one would wish to ask whether there was not some psychological circumstance in her private life connecting her strong affection for her father, her apparent lack of strong sexual attachment to any possible partner, and her inability or lack of desire to portray the more serious passions. One might wish to explore in greater detail the "artlessly passionate quality" of her attachments to women, including her long and deep friendship with Annie Fields. The most exquisite care would have to be taken with such efforts, and we must remember especially how much the contemporary women's movement has taught us all about accurate readings in the lives of women writers and in the history of social relations among women. As far as I can tell, however, no one has yet, half a century after *Sarah Orne Jewett* was published, undertaken this task.[24]

From another point of view, one would wish to ask what the Puritan tradition had to do with Jewett's reticence about sexuality and other passions and how such Victorian diffidence affected her psychological state as well as her perception of herself as a woman. That Matthiessen never dealt with these and similar issues is at least one indication of the critic's still undeveloped capacities in 1929.

The problem does not end with the Jewett book. From a number of possible sources, including his own feelings about his homosexuality and a kind of fastidiousness that would not otherwise be out of character, came a failure to examine the personal sexual lives of the artists about whom he was writing in all of his work, although one must note one signal exception, his brief comments about Whitman's homosexuality. For the most part, the lack is not important, because most of Matthiessen's books are not, as was *Sarah Orne Jewett*, literary biographies. Furthermore, it has been only fairly recently that criticism in general has been willing to face such issues squarely. Recent feminist criticism has played a role in this development, of course, as has especially Leon Edel's standard-setting biography of Henry James. This lack of attention to sexual matters becomes serious again most sharply in Matthiessen's last work—his other literary biography—his book about Theodore Dreiser. It is worth noting here, however, that in his books about Sarah Orne Jewett, Henry James, T. S. Eliot, and Dreiser, Matthiessen wrote about people whose literary works might have been further illuminated had he examined their sexual histories. That he did not do so, it seems to me, is a limitation in his critical method, and especially so in *Sarah Orne Jewett*, where the subject presents itself most dramatically and where it kept Matthiessen from exploring and properly focusing on the Maine writer's sentimentality.

I believe that another reason for the lack of acuity in *Sarah Orne Jewett* stems from the fact that Matthiessen did not measure Jewett's art against the achievements of tragedy. Perhaps that was the result of Matthiessen's relative youth at the time he wrote the book. Through profound reading in the European symbolists, in Melville and Hawthorne, but most especially in Eliot, and of course from his growing up and living, Matthiessen developed a sense of the power of tragedy in life and hence in literature, which was to become a most important criterion in his work. But in 1929, at twenty-seven, such a conception had apparently not yet come to Matthiessen. It was on its way. In a 1930 review of Newton Arvin's *Hawthorne*, Matthiessen wrote:

> the reason why Hawthorne, in spite of all his stiff self-consciousness and the flimsiness of his allegory, could suggest so hauntingly the dark recesses of their [Ethan Brand's, Rappacini's, and Chillingworth's] fate was that he knew it to be his own. He realized in his imagination that he had failed to meet life squarely, that that was the great failure of America. There seemed to be no alternative to a ruthless individualism which preyed upon itself until the individual was destroyed, no normal society but only a lifeless standardization which drove the sensitive man farther back into himself. Both Hawthorne's life and his work are fatally marked with the limitations of such a condition, but his enduring importance lies in the fact that, although one-sided himself, he had the strength not to accept what he knew to be false, and to embody in his quiet prose a searing criticism of what was, then as now, the dominant direction of American life.[25]

This is not yet the analysis of Hawthorne that was to become one of the graces of *American Renaissance*. It is, however, an analysis of American letters and of one of the major figures in American letters, which contrasts sharply with Matthiessen's uncritical acceptance of Jewett's untragic, sentimental, bittersweet donnée. But when Matthiessen wrote his book about Jewett he had not as yet grasped the central importance of the tragic vision, or at least he had not yet grasped it sufficiently to bring it to bear upon his subject's fiction.

His lack of awareness of the tragic or near-tragic content of American religious experience is related to Matthiessen's failure to discuss such experiences in *Sarah Orne Jewett*. Nowhere in that volume does he consider the religious life, feelings, or convictions either of the inhabitants of the South Berwick household or of the characters created in Jewett's books. He does not even comment on the rather striking absence of the church as a significant force in what, after all, he himself had described as a record of "the ordinary life in a Maine coast settlement of the last century." The critic who was to show us with such power how the influence of Puritanism and Unitarianism had shaped an Emerson, a Hawthorne, a Melville, seems simply to ignore any religious conviction or absence of such conviction on Jewett's part. This is hardly in keeping with his review of Norman Foerster's works, in which he called for an understanding of how religion and education had shaped American culture. Matthiessen himself was a devout Christian, although an unorthodox one, at the time he wrote the Jewett book. Why, then, no discussion of the Christianity of Jewett and its effect upon her artistic vision? Perhaps the figure in the "garden" to which Bowron points can be seen as an indication that Matthiessen had not yet put together a view of Christianity and of tragedy so as to constitute the postlapsarian Christian ethos, which was to become important in his later work.

Since Jewett cannot deal with tragedy and Matthiessen, although conscious of the fact, does not seem overly troubled by it, and since Matthiessen has not yet fully perceived the connections between the tragic and the Christian-socialist convictions he was to espouse later, he finds Jewett's private garden perhaps believable and certainly appealing. It was a garden without lust, sinful desire, and passion, and therefore without sin and tragedy.

In a piece of juvenilia, a 1922 lead editorial in the *Yale Literary Magazine*, Matthiessen expressed with fervor and devoutness the need for a search for meaning in the life of Yale students, a need to accept the importance of Christianity or of religion in general. "And living thus entirely on the surface," he wrote, "we have inevitably grown to think of a philosophy of life as hardly an essential. 'What need have I for all this truck about religion?' we ask frankly, for we have not yet been brought face to face with the Truth that in order to realize our highest possibilities we must be utterly dominated by an ideal."[26] Matthiessen was never to give up the notion that people need "a place to stand," that they must "believe in something," as he said in the same editorial. But he was to see, before too long, that it was not easy to "realize our highest possibilities." The Jewett garden, faint odor of rose leaves included, was acceptable to a young man who could express such an optimistic, nontragic view. The Matthiessen of 1929 had not yet outgrown the Yale student of 1922.

When Bowron says that Matthiessen was not yet sure what the past was for and locates in this uncertainty a cause for the sentimentality of *Jewett*, he points to a matter of importance. It is not true to say that Matthiessen completely ignores Miss Jewett's essential distortion-by-omission of the past:

> There is a stark New England Sarah Jewett does not show, sordid, bleak, and mean of spirit. She looked at nature in its milder moods, and at mankind in its more subdued states of tenderness and resignation. But she did not live in an unreal paradise. She was aware of all these aspects, she simply did not emphasize them. . . . Miss Jewett does not generally deal with the central facts of existence. You do not remember her characters as you do the atmosphere that seems to detach from their rusty corduroys and the folds of their gingham dresses. Her township was on the decline, and to her eyes it was a place where emotion was recollected in tranquility.[27]

This may be redolent of the sentimental Van Wyck Brooks, but it must be remembered that the young critic is writing simultaneously with or just after the appearance of Parrington's informing work, which was to make a sociological "search for the past" one of the loci of American criticism. There was hardly time, when *Sarah Orne Jewett* was being written in 1927 and 1928, for Matthiessen to have absorbed Howard Mumford Jones's "tingling sense of discovery" about such a politically aware criticism.

It is also true, I believe, that Matthiessen had not yet developed fully, at the time he wrote *Jewett*, the vision of America that was to result largely from his later experiences in and with the nation—after the crash, after the thirties, after World War II. In a memorial to a friend, the poet Phelps Putnam, Matthiessen describes his own feelings during the 1920s in this way:

Europe might feel its cultural stability broken by the recent vast destruction, and already menaced by further violence ahead, but its losses were still three thousand miles away from us. As Americans we had always been used to change, and at that moment we were bursting with a new sense of untried vitality, of an untold wealth of possibilities. This cocky awareness, as expressed by Putnam, with a reckless gusto even in its cynicism, seems far closer to the quality of the nineteen-twenties as I remember them than the mood of empty dis-illusion often attributed to them during the more socially conscious 'thirties.[28]

It is not only that Matthiessen did not know, at the time he wrote *Sarah Orne Jewett*, what the past was for, but that he did not yet know what the present was like. This seems to me crucial, for any view of the past, in literature certainly, as well as in histori-ography, is affected by one's view of the present, as T. S. Eliot has made clear. A Matthiessen who still saw America in the terms indicated above could not very well have seen how serious a flaw in Jewett's work it was to fail to deal adequately with the "sordid, bleak, and mean of spirit." It was the experience of the economic collapse of the 1930s, of the bread lines and apple sellers of prole-tarian literature, and of the brutality of the struggle to organize labor, which was to lay to rest, probably forever, such a "cocky awareness," such a sense of "untried vitality" about America. Little wonder, then, that for four chapters at least of *Sarah Orne Jewett* Matthiessen was prepared to tolerate, indeed to praise, those sentimental, gentle anachronisms that we find disconcert-ing. The America of the urban crisis, of the denatured spirit, of the loss of faith in possibilities, though increasingly present, was not to be fully realized in Matthiessen's work until his last book. Only in *Theodore Dreiser*, writing about that utterly urban figure whom he had cited in *Sarah Orne Jewett* merely as an example of a clumsy stylist, did Matthiessen come to grips fully with the city. And then, having written that work, having perhaps internalized a bleaker, albeit more realistic vision, Matthiessen could no longer live in the world that created it—and jumped to his death.

Bowron's description of the fifth chapter of *Sarah Orne Jewett* is quite accurate and to the point, then, and it indicates Matthiessen's awareness of a problem with the book:

> But in chapter five Matthiessen turns almost angrily against the logic of all four preceding chapters. He wrecks the unity of his book, but he redeems himself. Stepping outside the placid "grandmother's garden" of Miss Jewett's personal New England, Matthiessen awakens from his own spell and points out a number of hard truths. One imagines them to be directed less to his readers than to himself. He becomes sharply aware that the writers and critics who shared Miss Jewett's (and his own?) nostalgia were literary and social reactionaries, "pathetically smug and futile." Even the best of them, Howells, was a "narrow" realist, insisting that literature confine itself to the "smiling aspects." And as he takes a good second look at "the men whose thought composed the intellectual atmosphere that Sarah Jewett breathed," Matthiessen confesses that Sarah herself dwindles.[29]

But lacking even in this fifth chapter is full awareness of the elitist and—in its most literal sense—reactionary nature of Jewett's nostalgia for the Dunnet Township of farm and fisher folk, as opposed to the New England of workingmen and working women who came from abroad to upset it. Although the sensibilities of the later critic begin to emerge in the fifth chapter of *Sarah Orne Jewett*, even that chapter, as the rest of the book, is still dominated, one cannot help but feel, by the Yale man, trying hard to ignore his own differences from the rest of the "crowd." Giles Gunn makes the matter clearer when he writes: "With the world about her becoming more enthralled, and thereby depleted, through its bondage to the historically inevitable, Matthiessen tends to argue that Miss Jewett had little choice but to shut herself off from the turbulent world outside and to cultivate the garden of her own private but historically valuable sensibility. He quotes, with apparent approval, her least attractive statement regarding the necessity of this stratagem [concerning the building of more fences to assure increasing privacy]."[30] In this sense as well, then, the critic working in the late 1920s had not yet outgrown the Yale student of the early 1920s. The living experiences, the reading, the political action of the 1930s had not yet sufficiently honed away the less salutary aspects of the Yale experience, so that Matthiessen could recognize to the full the nature of Jewett's retrograde and elitist vision. Thus Matthiessen's book is first-rate criticism in its clarification of the contribution Jewett has made and something less than first-rate in its inability to see the worm of reaction and snobbery in the heart of her rose.

Bowron is indeed right when he says that Jewett's garden stands as the prime symbol for what Matthiessen has done with her work. But he is only partially right when he sees Matthiessen's view primarily as the result of sentimentality, as a self-indulgent retreat to the womb. In part, the failure here is the result of Matthiessen's personal life. Perhaps more important, Matthiessen is taken in by Miss Jewett's skill as a stylist and by her therefore evocative depiction of Maine village life half a century before her own time. Because he is not yet fully conscious of the nature of tragedy in life or letters or of the growing ineffectiveness of older American values, he accepts with only limited questioning Jewett's depiction of a life without these "central facts of existence." The small-town America of which Jewett wrote at a time when Frederic's *The Damnation of Theron Ware* and James's *What Maisie Knew* were being written, captured Matthiessen with its bittersweet nostalgia, with its superficial view of goodness and evil, cause and effect. In that sense, at least, Bowron is right when he says that *Sarah Orne Jewett* points "backward towards Van Wyck Brooks."

But the corrective, a form of the tragic and the antisentimental, aware of the less "smiling aspects" of American life, was not far off. Smelling of whale oil and not roses, Chicago dives rather than firs, it was to strike Matthiessen with full force both from his reading and from his life experience. Eliot and James, the figures of his *American Renaissance*, and in time, Dreiser, the Great Depression, and World War II—these would be Matthiessen's teachers.

3 ❧ The Unified Sensibility:
Eliot and James

MOST of the weaknesses of *Sarah Orne Jewett* are not to be found in Matthiessen's next major piece of criticism, one of the earliest American works of significance about the poetry and critical work of T. S. Eliot. Published in 1935 and reissued in two later editions, one of them posthumously, *The Achievement of T. S. Eliot* gives us a fine index to the mature Matthiessen's mind. The work is connected with a later work, *Henry James: The Major Phase*, except for *American Renaissance* probably Matthiessen's best-known book and originally conceived in response to an invitation to give the Alexander Lectures at Toronto. The most significant similarities between the two volumes have to do with their purposes and with the methodology they employ in achieving those purposes.

It is as arguments for a particular view, albeit polite arguments, that both works can be seen. The Matthiessen who produced the gentle and accepting biography of Jewett had, by 1935, developed a critical position that he was never to abandon and that he was to amplify and extend throughout his life. The loci of that position may be indicated by the two epigraphs Matthiessen attached to the book on Eliot.

> What does the mind enjoy in books? Either the style or nothing. But, someone says, what about the thought? The thought, that is the style, too.
>
> Charles Maurras

> We begin to live when we have conceived life as tragedy.
> W. B. Yeats[1]

Style as an integral aspect of content, then, and an essentially tragic view of life, the two conceptions absent from the Jewett book, make *The Achievement of T. S. Eliot* a major work of criticism. Subtitled *An Essay on the Nature of Poetry*, the book is more than a study of T. S. Eliot; it is also, given some of the critical modes of the time in which it was written, an argument for a critical point of view. Matthiessen's introduction to the first edition makes quite clear what the target of his polemic is:

My double aim[2] in this essay is to evaluate Eliot's method and achievement as an artist, and in so doing to emphasize certain of the fundamental elements in the nature of poetry which are in danger of being obscured by the increasing tendency to treat poetry as a social document and to forget that it is an art. The most widespread error in contemporary criticism is to neglect form and to concern itself entirely with content. The romantic critic is generally not interested in the poet's work, but in finding the man behind it. The humanistic critic and the sociological critic have in common that both tend to ignore the evaluation of specific poems in their preoccupation with the ideological background from which the poem springs. All these concerns can have value in expert hands, but only if it is realized that they are not criticism of poetry. In combating the common error, my contention is that, although in the last analysis form and content are inseparable, a poem can be neither enjoyed nor understood unless the reader experiences all of its formal details, unless he allows the movement and the pattern of its words to exercise their full charm over him before he attempts to say precisely what it is that the poem means. The most fatal approach to a poem is to focus merely on what it seems to state, to try to isolate its ideas from their context in order to approve or disapprove of them before having really grasped their implications in the poem itself. Consequently, my approach to Eliot's poetry, and to poetry in general, is through close attention to its technique. I agree . . . with the assertion that what matters is not what a poem says, but what it *is*. That does not mean either the poem or the poet can be separated from the society that produced them, or that a work of art does not inevitably both reflect and illuminate its age. Nor does it imply that a poet is necessarily lacking in ideas, or that the content of his work . . . is without cardinal significance in determining his relation to life and to the currents of thought in his time. But even that significance is obscured, if not distorted, by the criticism that pays heed solely to the poet's ideas and not to their expression, that turns the poet into a philosopher or a political theorist or a pamphleteer, that treats his work as a specimen of sociological evidence, and meanwhile neglects the one quality that gives his words their permanence, his quality as an artist.[3]

The argument here is quite clearly directed against a whole host of critics who, if not dominant, were certainly important in American criticism at the time Matthiessen wrote *The Achievement of T. S. Eliot*. If *Sarah Orne Jewett* had been written too soon after Parrington's *Main Currents*, then *The Achievement of T. S. Eliot* was written with full awareness of Parringtonian criticism and of a rising American Marxist criticism of the simplistic kind to which Matthiessen is reacting. Add to this the still powerful current of humanist criticism and the very palpable presence of Van Wyck Brooks, and one finds the three aspects of the American criticism of his time against which Matthiessen is arguing.

When he writes his book about Henry James, as his "overage contribution to the war effort,"[4] in 1944, he is still fighting the same battle, although in somewhat less sweeping terms. After a discussion of some critical views concerning James that he considers useful, Matthiessen turns to the position he is opposing in this volume.

Yet the view of the wider public is still quite other. It is the view that—so far as American readers of history and literature are concerned—has been conditioned by Van Wyck Brooks and Parrington. Brooks' thesis, developed in *The Pilgrimage of Henry James* (1925), and not materially altered in his later evocations, is a very simple one. James was a writer of vivid and original talent who made the fatal mistake of becoming an expatriate, who thus cut himself off from the primary sources of his material, and whose works thereby lost freshness and declined until they became at last hardly more than the frustrated gestures of "an habitually embarrassed man." Parrington devoted two pages to "Henry James and The Nostalgia of

Culture." This was one of his least happy efforts to satisfy
the demands of his publisher by making his magnificent
account of the evolution of our liberal thought seem more inclusive than it really was, a general "interpretation of American
literature." Far more solidly influential than Brooks' impressionism, Parrington's work has been the cornerstone for subsequent interpretations of our intellectual history. But in the
case of James, Parrington did little more than follow Brooks'
lead in deploring the novelist's deracination and cosmopoli-
tanism. He granted some importance to his "absorption in the
stream of psychical experience," but concluded with a sentence
that reveals how far off base he was in his demands from the
novelist: "Yet how unlike he is to Sherwood Anderson, an
authentic product of the American consciousness!"

Such a sentence is eloquent evidence of what happens when
you divorce the study of content from form. Even more
startling conclusions can be reached when, like the later
Brooks, you neglect form and content alike, when you merely
allude to books instead of discussing and analyzing them,
and reduce literary history to a pastiche of paragraphs culled
from memoirs. It is my conviction that *The Wings of the Dove*
searches as deeply into the American consciousness as *Wines-
burg, Ohio*. But in order to appreciate either book, you must
be equally concerned with what is being said and with the
how and why of its saying. The separation between form and
content simply does not exist as the mature artist contemplates
his finished work. That separation is a dangerous short-cut
taken by critics, and its disasters are written large over the
history of James' reputation.[5]

Indicative of the man Matthiessen was, of his uncompromising
dedication to his positions, is that among the primary targets of
both of these literary stances are critics and political figures who
were likely to be his closest political allies, while on the other
hand, Eliot, at least, stood at quite opposite political poles from
him. By the time he wrote *The Achievement of T. S. Eliot*, Matthiessen's socialist convictions had matured and had become a
central part of his consciousness. This was especially so under

the impact of the depression and of the drive by the Congress of Industrial Organizations (CIO) to organize unskilled workers. He writes:

In '32, with the depression at its worst, I thought that here at last was a chance for the Socialists to regain the broad base they had developed under Debs, and I joined the party. Roosevelt's speeches during that campaign struck me as little more than the promises of a Harvard man who wanted very much to be President, and I had not gauged the sweep of middle and lower-middle class reaction against Hooverism that turned the rascals out. Roosevelt in office was something quite other than I had foreseen, and after he began to effect even some of the things for which Thomas had stood, I voted for him enthusiastically, though always from the left, until his death. . . . By 1935 Alan and Paul Sweezy, Bob Lamb . . . and a couple of dozen more of us at Harvard had responded to the spirit of the time to the extent of organizing a local of the Teachers Union at Harvard. We thereby joined the AFL. . . .

The nineteen-thirties now appear in retrospect as a period when a considerable number of intellectuals commuted to radicalism and back. It was a time when writers, shaken by the depression, became Communists overnight, in a way that I always found difficult to follow. . . . Whatever objective reasons compelled towards socialism in the nineteen-thirties seem even more compelling now, and it is the responsibility of the intellectual to rediscover and rearticulate that fact.[6]

I have discussed Matthiessen's politics earlier, but this passage will indicate with what fervor and obvious devotion Matthiessen was, by 1935 and throughout the remainder of his life, a staunch adherent of the views of the left. Had Matthiessen been a doctrinaire adherent of such left-wing views, had he permitted his literary views to be submerged and influenced by what he considered to be the "correct" politics of those of his contemporaries whom he found politically congenial and who were often Marxists, he would certainly have taken his stand with the left of the *New Masses*, with Michael Gold, with Calverton, with Hicks, or with non-Communist Marxists and, in related though different terms, with Parrington. Despite his political agreement with these figures, they were among the major targets of the Henry James and T. S. Eliot volumes.

But these figures on the left were not his only targets, for Matthiessen saw, as the introduction to *The Achievement of T. S. Eliot* shows, a kinship between the political left and the political right in regard to their critical postures. He saw that, in each case, the critic was primarily concerned with the views of the work's creator or with the "message" one might extrapolate from the work.

He is contending, then, for a central notion of the New Criticism, or at least for that aspect of it which insists that what the critic must do is to look at the work of art in all of its technical, language-based ramifications. The critic must consider first of all "the semantic approach to poetry as a species of language," as it was to be described by Ronald S. Crane.[7] What Matthiessen is objecting to is any notion that considers the work of art purely, or primarily, as social, cultural, or biographical document. But one must hasten to look at the other side of the coin, or, perhaps a better figure, the remainder of the coin's design, in that, entwined in the engraving is also the coin's value, its denomination. Matthiessen considers the style, the manner of the work, integral to, part and parcel of, its function, and insists on a holistic judgment and understanding of the work.

In a 1934 article devoted to Granville Hicks's *The Great Tradition*, Matthiessen makes quite clear what his quarrel with Marxist criticism or with any other purely sociological approach to literature, is all about. He respects Hicks's work because he feels it is scholarly and because the "sharp conclusiveness of Mr. Hicks' book makes it the challenge which criticism should be."[8] But Matthiessen's article is called "A Counterstatement" and his most telling counter follows quickly:

> The omission [of Mark Twain, Henry James, and Emily Dickinson from the "great tradition"] is deliberate, and clearly defines the limits of Mr. Hicks' conception of the nature of literature. For him literature is inevitably a form of action; and it has been one of the great services of Marxian criticism that

it has brought to the fore the principle that "art not only expresses something, but also does something." There are, however, various ways of defining what it does. There is, for instance, the form of action expressed by the political pamphlet, of which the writings of Thomas Paine are still our most effective example; and this is kindred to the form of action in the problem novel which focuses its whole attention on presenting the consequences of specific wrongs, and by the very strength of its recreation of them serves as a weapon in their destruction. But if art is to be adequately described as a form of action, it must be realized that action cannot mean simply the immediate righting of wrongs. The greatest art performs its most characteristic action in more subtle ways; it "does something" in the novels of Fielding or Proust, by bringing its reader a new understanding or a fresh insight into the full meaning of existence. It thus acts on life by giving it release and fulfillment.[9]

Matthiessen understands that literature not only *is* something but that it *does* something and that, as many Marxists have said, culture can be a "weapon." But *how* is it such a weapon, by what mode can it be useful in changing the way men and women can live? The poet's function, Matthiessen maintains, is quite different from that of the political orator or pamphleteer: "the lyric poet is at the vanguard of his time not in the same way as the political orator; that is not the poet's main function, though one he may sometimes fulfill incidentally, to define and proclaim a new program of action; but rather to give the most accurate account he can of the particular quality of life as he has discovered it to be by means of his mind and senses. The poet is thus, in F. R. Leavis' phrase, 'at the most conscious point of the race in his time,' in direct proportion to the extent to which he makes articulate what his contemporaries feel."[10]

That this matter was still a source of concern for Matthiessen in 1944 is made evident by a portion of his preface to a volume published in the same year as *Henry James: The Major Phase*. Matthiessen had collected James's short stories about writers and artists and had published them in one volume. In commenting, in the introduction, on James's views concerning the function of the arts, he quotes a famous Wells-James exchange of letters. Wells had attacked James, had received a letter from James concerning that attack, and had replied to that letter by drawing a distinction between what he considered James's approach to literature and his own: "To you," Matthiessen quotes Wells's words, "literature like painting is an end, to me literature like architecture is a means, it has a use." Matthiessen approvingly quotes James's reply: "there is no sense in which architecture is aesthetically 'for use' that doesn't leave any other art whatever exactly as much so. . . . It is art that *makes* life, makes interest, makes importance . . . and I know of no substitute whatever for the force and beauty of its process."[11]

Matthiessen is using James's words here to reiterate the distinction he had made in his counterstatement to Hicks. Art is indeed *for* something, it does *do* something, he maintains, but what it does is related to its own, its life-giving functions, and only incidentally to its service to anything else.

Matthiessen is echoing one of Eliot's most important critical principles in taking this position, one that, however, Eliot himself was to change considerably through the years. In a 1923 essay Eliot had said in one of his most famous dicta: "I do not deny that art may be affirmed to serve ends beyond itself; but art is not required to be aware of these ends, and indeed performs its function, whatever that may be, according to various theories of value, much better by indifference to them. . . . I have assumed as axiomatic that a creation, a work of art, is autotelic."[12] Although Eliot modified this position as he became more and more royalist and Anglican,[13] Matthiessen entirely concurs with it as Eliot originally described it.

But it is not only the Marxists and those close to Marxism whom Matthiessen has in mind with this caveat. His 1936 review of Van Wyck Brooks's *The Flowering of New England*, while on the whole kindly and desirous of paying proper respect to the man who "has made his role in the revival of American literature since 1912 something akin to that of Channing's a century before,"[14] nevertheless devastates, in sentence after sentence, Brooks's criticism, which "has always been extremely personal in the bias of its emotional intensity."[15] A few samples of Matthiessen's critique will make the point clear: "But as the evocative chapters cumulate, often with only oblique mention of the works which these writers were producing, one begins to wonder exactly what Mr. Brooks implies in stating that his subject is 'the New England mind.'" Or again: "when one turns to his treatment of the few major artists, one is forced to ask what Mr. Brooks conceived to be the scope of literary history. He devotes almost fifty pages to Thoreau. . . . But in all this space there is literally no analysis of *The Week* or of *Walden* as works of art."[16] It is Brooks, then, who is the "romantic critic . . . not interested in the poet's work, but in finding the man behind it," mentioned in the preface to *The Achievement of T. S. Eliot*.

That Matthiessen held to the same view at the time he was writing *Henry James: The Major Phase* some nine years later can be seen from his 1944 review of Brooks's *The World of Washington Irving*. If anything, he has deepened his opposition to a methodology like Brooks's, as the much sharper tone of his review indicates in part because Brooks's tendency toward the sentimental had become dominant. "The method is easy to describe," Matthiessen says, "since it follows the formula that Mr. Brooks developed for his New England series. He proceeds, not by analyzing the writers' works or ideas, but by biographical sketches."[17] Near the end of the essay, Matthiessen suggests that "Brooks' feelings have little to do with the proper function of the historian or critic. Neither his earlier dejected image of our past nor his present glowing one is anything like an objective interpretation of the complex and warring forces that make up human life at any period. Brooks is not really a critic but a lyric poet *manqué*, who endows selected aspects of our history with the overtones of his own sensibility."[18] Thus two of the targets of Matthiessen's polemic are clear: one of these is the group of content-oriented critics that includes Marxists and Parringtonians who share to some degree a common methodology; the other is the group of "romantic" critics, like Brooks, who put their emphasis on the writer rather than on the work of art.

There was a third target. Although the heyday of the humanists had been the 1920s, the peak period of the work of Babbitt and

More, the early Sherman and others, Matthiessen found the humanists still influential and thus important enough to include in the preface to *The Achievement of T. S. Eliot*. It is not surprising that he did so when one considers that one of his teachers was Irving Babbitt. He says of him: "By far the most living experience in my graduate study at Harvard came through the lectures of Irving Babbitt, with whose neo-humanistic attack upon the modern world I disagreed at nearly every point. The vigor with which he objected to almost every author since the eighteenth century forced me to fight for my tastes, which grew stronger by the exercise."[19]

But it is not only a continuation of that struggle that makes the humanists another of Matthiessen's targets. In the opening pages of *The Achievement of T. S. Eliot* he points to the similarity of approach, though certainly from different vantage points, which the humanists share with Brooks and, to a lesser extent, with the Marxists. "In America, Irving Babbitt, also indebted to Arnold (more, perhaps, than he recognized), was concerned with the relation of the artist's thought to society, but not at all with the nature of art."[20] This is precisely the same criticism—concern with the writer's biography rather than with the work—that Matthiessen had made of Brooks. In a footnote he expands the point: "I have cited only the outstanding figure. Paul Elmer More expounded the same general doctrine as Babbitt, with greater distinction as a stylist, but with less challenging vigor."[21]

The independent nature of the work of art is still a crucial concept to Matthiessen in 1944, as, once again, the introduction to *Stories of Writers and Artists* shows. In discussing James's story, "The Figure in the Carpet," Matthiessen points to the title as a critical phrase used by Gide and Eliot, and then says: "The impulse behind the phrase has quickened our awareness that the task of the critic today, *after a century of historical accretion*, is to see the artist's work not piecemeal, but in its *significant entirety*, to find his compelling portrait *in his works*."[22] It is clear, then, that Matthiessen's concern with a defense of the autotelic nature of art, to use Eliot's term, against humanist, Marxist, or romantic criticism, is an abiding one. The Maurras epigraph from *The Achievement of T. S. Eliot* is a decisive aspect of Matthiessen's critical credo.

But what of the epigraph from Yeats? What of the role of tragedy in that credo? It must first be said that the very choice of subjects— T. S. Eliot and Henry James—indicates a change from *Sarah Orne Jewett*, or at least a new emphasis in Matthiessen's work. What is most characteristic of Jewett's work, that which in the previous chapter I have described as the "garden," is Jewett's essentially rural orientation. Her Maine has little or nothing to do even with such relatively small cities as Portland or Bangor. It is exclusively concerned with Dulham and with Berwick, with Dunnet Township. But Eliot, on the other hand, especially before 1935, is almost exclusively the poet of London and the Continent, perhaps inspired by St. Louis or Boston. When he takes his sensibility into the countryside, on a few rare occasions, it is to explore through the eyes of a city man the landscapes of New Hampshire, of Virginia, or of Cape Ann. And James, of course, is above all the writer of Boston and New York, Paris, London, and Rome, whose characters move into the country only rarely, and then do so, like Strether and like Chad Newsome and Mme. de Vionnet in the famous recognition scene, as city people out for a brief excursion. In dealing with artists of such urban orientation, it is much more difficult to indulge in the very American, "garden" variety of sentimentality that so mars Jewett's own work and Matthiessen's critique of it.

Furthermore, in part because of her rural orientation, Jewett is occupied with the past, not with her own present, the present of the "electric cars," and she seeks no inspiration from that present. Eliot's "The Waste Land," on the other hand, is a purely contemporary one, though informed by the past, just as his "The Hollow Men" reflects his vision of the creatures of his own 1920s. James's milieu is essentially that of his own fin de siècle era and not of an earlier period about which one may so easily become sentimental. It is thus clear, even from his choice of subjects, that Matthiessen has left the nostalgic and the sentimental far behind in favor of these much harder, urban, contemporary themes, which, at the very least, tend to offset any tendencies toward sentimentality if only because it is much harder to become maudlin about one's own, present troubles than someone else's past ones.

This choice, however, provides only the beginning of the tragic orientation that the Yeats epigraph implies. It is apparent that, sometime after writing the book about Jewett, Matthiessen seems to have come to grips with the notion of tragedy in all its profundity. An article about Sarah Orne Jewett published in 1931 indicates his new awareness quite clearly, for there he says what he had failed to say in his book: "Sarah Jewett did not have a sense of tragedy, a limitation which defines her sphere. The daughter of a country doctor was well aware of the stark elements of human nature, but in her temperament these were subordinated to tender pathos and humor."[23]

What did Matthiessen mean by tragedy? No better answer can be provided than an examination of his discussion of the nature of tragedy in *The Achievement of T. S. Eliot*. He cites Eliot's discussion of Baudelaire's ability to see through Victor Hugo's optimism as an example of the artist's ability to achieve "a real perception of good and evil." Matthiessen then points out that, in *After Strange Gods*, Eliot defined such a perception as "'the first requisite of spiritual life.'" "[It] is very close to Yeats's mature discovery," the passage continues,

that we begin to live only "when we have conceived life as tragedy." For both Yeats and Eliot recognize that there can be no significance to life, and hence no tragedy in the account of man's conflicts and his inevitable final defeat by death, unless it is fully realized that there is no such thing as good unless there is also evil, or evil unless there is good; that until this double nature of life is understood by a man, he is doomed to waver between a groundless optimistic hopefulness and an equally chaotic, pointless despair. Eliot has learned from his own experience that the distinguishing feature of a human life consists in the occasions on which the individual most fully reveals his character, and that those are the moments of intense "moral and spiritual struggle." It is in such moments, rather than in the "bewildering minutes" of passion "in which we are all very much alike, that men and women come nearest to being real"—an affirmation which again underscores his inheritance of the central element in the Puritan tradition.

And he has concluded that "if you do away with this struggle, and maintain that by tolerance, benevolence, inoffensiveness, and a redistribution or increase of purchasing power, combined with a devotion, on the part of an elite, to Art, the world will be as good as anyone could require, then you must expect human beings to become more and more vaporous."

It is their penetration to the heart of this struggle between the mixed good and evil in man's very being, and thus to the central factors in human nature, which forms a common element between the three strains of poetry that have affected Eliot most deeply, between such writers as Dante, Webster, and Baudelaire.[24]

His application of the notion of tragedy to Henry James's work, in the 1944 volume, indicates how important this idea had become for Matthiessen. Matthiessen certainly admires James, no doubt a good deal more than he does Sarah Orne Jewett, but he is fully aware of James's relationship to tragedy. He notes it as a weakness, as well as, in its own way, one of James's peculiar strengths, in his discussion of *The Wings of the Dove*:

> It is revelatory of James that . . . he again uses an image from the French Revolution, this time an image entirely aristo-cratic in its associations. That will mark for many readers how far James was from being capable of projecting a real American tragedy of his own time. But the controlling facts of tragedy are neither time nor place, but the urgency with which we are made to feel life and death. James has reduced his ore to the last possible refinement, but what is left is the purest metal. It is not merely the "vague golden air" of Susan's enchantment; it is rather, as in Donne's image,
>
> like golde to airy thinnesse beate, . . .
>
> There is much more of pity than of terror in Milly's con-fronting of fate. Her passive suffering is fitting for the deuter-agonist rather than for the protagonist of a major tragedy, for a Desdemona, not for an Othello. But if James has shown again that the chords he could strike were minor, were those of

renunciation, of resignation, of inner triumph in the face of outer defeat, he was not out of keeping with the spiritual history of his American epoch. Art often expresses society very obliquely, and it is notable that the most sensitive recorders of James' generation gave voice to themes akin to his.[25]

It is clear, from this passage, how much Matthiessen's perception of tragedy had affected and changed his critical views since he had written *Sarah Orne Jewett*. There is no doubt that had he applied then the strictures he applies here to James, he would have written a far more profound work, one not marred by the sentimentality of the earlier volume.

Matthiessen, then, uses the poet's ability to perceive tragedy in life as a central concept in making a value judgment concerning the artist's work. How this separates him sharply from American Marxist, Humanist or Romantic critics will become clear if we examine the criteria he establishes, in this regard, for Eliot's poetry. Answering objections to Eliot's "narrowness"—the kind of objection every teacher has heard in the classroom when students are troubled by the "gloomy" view of so many of the writers they confront in literature courses—Matthiessen says: "Most of the force of that objection is lost, I believe, when it is understood that he [Eliot] is not thus characterizing the present as distinct from the past, but is probing the implications of certain tragic elements inherent in the very nature of life."[26] Matthiessen goes on to separate those writers with a sense of tragedy from the "lost generation" writers by contrasting the former (in what I find a surprising bit of critical blindness on his part) with the "powerful but narrowly dated" stories of Ernest Hemingway. Nevertheless, the general principle he endeavors to propound is highly significant:

There is a great difference between an understanding that tragedy is at the heart of life, and an adolescent self-pitying of one's own generation as being especially unfortunate. The anarchy and futility of war inevitably heighten the sense of horror in existence; but for this sense to have significance, it must be part of a total vision of the meaning of life.

The value of the tragic writer has always lain in the uncompromising honesty with which he has cut through appearances to face the real conditions of man's lot, in his refusal to be deceived by an easy answer, in the unflinching, if agonized expression of what he knows to be true. The effect of such integrity is not to oppress the reader with a sense of burdens too great to be borne, but to bring him some release. For, if it is part of the function of every great artist to transform his age, the tragic writer does so not by delivering an abstract idealization of life, but by giving to the people who live in the age a full reading of its weakness and horror; yet, concurrently, by revealing some enduring potentiality of good to be embraced with courage and with an ecstatic sense of its transfiguring glory. Through the completeness of his portrayal of the almost insupportable conditions of human existence, he frees his audience from the oppression of fear; and stirring them to new heart by his presentation of an heroic struggle against odds, he also enables them to conceive anew the means of sustaining and improving their own lives. Only thus can he communicate both "the horror" and "the glory."[27]

This is indeed an extended definition of tragedy, one that Matthiessen applies not only to the drama but to any sort of imaginative literature. Matthiessen's thought is obviously based, in part, on the classical Aristotelian definition of tragedy, especially on those aspects concerned with the evocation of fear and the eventual purgation that results. It is also, one can surmise, derived from Matthiessen's lifelong interest in Elizabethan drama, especially in Shakespearean tragedy. One must also see it, however, as a postlapsarian Christian view of man, if for no other reason than Matthiessen's need to assert his own Christianity. I have already pointed out that Matthiessen was not a Marxist and that he found it problematic to be both a Christian and a radical, since his Christianity made him reject Marxism. The specifics of this rejection, however, are important to an understanding of Matthiessen's views concerning tragedy. In *From The Heart of Europe* he writes:

I am a Christian, not through upbringing but by conviction, and I find any materialism inadequate. I make no pretense of being a theologian, but I have been influenced by the same Protestant revival that has been voiced most forcefully in America by Reinhold Niebuhr. That is to say, I have rejected the nineteenth-century belief in every man as his own Messiah, along with other aberrations of the century's individualism; and I have accepted the doctrine of original sin, in the sense that man is fallible and limited, no matter what his social system, and is capable of finding completion only through humility before the love of God.

Such doctrines have often been pronounced meaningless by my radical friends; and I, in turn, have felt a shallowness in their psychology whenever they have talked as though man was perfectible, with evil wholly external to his nature, and caused only by the frustrations of the capitalist system. Shakespeare and Melville are witness enough that man is both good and evil.

But I would differ from most orthodox Christians today, and particularly from the tradition represented by T. S. Eliot, in that, whatever the imperfections of man, the second of the two great commandments, to love thy neighbor as thyself, seems to me an imperative to social action. Evil is not merely external, but external evils are many, and some social systems are far more productive of them than others. Thus my philosophical position is of the simplest. It is as a Christian that I find my strongest propulsion to being a socialist.[28]

There is a difficult problem here. How does one reconcile views of life and letters as disparate as Christianity, socialism, and the "tragic"? Matthiessen extends his definition of tragedy in *American Renaissance*, when he feels it necessary to discuss tragedy at the very outset of his consideration of Hawthorne:

The creation of tragedy demands of its author a mature understanding of the relation of the individual to society, and, more especially, of the nature of good and evil. He must have a coherent grasp of social forces, or, at least, of man as a social being; otherwise he will possess no frame of reference within which to make actual his dramatic conflicts. For the hero of tragedy is never merely an individual, he is a man in action, in

conflict with other individuals in a definite social order. . . .
And unless the author also has a profound comprehension
of the mixed nature of life, of the fact that even the most perfect
man cannot be wholly good, any conflicts that he creates will
not give the illusion of human reality. Tragedy does not pose
the situation of a faultless individual (or class) overwhelmed by
an evil world, for it is built on the experienced realization
that man is radically imperfect. Confronting this fact, tragedy
must likewise contain a recognition that man, pitiful as he may
be in his finite weakness, is still capable of apprehending
perfection, and of becoming transfigured by that vision. But
not only must the author of tragedy have accepted the inevitable co-existence of good and evil in man's nature, he
must also possess the power to envisage some reconciliation
between such opposites, and the control to hold an inexorable
balance. He must be as far from the chaos of despair as he
is from ill-founded optimism.[29]

The conflict here between more inexorable views of tragedy
and the one he expresses is not Matthiessen's alone. The discussion by such critics as Francis Fergusson and Louis L. Martz
concerning T. S. Eliot's attempt to make of *Murder in the Cathedral*
a Christian tragedy is a case in point. Furthermore, the problem
is larger than that of Christian tragedy. It involves any tragic protagonist whose destiny is directed by a predetermining, salvation-
promising force and whose response to that destiny is equally
directed by the same force. For our purposes, such a protagonist
might occur in any drama that sees the forces of history as determining direction. If Aeschylus's *Prometheus Bound* is tragic, it is
not so because we, or for that matter Aeschylus's audience, have
any doubt as to the outcome of the play. The tragedy is inherent
in how the protagonist will respond to the inevitability of the
outcome, an outcome that is not based on any a priori notion of
justice.

A number of writers have commented on the issues of "reconciliation" and the "inexorable balance" between various forces in
tragedy. One of the most interesting of these is the French Marxist, Lucien Goldmann, whose ideas are especially germane to a

discussion of Matthiessen's effort to come to terms with tragedy. Goldmann's brilliant *The Hidden God*, concerning Racine, Pascal, and Jansenism deals with thinkers who faced a dilemma similar to that facing Matthiessen, that is, how to reconcile God-centered and tragedy-centered views of human life when both the existence of God and the tragic condition seem to be the givens of experience. Goldmann, who considers that "authentic tragedy . . . makes its first appearance with the work of Sophocles," contrasts that work with Aeschylean tragedy. In Aeschylus, he points out, matters are eventually resolved, though the playwright "needs a whole trilogy in order to re-establish the balance which has been disturbed by the hubris of both Gods and men."[30] In Sophocles, however, there is no such balance. Goldmann writes:

> In my view, the basic meaning of his work is to be found in the expression which it gives of the unbridgable gulf which now separates man—or, more accurately, certain privileged and exceptional men—from the human and divine world. Ajax and Philoctetes, Oedipus, Creon and Antigone all express and illustrate the same truth: the world has become dark and mysterious, the Gods no longer exist side by side with men in the same cosmic totality, and are no longer subject to the same rule of fate or the same demands of balance and moderation. They have cut themselves off from man and taken it upon themselves to rule over him; they speak in deceitful terms and from afar off, the oracles which he consults have two meanings, one apparent but false, the other hidden but true, the demands which the Gods made are contradictory, and the world is ambiguous and equivocal. It is an unbearable world where man is forced to live in error and illusion, and where only those whom a physical infirmity cuts off from normal life can stand the truth when it is revealed to them: the fact that both Tiresias, who knows the will of the Gods and the future of man, and Oedipus, who discovers the truth about himself at the end of the tragedy, are both blind is symbolic of this. . . . For the others—Ajax, Creon, Antigone—their discovery of the truth does nothing but condemn them to death.[31]

Such a tragedy is not to be easily realized, given either a Christian or a social-determinist view. If human beings can be saved by submitting to God's will, or, if human beings can become "good" because they understand a stream in history in accordance with which they act, then full tragedy in the Sophoclean sense becomes impossible. Susan Sontag has discussed the matter cogently, in a generally favorable review of Lionel Abel's book, *Metatheatre: A New View of Dramatic Form*:

> . . . Abel considerably oversimplifies, and I think indeed misrepresents, the vision of the world which is necessary for the writing of tragedies. He says: "One cannot create tragedy without accepting some implacable values as true. Now the Western imagination has, on the whole, been liberal and skeptical; it has tended to regard *all* implacable values as false." This statement seems to me wrong and, where it is not wrong, superficial. . . . What are the implacable values of Homer? Honor, status, personal courage—the values of an aristocratic military class? But this is not what the *Iliad* is about. It would be more correct to say, as Simone Weil does [in *The Iliad or the Poem of Force*], that the *Iliad*—as pure an example of the tragic vision as one can find—is about the emptiness and arbitrariness of the world, the ultimate meaninglessness of all moral values, and the terrifying rule of death and inhuman force. If the fate of Oedipus was represented and experienced as tragic, it is not because he, or his audience, believed in "implacable values," but precisely because a crisis had overtaken those values. It is not the implacability of "values" which is demonstrated by tragedy, but the implacability of the world. . . . Tragedy is a vision of nihilism, a heroic or enobling vision of nihilism. . . .

As everyone knows, there was no Christian tragedy, strictly speaking, because the content of Christian values—for it is a question of what values, however implacably held; not any will do—is inimical to the pessimistic vision of tragedy. . . . In the world envisaged by Judaism and Christianity, there are no free-standing arbitrary events. All events are part of the plan of a just, good, providential deity; every crucifixion must be topped by a resurrection. Every disaster or calamity must be seen as either leading to a greater good or else as just and adequate punishment fully merited by the sufferer. This moral adequacy of the world asserted by Christianity is precisely what tragedy denies. Tragedy says there are disasters which are not fully merited, that there is ultimate injustice in the world.[32]

The point is well made. If *Murder in the Cathedral* fails as tragedy, it fails largely because Becket's basic values are never in question. His is no nihilistic universe in which he must make his own values or accept the fact that there are none. Although the world may be temporarily disarrayed, it is *not* a world, in Goldmann's terms, which is "unbearable." Unlike the Greek's warring godly factions, which make decisions on arbitrary and capricious grounds, the Christian god is a constant value in Becket's drama. In the same way, Marxist conceptions of human beings and of history, at least until fairly recently, are constants, and the victory of the revolution is certain. In American literature we can look to Odets's or John Howard Lawson's drama of the 1930s for verification of this notion, and even such a master of literature as Malraux posits the victory of the revolution and the righteousness of its cause as the certainties that permit Kyo and especially Katov in *Man's Fate* to die horribly—but victoriously—assured that justice will prevail. Thus most Christian and most socialist ideologies assume the existence of some known good, some ultimate justice in the world, which makes the fate of believing protagonists "bearable" and which provides for a world that is precisely not "ambiguous" and not "equivocal." The problem for Matthiessen and others, as Christians or as socialists, is how to account for the greatness of tragedy, tragedy that they see as providing for an "inexorable balance," in light of tragedies that deny such balance.

There are several ways in which attempts have been made to resolve the problem. One way assumes that somehow, within the framework of a world both good and bad, it is possible to arrive at a "satisfying" ending, or, as Matthiessen says, to forge a "reconciliation between such opposites." That is also Arthur

Miller's solution, as he explains in his famous essay, "Tragedy and the Common Man":

> There is a misconception of tragedy with which I have been struck in review after review, and in many conversations with writers and readers alike. It is the idea that tragedy is of necessity allied to pessimism. Even the dictionary says nothing more about the word than that it means a story with a sad or unhappy ending. This impression is so firmly fixed that I almost hesitate to claim that in truth tragedy implies more optimism in its author than does comedy, and that its final result ought to be the reinforcement of the onlooker's brightest opinions of the human animal.
>
> For, if it is true to say that in essence the tragic hero is intent upon claiming his whole due as a personality, and if this struggle must be total and without reservation, then it automatically demonstrates the indestructible will of man to achieve his humanity.
>
> The possibility of victory must be there in tragedy. Where pathos rules, where pathos is finally derived, a character has fought a battle he could not possibly have won. The pathetic is achieved when the protagonist is, by virtue of his witlessness, his insensitivity or the very air he gives off, incapable of grappling with a much superior force.
>
> Pathos truly is the mode for the pessimist. But tragedy requires a nicer balance between what is possible and what is impossible. And it is curious, although edifying, that the plays we revere, century after century, are the tragedies. In them, and in them alone, lies the belief—optimistic, if you will, in the perfectibility of man.[33]

That is one aspect of Matthiessen's approach to tragedy. When he says that man "is capable of finding completion only through humility before the love of God," he attempts to indicate how the victory in tragedy that Miller calls for is possible.

The difficulty is, however, that if such a possibility exists, then the inability of the individual to realize that fact is tragic. If all human beings know that they can find completion by being humble before God, then their failure to act on that knowledge stems either from an inability to overcome their pride or from their stupidity, folly, or weakness. Those failures make them something quite different from a tragic protagonist such as Oedipus who, after all, has no means of escaping from his dilemma. The Theban king must either doom Thebes or doom himself. There is no way, given the fate decreed for him, by which Oedipus can find fulfillment. By such a device, then, Matthiessen makes tragedy have a somewhat different meaning than it had for the Greeks or than it has for others who theorize about tragedy.

Some theorists pose another kind of solution, one that they believe will retain the tragic mode while it provides a set of moral values acceptable to them, but still compatible with tragedy. We can logically assume that the tragic lies in the inability of human beings to achieve that which they know to be necessary, despite a valiant struggle to do so. It is toward such a resolution of the problem that Matthiessen points by his reference to Reinhold Niebuhr and original sin. Such a resolution is much more complex than the one proposed by Miller and comes much closer to solving the problem. Giles Gunn makes the point clear:[34]

> To suppose that Christianity assumes a world in which all suffering is deserved and all events are preordained and fundamentally just is as fatally misleading and historically inaccurate as to argue that tragedy assumes a world in which the deepest suffering is unmerited and the most important events are unjust and arbitrary. As tragedy admits of more than one kind of form, so Christianity admits of more than one theology or view of the whole. More important, however, Matthiessen knew that Christianity has its tragic component just as tragedy has its redemptive. The Christian, as he stressed in a discussion of the later Eliot, is no more adept at overcoming or escaping or transcending the human condition than the next man. He simply has a slightly better chance of surviving that condition if he is willing to pay the price—a price, as Eliot insisted in the *Four Quartets*, "Costing not less than everything." The choice, as Eliot posed it, is simple but stark: "We only live, only suspire / Consumed by either fire or fire."

Such a choice, which Eliot called "an occupation for a saint," could be viewed as the tragic hero's occupation as well, only changed because the saint, unlike the tragic hero, may be said to receive by an act of grace a return on his investment, which he in no sense deserves. But like the tragic hero, he has no guarantee on his "something given / And taken, in a lifetime's death in love, / Ardour and selfless and self-surrender." The Christian hero, like his counterpart in tragedy, must simply learn with Eliot's Becket that "action is suffering and suffering is action" and wait for the rest, for whatever may follow "prayer, observance, discipline, thought and action," for "hints and guesses, / Hints followed by guesses."[35]

But the slight differences Gunn mentions are crucial in marking the distinctions between Matthiessen's Christian conception of tragedy and other, less meliorative, versions. Lucien Goldmann argues, for example, that the world of tragedy does indeed suppose that the most important events are unjust and arbitrary, that the deepest suffering is indeed unmerited, and, moreover, that there is no explanation available to human beings for that suffering. Such a view is incompatible with Christianity or with most socialist views. Goldmann says so quite directly: "Many forms of religious and revolutionary consciousness have insisted upon the incompatibility between God and the world and between values and reality. Most of them, however, have admitted some possible solution, if only that of an endeavour which can be made in this world to achieve these values, or, alternatively, of the possibility for man of abandoning this world entirely and seeking refuge in the intelligible and transcendent values of the city of God. In its most radical form, tragedy rejects both these solutions as signs of weakness and illusion, and sees them as being either conscious or unconscious attempts at compromise."[36]

We find such compromises in much of Shakespeare and certainly in Eliot's Becket. The possibility of Christian grace gives to the hero who believes he may attain it—whether he does or not—a "refuge" in hope. The belief, unshaken until the end, that one's work and suffering will have value, in Christian morality or in the establishment of a future socialist or other "good" society, gives the tragic protagonist a reason for the darkness and the horror of his fate. In modern terms, the figure who comes closest to rejecting any such compromise is Camus's Sisyphus, whose only triumph comes as he looks his never-ending despair full in the face at the moment he is about to undergo his torture once more: "His scorn of the gods, his hatred of death, and his passion for life won him that unspeakable penalty in which his whole being is exerted toward accomplishing nothing. . . . At each of those moments when he leaves the heights and gradually sinks toward the lair of the gods, he is superior to his fate. He is stronger than his rock. If this myth is tragic, that is because its hero is conscious."[37] Goldmann notes this particular quality in modern existentialism when he writes: "On a social as well as on an individual plane, it is the sick organ which creates awareness, and it is in periods of social and political crisis that men are most aware of the enigma of their presence in the world. In the past, this awareness has tended to find its expression in tragedy. At the present day it shows itself in existentialism."[38]

In a long and interesting footnote, Goldmann acknowledges his debt to Georg Lukács, and on the basis of Lukács's discussion of the place of tragic art and thought, writes: "One could thus define tragedy as a universe of agonising questions to which man has no reply."[39] Most Christian and most socialist protagonists do have a reply. They know why they suffer—because they have sinned, or for the greater eventual glory of God; because the class struggle requires it, or because the class enemy is implacable and cruel. Some characters in what I think we can call modern tragedies, however, do face entirely unanswered questions. When Ernie Levy deliberately goes to his death in André Schwarz-Bart's *Last of the Just*,[40] it is because he no longer wishes to live in the world that has created the concentration camps and that has deprived him of every human feeling, and not because he has suddenly accepted his role as the *Lamed Vov*, the last just man. The absolute brutality he sees, which has turned him into a human dog, a nonperson, is not in any way explicable. Ernie's action earlier in the novel, when he crushes bugs with his hands, as God or the world crushes humanity, for no reason at all—that is reality. Jerzy Kosinski has given us, if not heroes, then at least figures who see no value at all in any moral action. In Kosinski's world, there is no morality, no justice, no answer. Men and women become victims or victimizers, without rhyme or reason, that is, in either case they become monstrous. To paraphrase Adorno—after Auschwitz, no more poetry, only uncompromising tragedy, only darkness and ambiguity and death.

Matthiessen's sense of the tragic rejects so implacable a view of the world. His vision, it seems to me, is determined by protagonists who have some hope for grace, or for victory in struggle, or for justice. Although he points to the Greek tragedians, it is, I suggest, socialist, other radical, and Christian protagonists who dominate his vision. Othello wants his accomplishments known, because he hopes for understanding: "I have done the state some service, and they know't. / No more of that. I pray you, in your letters, / When you shall these unlucky deeds relate, / Speak of me as I am; nothing extenuate, / Nor set down in malice." Perhaps Othello even hopes for more than understanding, for justice, as Iago's role becomes clear. There is hope in the desire that posterity may know the truth. It is Horatio's wish that Hamlet be given an honorable funeral, because he wants his cause made clear. These heroes, from a Christian pen, can find explanation for their suffering; at least the plays suggest a rational universe. Malraux's Kyo and Katov can die with hope for revolutionary victory, and, in the American context, Steinbeck's Tom Joad achieves a new vision of working people united in struggle at the very moment when he most needs to understand Preacher Casey's death and his own impending exile. There are no such meliorations for Oedipus, for Sisyphus. For them, all that remains is their willingness to accept their suffering as everything. That Matthiessen, whose own life was to end with an acknowledgment of his inability to feel that he could continue to be of use, could not accept as complete so harsh a vision is not surprising.

Perhaps one other point needs to be made here, because Matthiessen's vision is so shaped by his Christianity. Is a Christian tragic vision possible that is as implacable as the one projected by Sophocles or by Camus? Lucien Goldmann argues that such a vision is possible. It would be beyond the scope of my work to examine in any detail Goldmann's argument, but he does seem to be directly on point in exploring the "slightly better chance" the Christian has, as Gunn suggests, of surviving the tragic condition. In discussing what appears to be Pascal's turn from Jansenism late in his life, Goldmann suggests that instead he had, in fact, "accepted a much more radical and a much more coherent position." This position points to the possibility for a Christian tragedy as stark as that conceived by the non-Christian writers I have mentioned. The core of such a position rests on the question of grace. Goldmann writes:

> But, for them [that is, for Jansenists] the existence of a God who watched all their actions was a certainty, a fixed and immovable point in their intellectual and spiritual make up; the element of doubt, the need to make a decision, the Pascalian idea of the "wager" came only afterwards, when the problem arose of whether or not this God had granted the grace to persevere, of whether a particular person was simply a just man, or "a just man to whom grace had been refused," or a just man who had been damned and fallen into a state of mortal sin. Pascal carried Jansenism to its logical conclusion when he ceased to wonder whether a particular individual was damned or saved, and introduced doubt as to whether or not God himself really existed. By deliberately choosing the paradoxical position of the "just to whom grace has been refused," by giving up the attempt to be an angel in order to avoid becoming a beast, Pascal, "more Jansenist than the Jansenists themselves," became the creator of dialectical thought and the first philosopher of the tragic vision.[41]

This notion of "a just man to whom grace has been refused" removes, of course, any element of hope from even a Christian vision of the universe. If the protagonist of such a tragedy has no hope for grace, then he or she has no hope for a just world and has no basis for seeing the world as rational. If grace is refused on grounds as arbitrary as those on which the Greek gods decided to punish Oedipus, then there is a possible tragic vision like Sophocles' in the world of the Christian thinker. Of course, such a notion was completely foreign to Matthiessen's thought—though one wonders about the feelings of the man who finally found only in destruction of the self, perhaps in the suicide of a "just man," a way out of *this* world.

One source for Matthiessen's conception of tragedy is the work of Reinhold Niebuhr, the theologian who played such an important role in American Christian thought in the last several decades. Niebuhr is more aware than Matthiessen seems to be that his conception of tragedy is not the classical one. In his 1937 essay, "Christianity and Tragedy," he writes:

> Jesus is, superficially considered, a tragic figure; yet not really so. Christianity is a religion which transcends tragedy. Tears, with death, are swallowed up in victory. The cross is not tragic but the resolution of tragedy. Here suffering is carried into the very life of God and overcome. It becomes the basis of salvation. . . . Christianity and Greek tragedy agree that guilt and creativity are inextricably interwoven. But Christianity does not record the inevitability of guilt in all human creativity as inherent in the nature of human life. Sin emerges, indeed, out of freedom and is possible only because man is free; but it is done in freedom, and therefore man and not life bears responsibility for it. It does indeed accompany every creative act; but the evil is not part of the creativity. It is the consequence of man's self-centeredness and egotism by which he destroys the harmony of existence.[42]

In this second resolution to the problem both Matthiessen and Niebuhr reduce the level at which the tragic hero carries on the struggle. He is no longer fighting implacable outside forces, with no chance of winning, but he is warring with himself and his own inability to do what must be done. The tragedy takes place, if there is one, at a less than cosmic level, somewhere in the soul of the protagonist. This struggle is ennobling indeed, but it is not the struggle of Prometheus, or Oedipus, or the vision of Sisyphus provided for us by Camus. The struggle suggested by Niebuhr and Matthiessen is essentially hopeful, regardless of its specific outcome, as is the struggle of the social activist. We have no precise word that I know of for this form of tragedy, which offers a less harsh vision of the universe than do Sophocles or Camus.

If I call it, then, a "reduced" tragedy, I imply no pejorative connotation by the term. I seek only to make a distinction between modes of tragic expression. Giles Gunn is right, of course, when he suggests that tragedy has more than one kind of form and Christianity more than one theology. But I think the larger distinction within forms of tragic thought or Christian theology can be determined by this question: Is there a hopeful, reasonable, ultimately just universe on which the tragic hero can rely, regardless of his or her own agony, or is there only Kurtz's ultimate "the horror! the horror!" in Conrad, or the meaningless "ou-boum" Mrs. Moore hears in Forster's *A Passage to India*? Matthiessen could not, at least in his writings, conceive of a world of the horror and the ou-boum. The mode of tragedy he conceived is neither as desperate as Mrs. Moore's or Kurtz's nor as difficult as the one ascribed to Pascal by Goldmann. Matthiessen's view, then, is what we can conveniently call "reduced" tragedy.

What Matthiessen did with his definition of the tragic, although we may quarrel with his term, is to find another standard for critical purposes that comes as close to the tragic as possible, given his world view. If classical tragedy is dead, as Susan Sontag suggests and many maintain, then there remains in post-Renaissance literature a drama very close to tragedy, one that does partake of the balance of good and evil on which Matthiessen insists so strongly. It is not the product of Bertrand Russell's "indifferent universe" nor is it the product of Camus's notion of the "absurd," but it is a moving near-tragedy, a "reduced" tragedy, which derives its force from the near-impossibility of achieving grace and salvation. It is in this sense that Matthiessen uses the word "tragic" and connects Christianity and tragedy.

Such near-tragedies can be found far more abundantly in our time than those that hark back to the classical model. Arthur Miller's *View from the Bridge*, in which the givens stem from psychoanalysis and from folk mores, is a case in point, as is *Murder in the Cathedral*, in which Becket's failure, if such it is, stems from hubris-caused temptation to seek martyrdom, thus avoiding the essential humility. Matthiessen finds such tragedies in Melville and Hawthorne, as we shall see, where the source of the tragic is the profound isolation of the individual from the Christian-democratic community. Matthiessen used his notion of tragedy for good critical purposes. It is only of secondary importance for the critic concerned with the practical task of considering works of literature that this definition is different from the more usually accepted classical definition.

Others might well hold the same view of the tragic, even if it is derived from quite different sources. For our purposes, however, it is important to understand Matthiessen's source and to see how the idea of tragedy separates him from many other critics of his time—from the Brookses and the Hickses and the Parringtons and their followers—in as significant a way as does his conception of the function of art.

One example of how his idea of tragedy separates Matthiessen from the sociological critics can be found in the following footnote from *The Achievement of T. S. Eliot*:

John Strachey, in his plausible but summary account of contemporary literature in *The Coming Struggle for Power* (New York, 1933), though perceiving that the tragic view of life "is the one thing which all the great writers of all ages have had in common," nevertheless objects to what he conceives to be an inferiority in the work of present tragic writers owing to the fact that they confuse the unavoidable tragedies of human existence in general with the entirely avoidable tragedies of the decaying capitalistic system. His principal charge against them is that "since they do not extricate themselves from present-day society, since they are unable to stand outside of it, conceiving of a new basis for human life, they are themselves, inevitably, infected by their surroundings of decay." . . . But the assumption that the tragic writer can stand outside his age abstractly conceiving a new basis for human life, and at the same time create a vision of life as he has known it, seems to me inhuman; indeed, it seems purely verbalistic. Yet it is one of the most widespread contemporary fallacies that confuse the nature of art.

An individual sees tragedy in the life surrounding him; if he is greatly perceptive, like Dante, he may be able to endow that tragedy with universal significance. He may be appalled by the horror of life in his age like Swift or Baudelaire or the creator of Stephen Dedalus. He may fight bitterly against his age like Milton or Tolstoy or Lawrence, and reveal the evil resulting from its assumptions. But insofar as he conceives new possibilities for mankind, he can give those imaginings an illusion of reality only if he remains integrally a part of his age, only, that is to say, if the tragedy which he creates in words corresponds to the potential elements in existence as he himself has experienced it. . . .

If the writer stands outside his age, he can envisage an ideal state like Rousseau or Marx; indeed it is only by such *abstraction* that philosophical or political thought becomes possible. But the first requisite for the tragic poet or novelist is to comprehend and portray *concrete* experience. He may heighten and idealize it like Sophocles; but he must not thereby lessen the real existence of both evil and good. But such is at once the effect if he takes refuge in the abstraction of "a new basis for life." . . .

I do not mean by these remarks to deny the value of propaganda; or to make an impossible separation between it and art. . . . My point is simply once more the chief assumption of my essay: that the poet and the political theorist, the artist and the philosopher, though all relating integrally to the age which produces them, express that relation in different ways. That does not impute a necessary superiority in value to the expression of the artist over that of the others.[43]

Since Matthiessen derives from his version of Christianity both a tragic view of life and his sympathetic view of socialism, his Christianity becomes an important source for his position both as a tragedy-conscious "New Critic" and as a socially conscious cultural historian.

Two central informing notions, then, that Matthiessen developed in the two works under discussion here are that form is an integral part of the "meaning" of the work of art and that tragedy is the highest form of that art.

In a less broadly aesthetic, more specifically literary, sense, there is another concept at work here, one Matthiessen derives from Eliot and uses as an important tool in his critical writings.

What Eliot had called the "objective correlative" was, for Matthiessen, the *means* through which he could relate the poet to the society out of which he came, a means by which he could connect the seemingly private sensibility to the sources from which it sprang in the novelist's or poet's total social experience. Furthermore, it is by means of the "objective correlative" that Matthiessen moves from his "New Critical" inclinations to a fuller, less parochial plane. "From Arnold, so Matthiessen's epigraph to Chapter III [of *The Achievement of T. S. Eliot*] would seem to suggest," writes Richard Ruland, "came the seed of Eliot's 'objective correlative,' a formulation which served Matthiessen as his central critical tool. . . . For Matthiessen, Eliot's own sensory perception—particularly his 'auditory imagination'—is eminently successful in supplying his poetry with the requisite concrete external facts, and, along with the writing of Donne, Browne, Marvell, and other Metaphysicals, it gave Matthiessen the touchstone he needed for his examination of the American literary past."[44]

Matthiessen sees the objective correlative as the means by which the poet can, in the first place, render emotion rather than thought, and by which he can, secondly, express his own emotions as a part of the emotional tone of his epoch. Again, we can see here a significant unity in Matthiessen's thought. The critic who has rejected the demand for immediate, programmatic function in the work of literature has found, through Eliot, a means by which art can serve another use, that which he described in his essay about Hicks and which is "to give the most accurate account he [the poet] can of the particular quality of life as he has discovered it to be by means of his mind and senses." In defending Eliot against the charge of being too intellectual, Matthiessen says: "He [Eliot] has himself taken pains on many occasions to point out that the concern of the poet is never with thought so much as with finding 'the emotional equivalent of thought'; that the essential function of poetry is not intellectual but emotional; that the business of Dante or Shakespeare was 'to express the greatest emotional intensity of his time, based on whatever his time happened to think.'"[45]

The crucial words here are "based on whatever his time happened to think." In discussing Eliot's "The Waste Land," for example, Matthiessen writes:

> On his [Tiresias, the "central observer" of the poem] infinitely sensitive power to "foresuffer all" could embrace the violent contrasts (and samenesses) that are now packed into the compass of a few square blocks: the dead luxury of the upper class, the vast uninspired bourgeois existence, the broken fragments of the talk of the poor overheard in a bar. Incidentally, the clearest perception of Eliot's range in ability to fit his style to his subject is furnished by the remarkably different manners in which he presents these three classes of society. Perhaps the sharpest dramatic effect in the whole poem lies in the contrasting halves of "The [sic] Game of Chess," the abrupt shift from an elaborately sensuous style that can build up an atmosphere of cloying richness to one which catches the very cadences of Cockney speech in a pub. And then, in the next section, in order to suggest the huge commercialized world that lies between these two extremes, Eliot portrays the characteristic scene between the typist and the clerk, and suggests the denatured quality of their life by a deliberate mechanization of his rhythm, as well as by the first continuous use of rhyme in the poem, which, being unexpected, contributes to heighten his effect. At the same time, beneath all these contrasts in appearance, are being stressed the similar human situations in which all these different people are found: they are all playing the same stale game, burning alike with sterile desire.[46]

Eliot has rendered, Matthiessen shows, not only an emotional state but also the social situations and the artifacts in the social situation that indicate the sources of the emotional state. One is struck, especially, by Eliot's catalog of objects in the opening passages of the "A Game of Chess" section, as he describes the rich, antique, classically inspired objects that surround the woman in that section. In his use of the Philomel legend as a painting over the mantel Eliot conveys not only the richness of the surroundings but also their contemporary social inconsequence by closing his description with:

> And still she cried, and still the world pursues,
> "Jug Jug" to dirty ears.
> And other withered stumps of time
> Were told upon the walls; staring forms
> Leaned out, leaning, hushing the room enclosed.[47]

Matthiessen points to Eliot's use of the objective correlative as a means for describing precisely the social situation in which the poet finds the source for his particular vision of society and the emotions that the vision arouses. Sophisticated Marxist and other sociological critics conceive of the function of the artist in much the same way—see, for example, Georg Lukács, surely among the most sophisticated Marxist critics, on the works of Thomas Mann.

But Matthiessen does not rest here. He wants to specify in relation to Eliot, and, in general, *how* the artist is to perform this function. He proposes that the artist must first of all *see* as clearly as he possibly can. In a section of the work on Eliot that sounds a good deal like his discussion of Emerson in *American Renaissance*, Matthiessen stresses the "prime importance of concrete presentation of carefully observed details" and then goes on to discuss the importance of *seeing* in modern painting "from Cézanne to Picasso" as well as in modern poetry. But whatever the poet sees must in time be transformed into emotion, he argues, so that the emotion can become the source for the exact image. It is at this point in his discussion that Matthiessen relates the poet's emotional state, via the "objective correlative," to his larger, his social, functions:

> To be sure, Eliot's observations are not primarily of physical objects; his most sustained analysis is applied to states of mind and emotion. But he holds none the less that permanent poetry is always a presentation of thought and feeling "by a statement of events in human action or objects in the external world." In his view the poet's emotions are not *in themselves* important; as he remarked in elucidation of Valéry, "not our feelings, but the pattern which we make of our feelings is the centre of value." The lasting poem is not the result of pouring out personal emotion, for "the only way of expressing emotion

in the form of art is by finding an "objective correlative'; in other words, a set of objects, a situation, a chain of events which shall be the formula of the *particular* emotion; such that when the external facts, which must terminate in sensory experience are given, the emotion is immediately evoked." This passage will not yield its full significance without careful reading; but it is already a *locus classicus* of criticism.[48]

Matthiessen saw a relationship, in this regard, between Eliot and James as far back as the first edition of *The Achievement of T. S. Eliot*. In discussing Eliot's use of Tiresias as the consciousness that can best see, in "The Waste Land," he suggests that such an observer is "a device which Eliot may have learned in part from Henry James's similar use of Strether in *The Ambassadors*."[49] Matthiessen comments on this relationship between the two authors further: "The more one thinks of Eliot in relation to James, the more one realizes the extent of the similarities between them. They are similarities of content as well as of method. Both James and Eliot, no less than Hawthorne, are mainly concerned with what lies behind action and beneath appearance. In their effort to find the exact situation that will evoke an impression of the inner life, they are occupied too in expressing like states of mind and feeling."[50] At least one similarity between them is their search for the "exact situation" that will express emotion through an objective correlative.

When Matthiessen turns his attention to James in 1944, he points to the novelist's use of imagery in such a way that once again demonstrates the closeness of James's method to that of Eliot. James "did not, like Mallarmé, start with the symbol," says Matthiessen, in contrasting James's work with that of the symbolists. "He reached it only with the final development of his theme, and then used it essentially in the older tradition of the poetic metaphor, to give concretion, as well as allusive and beautiful extension, to his thought."[51] That is as close to a definition of the objective correlative as one can find, especially if one emphasizes the word "concretion."

The objective correlative is a critical tool for Matthiessen. But the idea is a complex one and requires further explication, espe-

cially if it is considered in relation to such older and more standard critical terms as the symbol and the metaphor. It might be
said that the term "objective correlative" is simply another way
of saying "symbol," and that what Eliot, and, by extension, Matthiessen mean by the term is some form of what C. S. Lewis has
called the effort to "represent what is immaterial in picturable
terms."[52]

The problem of what constitutes a symbol, what its source is
and what its function, is clearly one of the most difficult confronting not only literary criticism but aesthetics in general. Eliot and
Matthiessen seek to remove the mystery from the term, or from
the closely related word "metaphor," and to substitute "objective
correlative," because Matthiessen as practicing critic, and Eliot as
practicing critic and poet, require a term that describes what in
practice writers do when they find such "picturable terms." In a
sense, this is what Northrop Frye does when he defines "symbol"
as "any unit of any literary structure that can be isolated for
attention,"[53] a definition, however, so inclusive as to serve little
practical use. Unlike Frye, however, and other framers of theories
of literary criticism, Matthiessen does not attempt to provide a
consistent theoretical definition of his term and neither does
Eliot. Neither the critic nor the poet in this case is basically a
system maker. It suffices, for their purposes, to demonstrate that
the artist must find some cogent, highly evocative form in object
or action through which he or she can make an emotional response palpable to the reader. Matthiessen means by objective
correlative precisely what Eliot means by it, and he means the
same thing when he speaks in a general way of the metaphor and
the symbol.

But this very approach to the problem of the symbol relates to
the uses of literature that Matthiessen wrote about so eloquently.
For both Eliot and James, as Matthiessen points out, use the
objective correlative in order to make clear the artist's individual
response to his own time and his own emotional state in that
time, and thus, through it, as artists they reveal "the greatest
emotional intensity of [their] time." It is through an examination
of the *kind* of objective correlative that artists choose that "aesthetic criticism, if carried far enough, inevitably becomes social

criticism, since the act of perception extends through the work of art to its milieu,"[54] as Matthiessen says. It is through critical analysis of *how* artists choose to relate the emotions of their time, that is, of their own emotions as those of inhabitants of their own epoch, that we may see what they have done and said as social criticism.

An example of how Matthiessen does this will, perhaps, make the point clearer. In following the fortunes of the physical golden bowl that gives title to James's novel, Matthiessen gives us a fine example of his virtuosity in "close reading." But his reading is exactly like that which any highly skilled contemporary follower of Brooks and Warren might exercise, until Matthiessen moves beyond the immediate, plot-related questions raised by the bowl to its larger connotations:

> The expertness with which James has brought out so many connotations latent in the bowl has kept that symbol from ever becoming frozen or schematized. He has thus unquestionably succeeded in making an *objet d'art* the cohesive center of his own intricate creation. But other questions are raised by those curiously mixed final images. When there is so much gold that it pervades even the vocabulary of love, is that a sign of life or death? What sort of world is being portrayed, and how are we to judge it?[55]

Matthiessen goes on to point out James's weaknesses in this novel, citing among the most important his inability to portray a businessman like Verver, whose "moral tone is far more like that of a benevolent Swedenborgian than it is like that of either John D. Rockefeller or Jay Gould;"[56] the fact that James, in never questioning the extremely close relationship between Maggie and her father is "oblivious to sexual distortions which would seem an almost inevitable concomitant of the situation he posits;" that, in sum, "James' characters tend to live, as has often been objected, merely off the tops of their minds."[57] But after the weaknesses of the novel are exposed, Matthiessen returns again to examinations of its objective correlatives as indexes to its social vision:

Or perhaps the unsatisfactory nature of the positive values in this novel may be better described through the contrast between victory and defeat. In both *The Ambassadors* and *The Wings of the Dove* we are moved most deeply by loss and suffering. But there is an intrusion of complacence when Maggie, imaged repeatedly as a dancing girl, is said to be having "the time of her life" in her sustained act. One reason why James was less convincing in imagining success was that he was unable to conceive it in any heroic form. In this he was a sensitive register of a time when American success was so crassly materialistic that, as we have noted, nearly all the enduring writers from that time voiced their opposition. . . .

Or we may put it technically, that he did not find the "objective correlative" for his theme.[58]

Matthiessen's final judgment of *The Golden Bowl* is that it is essentially a decadent novel. But he has arrived at this judgment through his examination of the objective correlative, the bowl itself and other images, as seen in the context of the entire work and in the context of the period of its composition.

Richard Ruland has commented on this aspect of Matthiessen's work, which on the whole he considers useful and important, in what appear to me rather condescending terms:

But while Matthiessen does make every effort to deal sensitively with Eliot's poetry and with the work of the writers who occupy him in his later books, his method is more a culmination of earlier cultural commentators than it is an anticipation of New Criticism. He is master of all the analytic techniques *Understanding Poetry* worked to foster, and there are passages in the later books which rival the best New Criticism has done in respecting the value and integrity of the poem itself. But Matthiessen the man-of-many-commitments, bent on being—to cite his favorite words from James—"one of the people on whom nothing is lost," Matthiessen the Christian-Socialist could never bring himself to recognize the autonomy of art and leave it at that. He is continually being led further into the relation of the poem to its author, his life and the life of his time, and the suggested analogies to the poem from past and present. The Eliot essay, with all its talk of influences, parallels, and theoretical underpinnings, is not so much about Eliot's poems as it is about what went into them, what made the man who has written as he has, and what made the age that made the man and that has responded to his poems. As we shall see demonstrated on a much larger scale in *American Renaissance*, once Matthiessen has shown that he can read as sensitively and perceptively as any New Critic might wish, he immediately moves outward to the role he finds more congenial and altogether more consistent with the social obligations of the scholar. He functions, in his own phrase, as a cultural historian.[59]

Ruland's language would lead one to believe that it was Matthiessen's position that art had no social function but was merely autotelic, that his views concerning art's relations to life were somehow brought in by subterfuge. But he never did hold to such a position, and neither did T. S. Eliot, as I have shown earlier. In fact, the more Eliot developed his own political and social and even religious views, the more did he move away from any pure autotelicism.

Matthiessen insisted almost from the beginning of his career, as his review of Hicks's work shows, that there is indeed a use for art, and that this use is that the work of art ought to be the most accurate account the artist can give of the quality of life in his or her own time. The artist's account of such qualities can only be understood if we treat what he or she does with the respect it deserves and if we understand that the work is as much its form as its message, that its form is, in fact, a part of what it has to say. Respect for the work, then, is the primary function of the critic— hence, he or she must give it a sensitive and perceptive reading. But equally important is the attempt to understand the *sources* of the artist's perceptions, the attempt to comprehend to what emotional state the objective correlative corresponds, and further, the attempt to comprehend what, in the artist's time and his or her relation to it, causes this emotional state. In this sense, the important artist is a representative of all human beings in his or her time, although he or she is also one unique person. The artist is "representative" in Emerson's sense of that term. Matthiessen's use of the techniques of New Criticism stems from his respect for the work of art, for the poem as, to use Eliseo Vivas's interesting phrase, "a linguistic artifact whose function is to organize the primary data of experience that can be exhibited in and through the use of words."[60] But an artifact is, by definition, an object showing human workmanship and modification, modification deriving from the interaction between individual and society. Matthiessen seeks the source and meaning of such workmanship —hence he must necessarily function as a cultural historian in order to function as total critic. In a limited sense Matthiessen anticipated developments in semiotics that were not to occur till after his death.

We shall see more fully how Matthiessen used this notion in examining his work concerning the major figures of our mid-nineteenth-century literature. He made it clear at the start of that work. In his introduction to *American Renaissance*, Matthiessen asserts the following: "An artist's use of language is the most sensitive index to cultural history, since a man can articulate only what he is, and what he has been made by the society of which he is a willing or an unwilling part."[61] His effort to prove this assertion was a motivating force behind *American Renaissance*, and from this effort stems the linking together of literature, the work of our genre painters (Mount and Eakins in particular), of our architects, and of still other artists in a further effort on Matthiessen's part to indicate what they have been made by the society of which they are a part.

From this point of view one can easily understand Matthiessen's rejection of those Marxist and neohumanist critiques that tend to blame a writer for not having written some other book than the one he has written. I have already cited Matthiessen's rebuke to Parrington for his curt dismissal of James. Matthiessen took the matter up again, though less directly, when he says of *The Golden Bowl* that in it "James was again bent on conjuring up a world of magical enchantment. If we want to understand his aims, we had better follow the first rule of criticism and turn to what he has done rather than what he hasn't. Instead of belaboring further his social and psychological limitations, it is more revelatory to examine the positive values which he found in such a world."[62] And that is precisely what Matthiessen does—he seeks to understand what the Jamesian artifact is. By applying to it a sensitivity to and awareness of form, and by applying to it the test of his tragic perception of life, he finds in James's latest phase those attributes that have made Matthiessen's description of it as the "major phase" almost universally accepted.

I have said earlier that it is their methodology and their polemical qualities that connect Matthiessen's *The Achievement of T. S. Eliot* and his *Henry James: The Major Phase*. When the targets of the polemics and the nature of the methodology are seen together, they constitute major aspects of a critical theory. Matthiessen believed that the work of art requires the critic's undivided and sensitive attention in and of itself as a discrete, self-contained, and self-serving object. The poem or novel does whatever it does best when it is approached that way, and thus the responsibility of the artist is to create a work of art that is successful in its own terms. But the critic's function goes beyond merely understanding the work in this fashion. To put it another way, close reading and consequent understanding is only the beginning of the critical function. For it is also the critic's responsibility, by examining in particular the objective correlatives that the artist chooses, to understand the human qualities of the artist. This is necessary because the artist acts, if he or she is a good artist, as the most sensitive perceiver on the one hand and as the most skillful renderer, on the other, of the emotional states of his or her own time. The greatest of artists, Matthiessen would insist, perceive the fundamental fact that the human condition is a tragic one. Because of this knowledge artists escape the narrowness of the merely timely and, through a sensitive awareness of their own epoch, render for us that which is more long-lasting. Matthiessen would have us see the artist as that human being who can best perceive emotionally both the particular and the social tragedy of the moment. The artist indicates the way in which that tragedy relates to the tragedy inherent in being human and can make us feel these interrelated tragedies by finding the event, the action, or the object that can best render the emotion he or she feels.

The critic who can point the way to understanding the artist so clearly must be, as Ruland has said Matthiessen wanted to be, "one of the people on whom nothing is lost." He must be possessed of a sensibility both exquisite and unified. He must understand not only the history of letters and the techniques of fiction, poetry, and drama, but he must also know a great deal about his own culture and his own time. Perhaps Matthiessen tells us what he thinks the critic, or, for that matter, any intellectual most requires when he notes, approvingly, Malraux's "putting into the mouth of Garcia, the intellectual Communist in *Man's Hope*, the statement that the aim of all life's purposive action should be the conversion of as much experience as possible into conscious thought."[63] Because of the critic's need to feel and then to understand the artist's work and to understand its sources, Matthiessen requires of his critic a totally unified sensibility. In his most theoretical essay, "The Responsibilities of the Critic," Matthiessen says:

> There is a basic distinction between bringing everything in your life to what you read and reading into a play of the past issues that are not there. All I am suggesting is the extent to which our awareness of ourselves as social beings is summoned by the greatest art. That is the root of my reason for believing that the good critic becomes fully equipped for his task by as wide a range of interest as he can master. . . . the critic should freely grant that the artist writes as he must. But for his own work the critic has to be both involved in his age and detached from it. This double quality of experiencing our own time to the full and yet being able to weight it in relation to other times is what the critic must strive for, if he is to be able to discern and demand the works of art that we need most. The most mature function of the critic lies finally in that demand.[64]

Matthiessen attempts, with much success, what too few critics of our time have been able to do—he bridges the gap between social criticism and aesthetic criticism, between Parrington and Hicks, on the one hand, and Brooks and Ransom, on the other.

I feel obliged to raise one final question concerning Matthiessen's obviously favorable approach to Eliot and James, and especially to Eliot. George Abbott White has raised the question most forcefully, and he has provided certain kinds of answers[65] to the question of how Matthiessen could be so obviously fond of a man like Eliot whose politics were so contrary to Matthiessen's own left-wing socialist ideas. Answers might come from personal relations between the two men, of course. They knew each other and corresponded warmly.[66] However, I have already indicated Matthiessen's honorable ability to separate personal friendship or sympathy from critical standards in the case of his left-wing friends. In Eliot's case, the same thing should have applied, and I believe it did apply. That is, it seems to me that no matter how much Matthiessen might have liked Eliot, no matter how much he might have felt that he shared personal problems with the poet—or, for that matter, with the novelist Henry James—his critical integrity was such that he would have taken negative views of their works, or no views at all, if he had not found something important in them.

What he found, I think, are precisely those qualities that I have suggested are the subject of his polemic in the two volumes under discussion here. He found a vision of tragedy that he could accept. He found an emphasis on the work of art as autotelic and an understanding of the importance of the objective correlative, both of which were central to his critical method and to his effort to create a socially conscious, societally aware but artistically sound, criticism. He found, in brief, in Eliot and in James, perfect representatives of the two epigraphs to the Eliot volume that constitute important cornerstones of his critical position.

It is to Matthiessen's credit that he was able to avoid falling into Parringtonian or vulgar Marxist traps, which deny validity to a work of art because the author's political or social views are unacceptable. If, despite his radicalism in politics, Matthiessen could help us to appreciate Eliot and James, it is similarly to his credit, as I shall attempt to show later on, that he was able to help us to appreciate Dreiser, despite his concerns about form. Nothing in Matthiessen's career makes clearer his devotion to an understanding of the importance of art as central to human experience than his ability to appreciate, and to help others to appreciate, *both* James and Dreiser. Nothing demonstrates more clearly the bridging function he performed between the primarily social and the primarily aesthetic critic than such a catholicity of taste. Perhaps Stephen Spender has told us with the greatest clarity precisely what Matthiessen saw in Eliot's work: "Eliot required not only to be a poet but also to be a penetrating analytic critic both of the past and of the present; a critic who, while guarding the integrity of literature, saw literature as still living past values operating within contemporary life."[67] That was what Matthiessen was interested in—criticism of society past and present, the guarding of the integrity of literature, and the combination of these two important endeavors.

4 ❦ American Renaissance

merican Renaissance is F. O. Matthiessen's masterpiece. It is his longest work, the one for which he is best known, and the one that took him the longest to write—ten years, according to his own testimony.[1] Its range is remarkable. The book, which begins with Matthiessen's "realization of how great a number of our past masterpieces were produced in one extraordinarily concentrated moment of expression" (p. vii), uses for comparison the works of a seemingly infinite number of artists, ranging from figures of the European Renaissance to those of Matthiessen's own day, from Shakespeare to Wallace Stevens. It brings together from the American 1850s the work of genre painters and builders of clipper ships, architects and politicians—in brief, it is a truly protean book.

It is also a very complex work. Divided into four books, respectively titled "From Emerson to Thoreau," "Hawthorne," "Melville," and "Whitman," it has sections that deal with Louis Sullivan and Horatio Greenough, with Mount, Millet, and Eakins, and it deals as much with Melville in the "Hawthorne" section and the "Whitman" section as in the "Melville" section. Thus its persons and themes are legion. One reviewer comments:

> One will of course find a host of other writers entering these
> pages, in ancillary chapters, or with briefer mention showing
> their connection with the main subject. Sir Thomas Browne,
> William Blake, George Herbert, De Quincey, Nietzsche,
> Byron, D. H. Lawrence, Henry James, these necessarily from
> among the shades. T. S. Eliot, Ezra Pound, Santayana,
> Thomas Mann, Jung and Freud of more recent days.
> Analyses of thought and emotion, of the mind's life and
> the body's life, the isolation of the individual, and the obli-
> gations that tie him to his fellow-men, the significance of
> symbols and myths, the search of the human spirit for
> authority, the necessity to experience facts, the nature of

the creative process in writing, American idealism, the
definition of romance, imagination as mirror, man finding
himself in the study of nature, character as action and action
as plot, the technique of trade, the dignity of common
humanity—here, mentioned at random, are but a few of the
themes entering into Mr. Matthiessen's significant volume.[2]

The very size and complexity of the work, which make it intellectually stimulating, make it also a difficult book to discuss.
"There ensues a vast and intricate structure which one cannot
think entirely successful if one values simplicity in form," comments another reviewer.[3] The book, like a work of art, can be
known only by being read—absorbed, really—in its totality.[4]
Because it is so much like a work of art, and because it is a complex and, in Eliot's sense, a "difficult" work, any discussion of it
will be less than the book itself.

It is in this work that Matthiessen announces what he considers to be his particular critical role. His introductory chapter,
"Method and Scope," probably as widely quoted as any of the
substantive portions of *American Renaissance*, brings together all
the aspects of critical function we have seen partially at work in
the studies discussed previously:

> My aim has been to follow these books [those of his five
> major authors] through their implications, to observe them as
> the culmination of their author's talents, to assess them in
> relation to one another and to the drift of our literature since,
> and so far as possible, to evaluate them in accordance with
> the enduring requirements for great art. That last aim will
> seem to many only a pious phrase, but it describes the critic's
> chief responsibility. His obligation is to examine an author's
> resources of language and of genres, in a word, to be pre-
> occupied with form. . . . My prime intention is not Sainte-
> Beuve's; to be a "naturalist of minds," to relate the author's
> work to their lives. I have not drawn upon the circumstances
> of biography unless they seemed essential to place a given
> piece of writing; and whenever necessary, especially in the
> case of Melville, I have tried to expose the modern fallacy that
> has come from the vulgarization of Sainte-Beuve's subtle

method—the direct reading of an author's personal life into
his works.

The types of interrelations that have seemed most productive
to understanding the literature itself were first of all the obvious debts, of Thoreau to Emerson, or Melville to Hawthorne.
In the next place there were certain patterns of taste and as-
piration; the intimate kinship to the seventeenth-century
metaphysical strain that was felt by Emerson, Thoreau and
Melville, the desire for a functional style wherein Thoreau
and Whitman especially were forerunners of our modern interest. That last fact suggests one of my chief convictions:
that works of art can be best perceived if we do not approach
them only through the influences that shaped them, but if
we also make use of what we inevitably bring from our own
lives. . . . The phase of my subject in which I am most interested is its challenge to pass beyond such interrelations to basic
formulations about the nature of literature. [pp. xi, xii, xiii]

Essentially the same critical strictures that have already emerged
from our examination of Matthiessen's work concerning James
and Eliot can be seen here, but they are now woven into a larger
scheme, a kind of grand design, the lack of which was apparent
in those other works. To isolate various components of this design is not simple, and is perhaps somewhat arbitrary, but for my
purposes, the following will suffice:

1. *The interrelations between art and the intellectual background
within which it develops.* Matthiessen is concerned with elucidating
the social and economic situations that give rise to such an intellectual background, without making that background the primary subject of his work. He might have said, with some justice,
that he was not writing a book in the tradition of Taine, any more
than one in the tradition of Sainte-Beuve, and he did say that he
was not writing a Parringtonian one.[5] But the intellectual background and its sources remain an important concern for Matthiessen, and they are among the dominant components of *American
Renaissance.*

2. *The influence of art upon art and of theories of art upon the work of
the artist.* Although this is a specialized and specific application of
my first point, it assumes a crucial role in Matthiessen's book.

3. *A concern with form—language for the most part, but the painter's, sculptor's, and architect's analogous concerns also—as the base upon which to build critical judgments and as the clearest indicator of the intent and achievement of the artist.*

4. *Tragedy as the ultimate measure of the artist's perception of the human situation.*

5. *The function of allegory and symbolism.*

6. *The role of the artist's work in the growth and development of democracy, whatever that difficult term may mean.*

Through an examination of these categories, we can evaluate Matthiessen's application of such critical concerns to one or another aspect of the work of important American writers of the 1850s and thus make an estimate of the overall impact of the book. Such an evaluation should further reveal Matthiessen's critical method, should make possible an estimate of the weaknesses and strengths of that method, and should demonstrate the relationship of that method to the extraliterary concerns Matthiessen brought to it—his Christianity and his devotion to the idea of a better society.

Art and the Intellectual Background

It is one of the complicating aspects of *American Renaissance* that Matthiessen divides his work into chapters dealing with intellectual modes typical of, though not peculiar to, mid-nineteenth-century America. Beginning in Book One with a discussion of Emerson and transcendentalism as the principal thought of the period, against which all other ideas react or with which they interact, he calls his first chapter "In the Optative Mood." Matthiessen means by "optative" the Emersonian kind of search for possibility in man, and a conviction that the search can be successful, that derives from Coleridge, from Wordsworth, from the early Shelley, and from Carlyle. In the 1850s such ideas were still very much a part of the Victorian intellectual landscape, although they were expressed in many different forms.

"The revolution in which Emerson shared," says Matthiessen, in discussing Coleridge's role in introducing Hartleyan psychology into criticism, "was primarily the one that was waged against the formulas of eighteenth-century rationalism in the name of the fuller resources of man. Coleridge had stressed what was to be one of Emerson's recurrent themes, 'the *all in each of human nature*,'—how a single man contains within himself, through his intuition, the whole range of experience" (p. 7, italics are Matthiessen's). It is from this epistemological view, from the idea that the individual man can know all there is to know and that once knowing he will act, that Emerson derives the kind of "optimism" that has so often annoyed readers of a period later than his own. Matthiessen demonstrates Emerson's certainty about the possibility of goodness in man as follows:

> On his way home from Europe in the fall of 1833, when asked what he meant by morals, his only answer was, "I cannot define, and care not to define. It is man's business to observe, and the definition of moral nature must be the slow result of years, of lives, of states, perhaps of being." But he was not at all unsure of the drift of his inner existence: "Milton describes himself in his letter to Diodati as enamored of moral perfection. He did not love it more than I. That which I cannot yet declare has been my angel from childhood until now . . . What is this they say about wanting mathematical certainty for moral truths? I have always affirmed they had it. Yet they ask me whether I know the soul immortal. No. But do I not know the Now to be eternal? . . . I believe in this life . . ."
> [p. 11, Matthiessen's ellipses]

Matthiessen goes to some pains to relate these views to the work of many of Emerson's contemporaries. That he cites the luminaries of transcendentalism from Ripley to Brownson and Alcott is hardly surprising in this connection. But much more interesting, and typical of Matthiessen's method of sketching in the intellectual background of his writers, is his sudden-seeming turn, in chapter IV to a section about the sculptor Horatio Greenough.

Although the primary thrust of this section concerns the elucidation of Coleridgian notions of the organic theory of art and of a "democratic" ideology, it also concerns itself with the meliorist view I have ascribed to Emerson. "In the final extension of his three divisions [from beauty, to action, to character], Greenough read into them a religious significance that mounted from 'faith of future action' and 'hope of future character' to 'the divinity of character' that gives itself 'in charity . . . to God, in sacrificing self to humanity.' What saved this identification from being merely verbal or from dissolving into uplift was Greenough's robust dislike of all transcendental millenniums. When he spoke of the potential divinity of man, he did not forget his artist's knowledge that the human body is 'a multiform command,' 'the most beautiful organization of earth' (p. 150)."

Matthiessen goes on to examine similar considerations in the work of Thoreau and Hawthorne, both of whom react against, as well as interact with, so sanguine a view of man's possibilities. In his discussion of Melville such Emersonian hopefulness becomes even more important, as Matthiessen points out how it provides an important stimulus for Melville, by way of opposition, for his novels. For Melville created Ahab, Matthiessen says, in part at least because he could not accept the potential "divinity in man" seen by Emerson and the other transcendentalists.

One reason why Melville was driven to magnify the relentless power of Fate is to be found in his reaction against Emersonianism. Emerson was too easy in his distinction when he said: "Our doctrine must begin with the Necessary and Eternal, and discriminate Fate from the Necessary. There is no limitation about the Eternal." Briefly, then, in one of the key passages in his essay on "Fate": "So far as man thinks, he is free," since thought partakes in the Eternal. "But Fate is the name we give to the action of that . . . all various necessity on the brute myriads, whether in things, animals, or in men in whom the intellect pure is not yet opened. To such it is only a burning wall which hurts those who run against it." But Melville apprehended in Ahab a man who thought, and yet conceived the white whale as an inscrutable wall shoved near him. The captain's insistence that "Truth has no confines" demanded that he thrust through the wall. Emerson would have agreed about the illimitability of truth, and, indeed, went on to say that Fate involves "melioration." For "the one serious and formidable thing in nature is a will." Emerson's hero is the man of will who moves others forward by it, since "the direction of the whole and of the parts is toward benefit." But Melville's hero of formidable will swept his whole crew to destruction. [pp. 455–56]

In a footnote to this passage, Matthiessen explains how he feels reactions like Melville's work. Pointing out that "Fate" was not published until several years after *Moby Dick* was written, he nevertheless insists that "the diffused presence of transcendentalism in the work of Melville and Whitman shows that, by the end of the eighteen-forties, a man did not have to be thinking of a specific text in order to be conscious of the main doctrines of the movement. In both Melville and Whitman we can perceive the double process of assimilation and rejection of those doctrines, with the chief accent on the first by Whitman, on the second by Melville" (p. 456, n. 3).

In a summary way, Matthiessen returns to the problem under discussion here at the very end of his book when, in the "Full Circle" portion of the chapter entitled "Man in the Open Air," he closes his discussion of Whitman by writing:

Whitman had neither Thoreau's lucidity nor firmness. By cutting himself loose from any past, he often went billowing away into a dream of perfectibility, which tried to make the human literally divine and was hence unreal. But because he was more porous to all kinds of experience, he gave a more comprehensive, if confused, image of his fluid age than Thoreau did.

The cult of perfection was an inevitable concomitant of the romantic cult of the future. The attitude behind both received its most searching contemporary analysis from Hawthorne. He sensed that Emerson's exaltation of the divinity in man had obliterated the distinctions between man and God, between time and eternity. [pp. 651–52]

This series of comments is an example of the way in which Matthiessen takes an important idea and deals with it throughout his work. Although only peripherally concerned with the particular social conditions that produce any given idea, he is concerned with tracing the ideas themselves and their effects on works of art in a way that makes his work a part of one of the critical currents of his time, one that I have not yet mentioned. Arthur O. Lovejoy had published, beginning at a time before Matthiessen was born, any number of papers that attempted to trace the workings of an idea through many of its forms. The History of Ideas Club had been founded at Johns Hopkins in 1923 when Matthiessen was a Rhodes Scholar in England.[6] There can be little doubt that he was heavily influenced by Lovejoy's approach. In fact, he calls him "the most searching historian of romanticism" (p. 380), an accolade he surely did not bestow lightly.

It would, however, be simplistic to see only Lovejoy's influence at work here. Certainly, Matthiessen was aware of the work of his colleague Perry Miller, whose exploration of American intellectual history is exemplary. Matthiessen was also influenced by the work of other scholars and by the presence in the intellectual "air" of the whole conception of the history of ideas, in part under the impetus of Marxist thought, in much the same way in which he saw the figures of the 1850s reacting to Emerson. It is surely no accident that Merle Curti's *The Growth of American Thought*, to cite just one example, was published less than two years after *American Renaissance* and that in the introduction to that volume Curti mentions Lovejoy and Parrington, Bury and Beard, Gabriel and Schlesinger, among others, as major influences in American thought.[7] Matthiessen was not by any means alone in seeing the value of intellectual history as a tool for the scholar and critic.

If all he had done in *American Renaissance* was to write an intellectual-critical history, Matthiessen would have made a useful contribution to American historiography, but he would have written a Parringtonian or a Lovejoyian or a Beardian book. That he did not do so points to his particular quality as a critic, for his intent was clearly to use intellectual history for the elucidation and understanding of literature and not, on the contrary, to use literature to document the writing of intellectual history. I have already cited his disclaimer of Parrington's method. He makes his aim even clearer in the following passage from *American Renaissance*:

> I have concentrated entirely on the foreground, on the writing itself. I have not written formal literary history—a fact that should be of some relief to the reader, since if it required a volume of this length for five years of that record, the consequences of any extension of such a method would be appalling. Parrington states in his *Main Currents of American Thought* (1927): "With aesthetic judgments I have not been greatly concerned. I have not wished to evaluate reputations or weigh literary merits, but rather to understand what our fathers thought . . ." My concern has been the opposite. . . . I am . . . suspicious of the results of such historians as have declared that they were not discussing art, but "simply using art, in a purpose of research." Both our historical writing and our criticism have been greatly enriched during the past twenty years by the breaking down of arbitrary divisions between them, by the critic's realization of the necessity to master what he could of the historical discipline, by the historian's desire to extend his domain from politics to general culture. But you cannot "use" a work of art unless you have comprehended its meaning. And it is well to remember that although literature reflects an age, it also illuminates it. Whatever the case may be for the historian, the quality of that illumination is the main concern for the common reader. [pp. ix–x]

It is interesting, in light of this avowed aim, to read at least one disagreement with it. Says Bernard Smith, in a review which begins with lavish praise of Matthiessen's book:

> I hope I may be forgiven a few words of comment on a peculiarity of the author's attitude toward his function as critic— a peculiarity which unnecessarily restricts the scope of his inquiry. He assures us—and he proves—that he is well aware of the social and intellectual currents ("the background") of the period, but he asserts that he has concentrated entirely on the foreground, on the writing itself. . . . He does nothing of the kind. . . . Professor Matthiessen knows perfectly well that he cannot "evaluate . . . in accordance with the enduring

requirements for great art" without at the same time estimating social and philosophical values; that he cannot explain
"*what* these books are as works of art" without at the same
time explaining *how* and *why* they came to be.

He does what should be done. His book is shot through
with social, political and even economic interpretations. . . .
This book is first-rate criticism; it does not divorce aesthetics
from thought, craft from culture. What, then, is the reason
for Professor Matthiessen's indecision about his own method,
his rather confused and certainly confusing statement about
what he is doing? That is for him to answer. Perhaps he has
studied T. S. Eliot too long and too affectionately. Perhaps he
has listened too politely to his academic colleagues. I know,
however, that if he had let himself go and devoted just a little
more space to social content and cultural relations, his book
would not have suffered.[8]

But Smith, it seems to me, misses Matthiessen's point. Matthiessen never asserted that background and "foreground" are
unrelated. Nor did he ever claim to evaluate without philosophical and social values. Rather, his book acts, in a significant sense,
as a corrective for what the Parringtons and the Hickses—not to
mention the Calvertons—had already done. It shifts the focus
of critical vision to another place without abandoning a "sociological" perspective. The problem of literary criticism, much more
so than that of scientific exploration, is always how to separate
things and ideas in such a way as to make their study possible.
The scientist, by the very nature of his subject matter, can separate out the behavior of compounds from the total body of all
physical states by means of the mass spectrometer. In the same
way, one can assume, the critic can separate out the works of
John Donne or Herman Melville from the body of writing in one
particular language and examine such works as discrete entities.
But as soon as the literary critic attempts to understand how the
works of such artists came into being, what effect they may have
had on other works of art, or how they illuminate the times in
which they were written, on the one hand, or the general human
condition, on the other, he strikes far greater complexities.

The problem Matthiessen addresses here, that of the relationship of the individual artist to the society in which he or she creates, has recently been addressed in somewhat similar fashion by what Geoffrey Hartman has called "a *'structuralisme génétique'* of Marxist inspiration."[9] Hartman cites Lucien Goldmann's work as the prime example of such a structuralism, and certain similarities between Matthiessen's late 1930s approach and Goldmann's 1966 comment on this matter are striking. Goldmann says:

> What I briefly tried to show in this analysis is that our research deals with intrasubjective structures with trans-individual subjects. If I am asked, not why Racine's tragedies could be written from Port Royal but why it was Racine who wrote them, that is a problem for the psychoanalyst. Among twenty-five or fifty Jansenists it was Racine who found in this world-view the possibility of expressing his personal problems in a coherent manner. . . . But the essential fact is that if I want to understand the meaning of Phèdre or of Genêt's plays, I must refer them not to Racine or Genêt but to the social groups who worked out the structures with which the plays (which have no symbolic meaning) have created a rigorously coherent universe, the same structures which on the practical level facilitated the group's possibility for living. Therefore the important thing is to know with which *collective subject* one is dealing.[10]

I do not mean to suggest that Matthiessen can be called a structuralist in any rigorous sense of the term or that his approach is precisely that of Goldmann. It does seem to me, however, that Matthiessen also attempted to deal with the "collective subject"— that is, the United States of the mid-nineteenth century and the artists who responded to the presence of transcendentalism—in such a way as to show us how each individual work of art reflects that collective subject. That he is not nearly as rigorous in the separation he makes as Goldmann suggests one might be reflects the state of critical thought of the period in which Matthiessen wrote. Furthermore, such rigor is fraught with difficulties. Goldmann's comment, in the same paragraph, concludes that "to transfer problems with an individual subject to a collective social context—and vice-versa—is absurd and dangerous even if the separation between the individual and the collective is clear only to the analyst." Matthiessen's effort was to keep the focus on the individual works of art and, at the same time, to find a method that indicates the relationship of those works to the "collective subject," and, what is more, he meant to accomplish that complex task without the oversimplifications or the purely historical approaches of some of his predecessors.

Matthiessen believed that what Parrington and others like him had done was of great value, but that it was not the central task that would have to be performed in order to understand the work of art as such. Here, as in the James and Eliot books, Matthiessen is attempting to provide another necessary way of separating out the materials of criticism, and he is using the introduction to *American Renaissance* as a polemic in the service of that effort. The background, the history of ideas, the social history of the period in which art is created must be understood, Matthiessen asserts, if we are to understand the literary period corresponding to the historical "age." But they cannot be the overriding considerations in understanding the works of art, which are, after all, among the most important data in understanding that age and which are the product of the unique and peculiar sensibility of one single artist. The works of art must be understood in their own terms, as separate entities, and must be judged, in part at least, by the literary and intellectual intentions of their authors, as "trans-individual parts" of an "intrasubjective structure." Matthiessen wrote:

> But "the history of an art" as Ezra Pound has affirmed, "is the history of masterwork, not of failures or mediocrity." And owing to our fondness for free generalization, even the masterworks of these authors have been largely taken for granted. The critic knows that any understanding of the subtle principle of life inherent in a work of art can be gained only by direct experience of it, again and again. The interpretation of what he has found demands close analysis, and plentiful instances from the works themselves. With a few notable exceptions, most of the criticism of our past masters has been perfunctorily

tacked onto biographies. . . . And such good criticism as has been written has ordinarily dealt with single writers; it has not examined the interrelations among the various works of the group. [p. xi]

Theory and Practice

Matthiessen calls his chapter IV "The Organic Principle," and with that title he points to the primary theory he will treat as he shows the "conceptions held by five of our major writers concerning the function and nature of literature" (p. vii). It is a commonplace of criticism in American letters to say that the mid-nineteenth century could only derive its literary theory from organic, Coleridgian notions of art. As Robert E. Spiller puts it: "The organic theory of literary art, upon which Emerson and Thoreau so fully agreed, was the only possible one for a nation that had so much new experience to shape into expression as did the young Republic."[11]

But for Matthiessen, organicism was a valued aesthetic theory only rarely attained in practice by the writers of the period. Very early in *American Renaissance* he says of Emerson: "Organic wholeness was what he admired most; he could suggest it metaphorically by saying that writers like Montaigne or Browne, 'when they had put down their thoughts, jumped into their book bodily themselves.' When he turned to his contemporaries and himself, he missed this ability to do justice to the solid as well as the ethereal" (p. 28).

Emerson's conception, Matthiessen shows, came essentially from Coleridge, and he quotes Coleridge's famous formulation as a basis for the discussion of organicism.

"No work of true genius dares want its appropriate form, neither indeed is there any danger of this. As it must not, so genius can not, be lawless; for it is even this that constitutes it genius—the power of acting creatively under laws of its own origination . . . The form is mechanic, when on any given material we impress a pre-determined form, not necessarily arising out of the properties of the material;—as when to a mass of wet clay we give whatever shape we wish it to retain when hardened. The organic form, on the other hand, is innate; it shapes, as it develops itself from within, and the fulness of its development is one and the same with the perfection of its outward form. Such as the life is, such is the form. Nature, the prime genial artist, inexhaustible in diverse powers, is equally inexhaustible in forms . . ." [pp. 133–34, Matthiessen's ellipses]

Going on to show how Thoreau and Emerson both derived their version of the organic idea largely from the growth of living things in nature, Matthiessen then indicates how the organic principle can be abused. "The manifest risk for art in such a doctrine is that its exclusive emphasis on the inner urge rather than the created shape can quickly run to formlessness, particularly when it insists on the same spontaneous growth for a poem as for a plant. In fact, it could be argued that the various degrees of formlessness in Emerson, Thoreau, and Whitman were owing to the varying lengths to which they carried this analogy" (p. 134).

Returning specifically to Emerson, Matthiessen cites Emerson's devotion to organic imagery, which is illustrated by his thesis that decoration can be reduced to "endlessly varied imitations of plant and animal life, such as the shapes of leaves, the wheat-ear, the pine-cone, the sea-shell and the lion's claw" (p. 135). Finally, Matthiessen turns from Emerson's theory to his poetry, and cites two examples, one successful and one unsuccessful, of Emerson's use of natural, hence "organic," imagery. He concurs with Yvor Winters that in "Woodnotes" Emerson has fallen prey to the "fallacy of imitative form," that is, he has attempted to imitate nature rather than to analogize it. But in "The Snow-Storm" Emerson has avoided the characteristic danger of his poetry that of "leaving it [material nature] behind altogether. His most fruitful work resulted from a poise in attitude between the two extremes, when the organic analogy between art and nature gave substance to his lines without causing him to lose sight of the fact that it was simply an analogy" (p. 138). Matthiessen then quotes "The Snow-Storm" in its entirety, concentrating his discussion on the second part of the poem, beginning with "Come see the north wind's masonry," which he considers Emerson's "most lucid and graceful expression of the doctrine of organic form. The rhythm is not so successfully sustained as in the more immediately descriptive stanza, and limps very badly in the next to last line, only to rally, to recapture once more the vibrating excitement that the poem has been designed to express. Emerson has suggested nature's inexhaustible plentitude, but has recognized its want of 'number' and 'proportion,' the very qualities with which any art of man must be concerned. In creating them here he shows how he could avoid the fallacy of literal imitation" (pp. 139–40).

This gives us the background against which Matthiessen will treat the use of the organic principle by his artists. As with his discussion of ideas in general, he turns first to Greenough, to the visual artist, before he goes on to other writers. Matthiessen sees in Greenough a representative both of the democratic tradition and of the strictest kind of organicism that will prepare the way, half a century later, for Frank Lloyd Wright.

> Greenough was clear in his insistence that notwithstanding the immediate ugliness, the meretricious by-products of scroll-work and brummagem, the right course for art was to accept the principles of the newly invented machines. If we compare the first form of one of these "with the perfected type of the same instrument, we observe, as we trace it through the phases of improvement, how weight is shaken off where strength is less needed, how functions are made to approach without impeding each other, how the straight becomes curved and the curved is straightened, till the struggling and cumbersome machine becomes the compact, effective, and beautiful engine." [pp. 147–48]

From this discussion of Greenough's prophetic vision of Bauhaus functionalism Matthiessen eventually gets to Thoreau, and in particular to *Walden*, which he considers a near-perfect example of the highest merging of organic form with the work of art:

The particular value of the organic principle for a provincial society thus comes into relief. Thoreau's literal acceptance of Emerson's proposition that vital form "is only discovered and executed by the artist, not arbitrarily composed by him," impelled him to minute inspection of his own existence and the intuitions that rose from it. . . . Thoreau demonstrated what Emerson had merely observed, that the function of the artist in society is always to renew the primitive experience of the race, that he "still goes back for materials and begins again on the most advanced stage." Thoreau's scent for wildness ferreted beneath the merely conscious levels of cultivated man. It served him, in several pages of notes about a debauched muskrat hunter (1859), to uncover and unite once more the chief sources for his own art. [p. 174]

Although this analysis of organicism in relation to Thoreau and Emerson is not now startling or unique, it demonstrates once again Matthiessen's virtuosity as a close reader and his ability to make clear the conversion of theory into practice. It is the same skill that makes him quite critical of Whitman in this regard, although he also asserts that in Whitman "we are now in a position to test the validity of Coleridge's organic principle in a more comprehensive context than when we were faced with . . . what it meant to Emerson and Thoreau. . . . Whitman, with no Yankee restraint, could push the analogy between art and nature to the farthest limits of recklessness and confusion. . . . Yet, at his best, he penetrated to the core of Coleridge's principle, and demonstrated what it could mean by his own creation" (p. 593).

When Matthiessen turns to Hawthorne and Melville, however, he is not nearly so concerned with examining their response to the organic principle. He does make the assertion that Melville had found, in the similes that Matthiessen identifies as Homeric, the epitome of organicism. "But what Melville had learned in *Moby-Dick* that he had not known in *Mardi*," adds Matthiessen, "came not from Homer, but from his own assimilation of the organic principle. He had learned how to make beauty out of natural strength. He had learned how to make it functional, for, unlike most borrowers, he did not let his Homeric similes remain mere ornaments" (p. 461).

Matthiessen believes that the organic principle does not apply in the same way to Hawthorne, claiming that Hawthorne fit into the Emersonian mold even less than Melville did. Hawthorne, for one thing, was not nearly so "inclined to the metaphysical speculation that absorbed Melville in his efforts to express the human tragedy involved in the doctrine of 'innate depravity' that he had inherited from his Presbyterian youth. Nevertheless, Hawthorne could not help being interested in ideas, if only on the level of meditation. . . . With all the forces conditioning his art that we have noted—the scantiness of material and atmosphere, his lack of plastic experience, his steady moral preoccupation—it is no wonder that the favorites of his childhood, Spenser and Bunyan . . . helped determine his bias to allegory" (pp. 243–44).

Matthiessen's distinction between allegory and symbol I will discuss more fully at another point. For the purpose of examining his estimate of Hawthorne's relation to the organic theory, it suffices to say that Matthiessen conceives of Hawthorne as essentially an allegorist and hence a writer with a nonorganic theory. In contrasting him with Melville he points out that Hawthorne is primarily interested in ideas and that his concern with a prior thought takes the form of a "predetermined habit of looking for emblems everywhere" (p. 244).

A second reason that Hawthorne is not involved with the organic theory extensively is that his sources, far more so than those of the other four writers, are deep in the eighteenth century. Matthiessen makes the point in many ways, both large and small in scope. For example, he discusses Hawthorne's diction and its eighteenth-century flavor—as when a "great old dog" in a sketch preliminary to "Ethan Brand" becomes in the finished short story "a grave and venerable quadruped," so that one can sense Hawthorne's "relish for the rounded period, and for the heightened dignity that the eighteenth century had believed must characterize serious art" (p. 213). He quotes Hawthorne himself as saying that his style "is, in fact, the style of a 'man of society,' by which quiet assertion he bears out my contention that many of his hidden roots are in the Augustan age" (p. 222). Matthiessen misses an important point here, in my opinion, in that he fails to comment on this kind of diction as a form of wit, as Hawthorne's sly and suppressed satire on his own day as well as on the Augustan age that gave us the "man of society" who was still a force in the nineteenth century and whose consciousness Hawthorne surely knew. Had he made this additional comment, however, Matthiessen's important point would only have been strengthened.

Thus Hawthorne's style is not organic in the sense in which Thoreau's and Melville's and, at times Emerson's and Whitman's, clearly are. Furthermore, Hawthorne was fully aware of his separation, in this connection—as in others—from his contemporaries. Quoting Hawthorne's introduction to *The Snow Image*, a volume in which he "reluctantly consented to a final gleaning from his fugitive pieces" (p. 220), Matthiessen concludes that "thus he announced his failure to meet the test which Thoreau had set up two years before in the *Week*, that a book should be so saturated with nature that it could stand the scrutiny of the unobstructed sun; to say nothing of what Whitman was soon to demand of his lines, that they should read as though they had been charactered in blood" (p. 221).

But Matthiessen does see a connection between the four "organic" authors and Hawthorne. It is a connection that comes through the effect of the Puritan concept of "remarkable providences," of the search for "emblems," devices most evident in Hawthorne's work and central to his literary method. Says Matthiessen:

> No art that sprang from American roots in this period could fail to show the marks of abstraction. . . . The tendency of American idealism to see a spiritual significance in every natural fact was more broadly diffused than transcendentalism. Loosely Platonic, it came specifically from the common background that lay behind Emerson and Hawthorne, from the Christian habit of mind that saw the hand of God in all manifestations of life, and which, in the intensity of the New England seventeenth century, had gone to the extreme of finding "remarkable providences" even in the smallest phe-

nomena, tokens of divine displeasure in every capsized
dory or run-away cow. [p. 243]

In this way Matthiessen connects the Neoplatonic sources, from
which Emerson and Coleridge derive their theory, to Hawthorne's
essentially allegorical method. The connection here points to the
similarity in origin of symbolic and allegorical devices, both of
which have roots in the notion that some event, vision, experience, or emotion is not merely sufficient unto itself but is an
indication of some other truth or another level, which is best
comprehended on the basis of the first event, vision, experience,
or emotion. This idea merely confirms the still-existing difficulty
in distinguishing easily and clearly between symbol and allegory, and it points to the relationship between the two modes of
"other-speaking," which concerns Matthiessen just as it concerns
contemporary critics, especially in light of challenges to earlier
notions that come from such thinkers as Derrida or Lévi-Strauss.

Matthiessen's discussion of the organic principle makes it clear
that he sees in the organic approach a source of strength for his
authors. Matthiessen himself, although transforming Victorian
notions into their more modern counterparts, believes that some
organic theory of art is the crucial component of a positive aesthetic. We have seen, in the earlier discussion of Henry James
and T. S. Eliot (both of whom are widely quoted in *American
Renaissance*), that what Matthiessen values almost above all else
as a criterion for good writing is the "unified sensibility." Such a
unification, Matthiessen shows us, derives for at least four of the
writers of his renaissance from the organic theory. Thoreau is pre-
eminent as a representative "organic" writer, for it is the native
Concord man who "proved on his pulses" the things that "others
were preaching" (p. 80).

Furthermore, "wherever Thoreau turned for fresh confirma-
tion of his belief that true beauty reveals necessity, he saw that
'Nature is a greater and more perfect art,' and that there is a
similarity between her operations and man's. . . . He held, like
Emerson, that 'man's art has wisely imitated those forms into
which all matter is most inclined to run. . . .' But Thoreau studied
more examples in detail than Emerson did . . . and when he

wanted his basic lesson in Coleridge's distinction between mechanic and organic form, all he had to do was to mould a handful
of earth and to note that however separately interesting its par-
ticles might be, their relation was one of mere lifeless juxtaposi-
tion. In marked contrast was the shape of even 'the simplest
and most lumpish fungus,' and the reasons for its fascination
crowded upon him: 'it is so obviously organic and related to
ourselves . . . It is the expression of an idea; growth according to
a law; matter not dormant, not raw, but inspired, appropriated
by spirit'" (p. 154). On the other hand, Matthiessen discusses
Emerson's failures, and more especially Whitman's, when these
two far less "earth-bound" writers took off on flights of uncon-
trolled fancy. Matthiessen might have said not only that they left
behind the organic style but also that their failure was a failure in
the unification of sensibility. Still another way he might have
expressed this view is that they had failed to find the appropriate
objective correlative, a notion that is intimately related to any
contemporary version of Coleridgian organicism. Thus we can
see a possible desire on the part of Matthiessen to look for the
permanent in aesthetics by finding sources for what he considers
great art in the middle of the nineteenth century that are similar
to those in his own time.

But this raises another matter in its turn, for we must ask if
Matthiessen's judgment that the organic style was a major source
of artistic strength is valid. In finishing his analysis of "The Snow-
Storm" Matthiessen says that

> the attitude towards art that Emerson takes in this poem is
> integral to the determination of the American writers of his day
> to speak out of a direct relationship to experience, and not
> through borrowed modes. Thoreau made the attitude more
> explicit when he voiced the satisfaction with which he read, in
> a report on farms by a group of Middlesex husbandmen, of
> the number of rods of stone wall and of bushels of corn and
> potatoes: "I feel as if I had got my foot down on the solid and
> sunny earth, the basis of all philosophy, and poetry, and reli-
> gion even." The implication again is of art as a natural growth,
> and since the solidity of both *Walden* and *Leaves of Grass*, as

well as the limitations of the one and the weaknesses of the other, can be charged to that conception, we may profitably carry our examination of it beyond Emerson's occasional remarks. [p. 140]

A further indication of the importance Matthiessen gave to the organic theory can be seen in his consideration of the genre painters of the last half of the nineteenth century. When he writes about nineteenth-century painting, in a portion of his Whitman chapter dealing with Eakins, Mount, and Millet, Matthiessen says of the first of these:

> The nearest approach he ever made to defining a philosophy of art was in another long letter to his father. . . . It has much bearing . . . on a further phase of the organic style, on what primary analogies between art and nature have continued to mean when freed from transcendental philosophy. "The big artist," Eakins wrote, . . . "does not sit down monkey-like and copy a coal scuttle or an ugly old woman like some Dutch painters have done, nor a dung pile, but he keeps a sharp eye on Nature and steals her tools. He learns what she does with light, the big tool, and then color, then form, and appropriates them to his own use. . . . if ever he thinks he can sail another fashion from Nature or make a better-shaped boat, he'll capsize or stick in the mud. . . ." As Lloyd Goodrich has put it, . . . "Eakins worked from the core of reality out into art." [pp. 606–8]

Matthiessen points to these views with approval on the whole, though he demurs at such extremes as Eakins's painting of the physicist Henry Rowland, which Eakins decorated with spectrum lines and mathematical formulae even on the frame. But he does contrast Eakins, as he does at least four of his writers, with those who did not share his organic views, and he asserts that organicism contributed more than anything else to making the work of these writers and artists great.

It seems difficult, at best, to defend a judgment that insists that only one theory can be or has been used successfully for the creation of great art in any given historical period. Spiller's phrase that the "organic theory . . . was the only possible one" seems an overstatement. One may argue, as Matthiessen successfully does, that the creators of a great literature shared a particular point of view. But to make that point of view causative for their success constitutes a step far more difficult to take. It is certainly possible, literary creation being the highly complex act we know it to be, that the aesthetic theory of the artist may be an after-the-fact rather than a before-the-fact concept—that is, the artist may develop a theory from the way his writing, his reading, his total life experience shapes his art rather than from any preconceived theory. Or perhaps the theory changes as the art does, and it is only in retrospect that we can pick out similarities and consistency. The history of literature is replete with examples of writers who created great poetry or fiction based on quite different theories, if they were aware of any theories at all. Such pairs roughly contemporary with one another as Shakespeare and Jonson, James and Twain, and Brecht and Beckett rather obviously make the point.

Yet Matthiessen's case for the organic theory as relevant to and perhaps descriptive of the work of at least four of his artists is certainly persuasive. His proof that they consciously adhered to such a theory is equally so. But he cannot give us, by these means, more than a suggestion that such a theory *causes* the greatness of their work, and perhaps he sets himself an impossible task when he attempts to do so. Even with the most conscious, most theoretically inclined artist, a Matthew Arnold for instance, the relationship between conscious theory and creative practice is always tenuous and open to question. Even Brecht, many will argue, wrote more epic theory than epic theater. We are close here, of course, to the problem of "intentional fallacy," which W. K. Wimsatt, Jr., and Monroe C. Beardsley have discussed and which suggests that though the artists of the American Renaissance may have adhered to an organic theory, it is difficult to demonstrate convincingly that it was their intentional use of that theory that gave their art its excellence. I think it fair to say that Matthiessen here betrays his own "romantic" biases to

the degree, at least, that such biases were not profoundly modified by what he had learned from Eliot and from New Criticism in
general.

But Matthiessen's effort is significant and useful, because it
demonstrates the importance of the organic theory in the 1850s
and for the artists of that period, and it suggests that one explanation for the particular kind of success these artists had may have
come from their efforts to produce an organic art. More important, it points to the simultaneous expression of organic theory
and the particular works of these writers as efflorescences of a
"spirit of the times," a "collective subject," in Goldmann's phrase,
which helps us to understand America in the mid-nineteenth
century and our literature subsequent to it. However, Hawthorne
proves that all successful writers of the period did not have to
adhere to such a view to write with excellence.

I have dealt with only one—albeit the most important—artistic
theory that Matthiessen discusses in *American Renaissance*. He discusses other theories as well. He comments, for example, on the
force and the influence of oratory upon his writers, and he ana-
lyzes the effect of musical comparisons they used as metaphor. It
is sufficient, however, to examine one theory to understand how
Matthiessen goes about showing us what influence "the conceptions . . . concerning the function and nature of literature" had
on his five writers.

The Importance of Form

Matthiessen's concern with language and form pervades *American
Renaissance* as does nothing else. He meant precisely what he said
when he announced in his introduction that "the avenue of approach to all these themes is the same, through attention to the
writers' use of their own tools, their diction and rhetoric, and
to what they could make with them. An artist's use of language
is the most sensitive index to cultural history, since a man can
articulate only what he is, and what he has been made by the
society of which he is a willing or an unwilling part" (p. xv).

On the whole, his efforts at this kind of analysis are quite successful and highly illuminating. There can be no question that Matthiessen was as sensitive to and as skilled at close reading as any of his New Critical contemporaries and that, steeped in the poetry of his own time as well as that of the English Renaissance and the American nineteenth century, he was as well equipped by training and experience as one could be to look carefully at style and to derive a great deal from that look. Matthiessen would no doubt agree with John Crowe Ransom's stricture that "the intent of the good critic [is] . . . to examine and define the poem with respect to its structure and its texture."[12] He would add, however, that one can apply the same intent to many kinds of serious prose.

Matthiessen's analysis of *Walden*'s style is a case in point, and is worth quoting in its entirety here, because it provides a good example of his use of stylistic analysis as an "index to cultural history." He quotes the passage in *Walden* that begins, "I went to the woods because I wished to live deliberately, to front only the essential facts of life . . . ," calling it "the core of his [Thoreau's] declaration of purpose," and then provides the following analysis of its style:

> The measured pace seems in exact correspondence with his carefully measured thoughts, and serves, as effective rhythm always does, to direct the fullest attention to the most important words. The satisfaction that we have seen him taking in the feel of syllables in the muscles of his mouth and throat is carried across to us by the placing of "deliberately": as the first long word in the sentence, followed by a marked pause, it compels us to speak it as slowly as possible, and thus to take in its full weight: deliberate = *de* + *librare*, to weigh. A kindred desire to bring out the closest possible relation between the sense of a word and its sound seems to operate in his placing of "resignation," for again the pause emphasizes its heavy finality. A clearer instance of his "philological" interest is the pun on "dear," which is not distracting since its basic sense of "beloved" is no less relevant than its transferred sense of "expensive." Hence it encompasses something of what Coleridge praised in the puns of the Elizabethans, a compressed and thereby heightened variety.

But the chief source of power here seems to lie in the verbs of action: "front," barer than the more usual "confront," is also more muscular. Behind Thoreau's use of it is the conviction that the only frontier is where a man fronts a fact. The extension of its range is reserved for the third sentence, where his metaphors shift rapidly but not in a way to interfere with one another, not until each has released its condensed charge. For the primitive act of sucking out the marrow is not incompatible with the military image, appropriate to this Spartan intensity, of putting to route life's adversaries. And as the campaign returns from the enemy to the pursuit of essence, both the range and pressure of Thoreau's desire are given fuller statement by the widened image of harvesting and the contracted image of closing in on a hunted quarry. With that final dramatic concentration, we are able to feel what it would really mean to reduce life to its lowest terms. The phrase is no longer a conventional counter since we have arrived at it through a succession of severe and exhilarating kinesthetic tensions. [pp. 95–96]

This is close analysis indeed, and it is useful close analysis. But more important, it is close analysis that indicates the connections between the "habit of mind" of the "collective subject," as it is manifested by Thoreau, and the language that expresses such habits. Thus we can see, in Matthiessen's analysis of Thoreau's use of language, how the organic theory works out in practice; we can further see quite clearly how Thoreau achieves the effects he desires. Just as we became aware, in the English Renaissance, of the difference in habit of mind reflected by the shift from the Ciceronian to the "loose" style,[13] so we become aware, in Matthiessen's reading of Thoreau, of the relationship between style and, in the broadest sense, "culture." We might provide many other examples of Matthiessen's analytical powers not only in regard to literature but also in regard to painting and sculpture and architecture. I have already mentioned his careful discussion of the work of Mount, Eakins, Millet, Greenough, and Louis Sullivan, to which we might add his more occasional discussion of the architecture of Samuel McIntire or the shipbuilding of

Donald McKay, whose portrait is the frontispiece for *American Renaissance*.

One more example of his analytic method, this time of poetry, will make his approach clearer. His chapter XIII, entitled "Only a Language Experiment," is replete with analyses of Whitman's language, a subject that, since the writing of *American Renaissance*, has received extensive treatment.[14] Matthiessen's extended discussion of "A Song for Occupations," for example, ends as follows:

> At times he [Whitman] produces suggestive coinages of his own:

> The blab of the pave, tires of carts, sluff of boot-soles, talk of the promenaders.

> Yet he is making various approaches to language even in that one line. "Blab" and "sluff" have risen from his desire to suggest actual sounds, but "promenaders," which also sounds well, has clearly been employed for that reason alone since it does not belong to the talk of any American folk. "Pave" instead of "pavement" is the kind of bastard word that, to use another, Whitman liked to "promulge." Sometimes it is hard to tell whether such words sprang from intention or ignorance, particularly in view of the appearance of "semitic" in place of "seminal" ("semitic muscle," "semitic milk") in both the 1855 preface and the first printing of "A Woman Waits for Me." Most frequently his hybrids take the form of the free substitution of one part of speech for another—sometimes quite effectively ("the sooth of the waves"), sometimes less so (she that "birth'd him"). [p. 528]

Enough has been said to indicate the nature, the extent, and the sensitivity of Matthiessen's stylistic analyses. But one is troubled by his approach for the same reason that one is always troubled by such analyses: by their very nature they depend on the particular reader's taste and judgment. What Matthiessen considers a "needless monstrosity" (in reference to Whitman's use of the word "savantism," p. 529) need not strike every other sensitive reader equally so. Surely the perception of the effectiveness of the poem's language is, after all, a necessarily subjective act on the part of the critic, and it tells us as much about the critic's sensibilities and the tastes of the historical moment in which the critic writes as about the poet's.

A third example of Matthiessen's method will demonstrate this problem more fully. In discussing *Mardi* and Melville's being "carried along by [Sir Thomas] Browne's desire to believe, more often than by his skepticism" (p. 123), Matthiessen quotes from a passage that begins, "In some universe-old truths mankind are disbelievers," then goes on to list a whole series of exemplary historical experiences from the deluge through the last items in the series, "I, the man in the iron mask: I, Junius." Matthiessen comments on the passage: "As he passes from example to example, led on by Browne's range, it becomes *apparent* that, in spite of Melville's enthusiasm for discovery and revolt, no depth of feeling has fused his instances with his abstraction. . . . Consequently, though some of them suggest the pressure of his widening interests, the series as a whole does not carry the conviction of standing for anything especially *relevant* or *central* for him. The difference is marked from Thoreau's close matching of thought and feeling in the passage on Ganges and Walden" (p. 124; italics have been added).

I do not really wish here to dispute Matthiessen's judgment but to question its basis. "It becomes apparent" merely means that it becomes apparent to that particular critic, not necessarily to every other reader. Nor can one add that it becomes apparent to "every sensitive reader," or some such other qualifier, and let it suffice. I am, further, not necessarily convinced by Matthiessen's mere assertion that the series as a whole does not carry the "conviction of standing for anything especially relevant or central" for Melville. There is no doubt in my mind that a critic willing to examine the series in the light of Melville's total work could, with a little ingenuity, come up with a reason—an *ex post facto* reason, of course—for why the particular elements in the series were chosen. Thus such an ingenious critic would conclude that the series is indeed relevant for Melville regardless of whether it carries the conviction of that relevance to his readers or not. To sum up, Matthiessen *may* be right when he makes such judgments, but his right is not necessarily every other reader's right.

In this sense, Matthiessen is, though not avowedly so, essentially Crocean in his method and thus a romantic. Croce writes: "Now, if another individual, whom we shall call B, is to judge that expression and decide whether it be beautiful or ugly, he *must of necessity place himself at A's point of view*, and go through the whole process again, with the help of the physical signs supplied him by A. If A has seen clearly, then B (who has placed himself at A's point of view) will also see clearly and will see the expression as beautiful. If A has not seen clearly, then B also will not see clearly, and will find the expression more or less ugly, *just as A did."* [15]

Some such theory, it seems to me, must lie behind Matthiessen's "apparent" and behind his assertion that Melville's list fails to carry the conviction of centrality or relevance. Matthiessen's view is not really surprising. The critic who depends as heavily as does Matthiessen on a notion like the objective correlative can be expected to make judgments based on his attempt to share the feelings of the artist as the latter tries to find those verbal structures that will most effectively convey his reactions to the world. The critic will then judge them effective or ineffective from the point of view of his ability to "get what the writer is driving at," that is, he will evaluate the artist's ability to evoke like responses in himself.

This position is not necessarily an inadequate basis for judging works of art, as its many defenders make obvious. I would assert, furthermore, that on the whole Matthiessen is quite successful in convincing us that his sensibilities are sound and that his responses to the work's forms help us to perceive it more fully. But it is important to remember that the limitations of such an aesthetic are the limits of any essentially subjective theory. It goes beyond the scope of this work, which seeks to understand Matthiessen's method, to ask if such subjectivism is not the only possible aesthetic. Suffice it to point out that although Matthiessen is extremely well equipped by training, experience, and inclination, his judgments remain nevertheless subjective judgments. It is certainly true that his judgments help all readers because they provide the insight of an intelligent, sensitive mind, and thus they offer observations that other readers can use as standards of comparison.

Tragedy

In a previous chapter I have described Matthiessen's ideas concerning tragedy as essentially a "reduced" view as opposed to a classical position. The tragic in the human condition, Matthiessen suggests, inheres in the striving of the individual toward a goal that is nearly unattainable, although it is theoretically within reach. It is a goal that constantly draws the individual onward, although very few will ever attain it—the word "grace" comes to mind as a name for the goal, if one does not take that name in any strict theological sense. Matthiessen believes that the writer of tragedy must understand that even though human beings are radically imperfect, they can nonetheless *perceive* perfection, and that the artist who wishes to create tragedy must understand the nature of good and evil as well as the relationship of the individual to society.

This theory received its most important test, as does so much else, in *American Renaissance*. My intent, therefore, is to see how Matthiessen uses his conception of tragedy to explicate more fully his view of the work of the writers in *American Renaissance*. His main concern, in this connection, is with Hawthorne and Melville. He conceives of Hawthorne as a writer of essentially tragic propensities, which, however, are offset by the idea of "romance." He makes clear Hawthorne's sharp differences from the tragic vision of classical drama. In discussing *The House of the Seven Gables* Matthiessen writes:

> Such an accumulation of oppressive evil upon the roof of one family hardly falls short of the terrible imagination of Aeschylus. Speaking from the great range of his reading, [Paul Elmer] More held (1904) that *The Seven Gables* was the one companion in modern literature "to the Orestean conception of satiety begetting insolence, and insolence calling down

upon a family the inherited curse of Ate." This kinship in
theme also throws into relief Hawthorne's difference from the
Greeks in conceiving the operation of a curse: not in sudden
violent disasters so much as in the prolonged "disease of inner
solitude." More recognized this as a consequence of Hawthorne's particular Christian tradition: "Not with impunity had
the human race for ages dwelt on the eternal welfare of the
soul; for from such meditation the sense of personal importance had become exacerbated to an extraordinary degree.
What could result from such teaching as that of Jonathan
Edwards but an extravagant sense of individual existence, as
if the moral governance of the world revolved about the
action of each mortal soul?" [p. 338]

This is not an entirely satisfactory conception. *The House of
the Seven Gables* is certainly a serious novel, despite its comic
elements, but it is difficult to see it as a tragic one. In fact, it is
difficult to see anyone in the novel—certainly not Clifford or
Hepzibah—as anything other than pathetic. As for Holgrave or
Phoebe, although they are not pathetic, they are at best a pleasant
young couple, aware and interesting, but certainly no Orestes
and Electra, or, for that matter, the Lord and Lady of Dunsinane.
And though Maule's curse has about it some of the *machinery* of
tragedy, it is, after all, about the ownership of a small piece of
land. Important though that may be to the Maules and the Pyncheons, it is hardly a grand tragic theme, equivalent, for example,
to Clytemnestra's curse on Agamemnon, or Lear's on Cordelia.
Matthiessen's conclusion, following logically from his citation of
More, seems warranted enough. He says that "the most compact
examination of theological history brings us to the very point that
we have already reached in noting the effect of American social
forces on an individual like Hawthorne, who was not content
with Emerson's new freedom of solitude" (pp. 338–39). However, this does not provide us with grounds for calling such a
work as *The House of the Seven Gables* tragic. Matthiessen does
not, after all, really call *The House of the Seven Gables* a tragedy,
although his Aeschylean comparison brings him dangerously
near to doing so.

At a somewhat later point in the same chapter, Matthiessen makes a more general assessment of Hawthorne in relation to tragedy and uses the more relevant *The Scarlet Letter* as his example. Here his definition of tragedy becomes plain, and it is the source for both the weakness as well as the strength of his attitude toward Hawthorne as a tragic writer. If we are to see that definition in action, it will be necessary to quote at length:

> Hawthorne's way of conceiving a rounded character thus demonstrates his own kind of response to the belief in the common man. It demonstrates likewise that the one-sided and broken figures who throng his most typical pages are seen against a human norm, that he was not so immersed in presenting distortion and defeat as to be incapable of imagining harmony. But his stature as a writer of tragedy cannot be attested even by this perception of the double nature of life, of the fact that there is no such thing as good unless there is also evil, or of evil unless there is good. For tragic power springs not from the mind's recognitions, but from the depth to which the writer's emotions have been stirred by what he has recognized, from the degree to which he has really been able to comprehend and accept what Edgar meant by saying,
>
> > Men must endure
> > Their going hence even as their coming hither:
> > Ripeness is all.
>
> The briefest description of the tragic attitude is the one Keats gave when he called it "the love of good and ill." . . .
>
> The testing of an author's possession of that attitude . . . can be briefly scrutinized . . . in his ability to hold an undismayed control between the pressures of conflicting forces. The kind of poise that is demanded is what enabled Hawthorne to say in the opening scene of *The Scarlet Letter* that if there had been a Papist among these Puritans he might have been reminded by his first glimpse of this beautiful woman, with her baby at her breast, "of that sacred image of sinless motherhood, whose infant was to redeem the world." Yet he would have been quickly disabused, for here, in bitterest contrast, was "the

taint of deepest sin in the most sacred quality of human life, working such effect, that the world was only the darker for this woman's beauty, and more lost for the infant she had borne." Nevertheless, throughout the book Hawthorne emphasizes the self-righteousness of the Puritan leaders, who pursue her with such relentless rigor. Her punishment and suffering are treated as inevitable; but you are never allowed to forget the loss involved in their sacrifice of her generosity and tenderness, by the lack of which their own lives are starved.

The purgative effect of such acceptance of tragic fate was reinforced in Greek drama by what Aristotle called the recognition scene, wherein the protagonist became aware of the inexorable course of the action and of his implication in it. . . . And this latter strain [as in Oedipus's inner, moral recognition] was developed to the full by Hawthorne. For his protagonists finally face their evil and know it deserving of the sternest justice, and thus participate in the purgatorial movement, the movement towards regeneration. These last phrases may seem an unwarranted transfer of the tragic catharsis from the audience to the protagonist, but though I would not presume such a formula would fit all tragedies, what I mean by purgatorial movement can be observed most fully in Shakespeare in Lear's purification through suffering; it also forms the basis for the rising inner action of Milton's Samson. Such too is the slow, heroic course by which Hester arrives at a state of penitence; such is the crisis that at last brings the wavering minister to confess his guilt and beg for mercy; such even is the desperate recognition by Chillingworth that he "a mortal man, with a once human heart," has become a fiend for Dimmesdale's "especial torment"—though by then his will has become so depraved, so remote from divine grace that he can only feel a revulsion of horror from the "dark necessity" that he cannot escape. [pp. 349–50]

It is doubtful whether Hester, at least, ever achieved the kind of "recognition" that Matthiessen attributes to her. That she has become the ministering angel of mercy by the end of the novel is true enough; that she retains the letter itself as a kind of badge of her trade (so that it became a sign for Angel for some, as was the A in the sky at the time of the first scaffold scene with Dimmesdale) is also true. But nowhere does Hawthorne lead us to believe that Hester has ever accepted some sense of her *moral* culpability for the liaison with Dimmesdale. In the penultimate paragraph of his novel, Hawthorne writes: "Earlier in life, Hester had vainly imagined that she herself might be the destined prophetess, but had long since recognized the impossibility that any mission of divine and mysterious truth should be confided to a woman stained with sin, bowed down with shame, or even burdened with a life-long sorrow."[16] There is much room for interpretation here. One need not assume that all three of the categories—sin, shame, and sorrow—apply to Hester. Certainly the last does. But her continued proud bearing and her hope that a newer day would "establish the whole relation between man and woman on a surer ground of mutual happiness" make her sense of sin and shame highly doubtful.

Insofar as Dimmesdale is concerned, it is certainly true that he comes to recognize his own culpability and stands upon the scaffold in the broad light of day. But his motivation for that action at the end of the book remains obscure, or, at least, ambiguous. Is he driven by a sense of guilt toward Pearl and Hester or, by his new awareness of his responsibility toward the Puritan community whose election sermon he has just preached so brilliantly? Are we to accept, without further psychological probing, the notion that he acts "by the grace of God?" Harry Levin writes, in this connection: "Characteristically his [Dimmesdale's] final action is surrounded with metaphysical uncertainties, leaving readers a choice of interpretations."[17]

It would seem that Matthiessen has resolved some of Hawthorne's ambiguities in a manner that makes *The Scarlet Letter* fit into his theory of tragedy. I do not want to say that he has made an "error." Given ambiguity, one may make choices. Given an announced theory, a ground on which he stands, the critic has a right to interpret the work he reads in accordance with it. Because of his position concerning the nature of tragedy, Matthiessen sheds useful light upon *The Scarlet Letter*. He gives us one way, at least, of understanding Hawthorne's resolution as the result of the writer's ability to see both good and evil, both the difficulty and the possibility of achieving grace. But it must also be said that Matthiessen is not entirely convincing and that one can feel the constraints by which he has shaped his reading of the novel to his a priori definition of tragedy.

Matthiessen recognizes another difficulty of interpretation, but he slides over it too easily to satisfy all of his readers. He does indeed "transfer the tragic catharsis from the audience to the protagonist" and thus solves one of his problems. It is interesting that Matthiessen must here shift his comparison from Aeschylus to Shakespeare, for by that very change he acknowledges, indirectly at least, that he is dealing with tragedy in a different sense from that which we find among the Greeks. Theodore Spencer, Matthiessen's close friend and contemporary, describes the Shakespearean world view in this way: "There was an eternal law, a general order—in the universe, the ranks of created beings, in the institution of government—and it was the business of thoughtful men to discover it and describe it so that through knowledge of it they could fulfill the end for which God had made them."[18] Matthiessen wrote that Spencer's purpose in this book was to "describe the tension between the forces of order and the forces making for chaos."[19] Thus Matthiessen has, in Shakespeare more readily than in Aeschylus or Euripides or Sophocles, found a comparison that works well, given his definition of tragedy.

In a discussion of Ahab as a Christian tragic hero, W. H. Auden makes clear the distinction between Christian and Greek tragedy, a distinction that, I am suggesting here, was an unresolved problem for Matthiessen. Says Auden:

> To sum up in advance, the conclusions I shall try to demonstrate are these: first, Greek is the tragedy of necessity; i.e., the feeling aroused in the spectator is "What a pity it was this way when it might have been otherwise"; secondly, the hubris which is the flaw in the Greek hero's character is the illusion of a man who knows himself strong and believes that nothing can shake that strength, while the corresponding sin of Pride is the illusion of a man who knows himself weak but believes he

can by his own efforts transcend that weakness and become strong.[20]

Matthiessen's effort, although he does not tell us so, is to subsume the idea of tragedy under a definition covering both the Christian and the classical versions, thus sliding over the crucial differences that Auden makes quite clear. Had Matthiessen indicated the distinction in terms somewhat like Auden's, we would have been less troubled by his approach and would then have accepted more readily his reading of Hawthorne and, as I shall show later, his reading of Melville's Ahab and Billy Budd.

Once we recognize the distinction Matthiessen failed to make, we cannot find his reading of The Scarlet Letter "wrong." Indeed, it may, and probably does, tell us precisely what Hawthorne wished to do. But the critic who approaches Hawthorne with a less fixed or an otherwise articulated definition of the tragic, with a less grace-oriented definition, might not wish to make quite so much of the one phrase Hawthorne gives us ("Here had been her sin; here her sorrow; and here was yet to be her penitence."),[21] which indicates that Hester had achieved a recognition of her "evil." For Matthiessen, that sentence makes of The Scarlet Letter a work in which catharsis, occurring in the protagonist, does indicate the balance of good and evil that is so important to his definition. When seen in the light of those of Shakespeare's tragedies that are most informed by a Christian world view, it can make of The Scarlet Letter a tragedy in Matthiessen's sense. Here again, if he is not entirely convincing, he is stimulating and provocative.

The same sort of difficulty occurs when Matthiessen applies his notion of the tragic to Melville. One of Matthiessen's several discussions of Ahab and Billy Budd, both of whom he considers tragic protagonists, can make the point clear. In a lengthy and highly interesting analysis of Ahab as a fatalist, filled with a "*hubris* [which] challenges instant *nemesis*" (p. 454), Matthiessen comes to the following conclusion:

> The result of Ahab's Fatalism is that his tragedy admits
> no adequate moral recognition. The catharsis is, therefore,
> partially frustrated, since we cannot respond, as we can in

Lear, to Ahab's deliverance from the evil forces in which he has been immersed. He is held to the end in his Faustian bond to the devil. Moreover, unlike both the sixteenth- and the nineteenth-century Faust, he never really struggles to escape from it. Although his tortured soul cries out in his sleep, during his waking hours his mind and will are dominant and inflexible. When talking with Pip and Starbuck, he perceives the human consequences of his action. He is momentarily touched, but he is not moved from his insistence that his course is necessary. In his death therefore . . . colossal pride meets its rightful end, and there can be no unmixed pity for him as a human being. [p. 456]

The comparison with *King Lear* rather than with one of the Greek plays is again telling. There is reason to think that Matthiessen was influenced in this choice by the work of his student, the poet Charles Olson, whose essay "Lear and Moby-Dick," a predecessor to his brilliant *Call Me Ishmael: A Study of Melville* (1947), appeared in 1938 while Matthiessen was deeply involved in the writing of *American Renaissance*. Olson's essay reveals, in part because of his study of Melville's reading of Shakespeare, the profound influence of *King Lear* upon *Moby-Dick*, and Matthiessen had access to Olson's work.[22] Olson demonstrates well that "a thorough and imaginative dissection of *Moby-Dick* will discover the deep impact of *Lear* upon Melville. The use of *Lear* is pervasive and, as far as any generalization can stand, the most implicit of any Shakespeare play."[23] Matthiessen is not without warrant, then, for choosing Lear as an apt work for comparison with *Moby-Dick*. Both Matthiessen and Olson use the connection between *Moby-Dick* and *King Lear* to construct a definition of tragedy that is essentially Christian. Olson writes, "Melville in Moby-Dick had worked out what may be called a concept of democratic prose tragedy." Melville, Olson writes, "weds democracy with Christianity because he seems to see both ideally freeing man from his own and his fellow's oppression, leaving man 'unshackled.' In this sense democracy practically implements the Christian ideal. Ishmael can, therefore, call to a 'great democratic God'—'though just Spirit of Equality'—to bear out the use of the whaler's crew, simple workers, skippered by a poor old whale-hunter for the purposes of a prose tragedy."[24] That Olson is here echoing Melville's own language from "Hawthorne and His Mosses," as does Matthiessen, is clear. Similar ideas had been suggested by Lewis Mumford about Melville, especially in his *Herman Melville*, where he writes that Melville's work "expresses that tragic sense of life which has always attended the highest triumphs of the race, at the moments of completest mastery and fulfillment."[25]

Such connections between Christianity, democracy, and tragedy are of course ready-made for Matthiessen's views of tragedy. But the fact that others hold a position similar to his does not resolve the difficulties Matthiessen's theory encounters. The issue is still that the theory—whether it be Matthiessen's, Olson's, Mumford's, or even Melville's—raises a difficulty in relation to the classical notion of tragedy that I have been comparing here to Matthiessen's. The connection between tragedy and Christianity provides a view of the world less implacable than the Greek view.

It is difficult, furthermore, to understand what Matthiessen's catharsis would have meant here, especially a catharsis transferred "from the audience to the protagonist." It would, of course, have made of Ahab a totally different character. If Ahab is to remain the man of indomitable will, the man who asks "Is Ahab, Ahab?," he cannot find catharsis of the sort Matthiessen seeks to ascribe to Hester Prynne. Melville makes this quite clear in the chapter "The Symphony," when Ahab answers Starbuck's last appeal to turn back:

> "What is it, what nameless, inscrutable, unearthly thing is it, what cozening, hidden lord and master, and cruel, remorseless emperor commands me; that against all natural lovings and longings, I so keep pushing, and crowding, and jamming myself on all the time; recklessly making me ready to do what in my own proper, natural heart, I durst not so much as dare? Is Ahab, Ahab? Is it I, God or who, that lifts this arm? But if the great sun move not of himself; but is as an errand-boy in heaven; nor one single star can revolve, but by some invisible power; how then can this one small heart beat; this one

small brain think thoughts; unless God does that beating,
does that thinking, does that living, and not I. By heaven,
man, we are turned round and round in this world, like yonder
windlass, and Fate is the handspike. . . . Where do murderers
go, man! Who's to doom, when the judge himself is dragged
to the bar?"[26]

Given such an Ahab, catharsis would contradict the very essence
of Melville's book.

Matthiessen is aware of this. He sees in Ahab's development as
a central character the embodiment of Melville's "most profound
response to the problem of the free individual will *in extremis*"
(p. 447), a point that he argues brilliantly and convincingly and
ties closely to "the matrix of Melville's age" (p. 447) and thus to
the "collective subject." Ahab's strength, Matthiessen asserts, as
an "ungodly" but nonetheless "godlike" man, was a kind of sign
of the period:

> Anyone concerned with orthodoxy holds that the spiritual
> decadence of the nineteenth century can be measured accord-
> ing to the alteration in the object of its belief from God-Man
> to Man-God, and to the corresponding shift in emphasis from
> Incarnation to Deification. Melville did not use those terms,
> but he had been responsive himself to that alteration, from
> belief in the salvation of man through the mercy and grace of
> a sovereign God, to belief in the potential divinity in every
> man. That alteration centered around the Crucifixion. By
> Melville's time, and especially in protestant, democratic
> America, the emphasis was no longer on God become Man,
> on the unique birth and Divinity of the Christ, who was killed
> and died back into eternal life; but on the rebel killed by an
> unworthy society, on Man become the Messiah, become
> God. [p. 446]

This analysis is illuminating and extremely useful for an understanding of *Moby-Dick*. But one is struck by the essentially Christian concept here (including the capitalization of such words as
"Crucifixion" and "Messiah"), and by the way such a reading of
intellectual history serves Matthiessen's tragic ideal. It does not,

however, explain away Ahab, and does not, therefore, make of *Moby-Dick* a tragedy in Matthiessen's sense, for it still does not provide for a vision of the "good" upon which Matthiessen insists. Rather, Melville is much closer to Aeschylus, that is, to Greek tragedy, in which there is no resolution and no catharsis for the main character and in which the audience must provide its own catharsis, as does Ishmael, through its experiencing of the chaotic and evil universe.

Matthiessen might have, had he so chosen, seen catharsis as occurring through the agency of another character and might then have compared *Moby-Dick* with *Hamlet*, arguing that someone in the novel might fulfill the function of Fortinbras in that play. The two possible candidates for such a role would have been Bulkington, buried by Melville in his self-conscious six-inch chapter, or Ishmael himself. But Matthiessen eschews such a solution and in fact insists on the inadequacy of "moral recognition" in the novel: "But Ahab's absolute domination carried Melville even farther; it caused him to drop what had seemed to be one of his major themes—the relation between Ishmael and Queequeg, to abandon all development or even subsequent mention of Bulkington, the barrel-chested demigod whom he had introduced at the Spouter Inn, as a natural seeker for truth. To a degree even beyond what Melville may have intended, all other personalities, all other human relations became dwarfed before Ahab's purpose" (p. 447).

But this statement points primarily to Matthiessen's insistence that full tragedy must fit the pattern he has deduced it to have. That pattern shows a balance of good and evil and suggests the possibility of the existence of grace, even though its achievement can never be reached by the protagonist. What Matthiessen is really confronting here is Melville's view of the universe compared with his own, or, in another sense, Melville's view of the nature of tragedy compared with his own—and here Matthiessen is decidedly the more "Christian," the less "Greek," of the two. Matthiessen's conviction that there must be purgation for the protagonist rather than for or in addition to the audience—a distinction he does not recall for us here—leads him once more to a point of view that is interesting and thought-provoking but not entirely convincing, especially to those who might adhere to a metaphysics different from his.

But in *Billy Budd* Matthiessen finds a work tailor-made for him. Here his theory stands him in better stead than ever, for it helps him to come very close to the probable purposes of Melville's last work. Matthiessen asserts, and his language is as indicative as its content, that in *Billy Budd* Melville had "conceived the idea for a purer, more balanced tragedy than he had ever composed before" (p. 500). "Pure" is the key word here, for Matthiessen sees in *Billy Budd* the work in which Melville "could now face incongruity; he could accept the existence of both good and evil with a calm impossible to him in *Moby-Dick*" (p. 512).

Matthiessen calls his chapter on *Billy Budd* "Reassertion of the Heart," and closes it with the following:

> How important it was to reaffirm the heart in the America in which *Billy Budd* was shaped can be corroborated by the search that was being made for the drift of significance in our eighteen-eighties and nineties by two of our most symptomatic minds. John Jay Chapman was already protesting against the conservative legalistic dryness that characterized our educated class, as fatal to real vitality; while Henry Adams, in assessing his heritage, knew that it tended too much towards the analytic mind, that it lacked juices. Those juices could spring only from the "depth of tenderness," the "boundless sympathy" to which Adams responded in the symbol of the Virgin, but which Melville—for the phrases are his—had found in great tragedy. After all he had suffered Melville could endure to the end in the belief that though good goes to defeat and death, its radiance can redeem life. [p. 514]

Here the Christian content of Matthiessen's view of the tragic becomes ineluctably clear. But in this case, since *Billy Budd* seems to fit the notion that both good and evil are part of the tragic moment, Matthiessen's theory is a major help to his criticism, rather than a limiting force, as it has been elsewhere. James E. Miller, Jr., to cite only one example, has seen the same quality in the novella as has Matthiessen. "Since Billy's disorder is that which springs from the dominance of an out-sized heart over an

almost non-existent intellect," he writes, "his fate, although cata-
strophic on earth like that of the others, [Taji, Ahab, Pierre, and
Mortmain] ultimately partakes of a spiritual transfiguration."[27]

Matthiessen's definition of tragedy, I believe, is at times a
liability to the fullest exercise of his critical powers and at times
it is an asset, a comment one might probably make about *any*
theory of tragedy that attempts to limit the genre. It is a liability
to the extent that Matthiessen looks for the kind of tragedy he
desires and does not provide sufficiently for other definitions of
tragedy—what might best be called "non-Christian" definitions.
The clearest case of such a liability is his approach to *Moby-Dick*.
His judgment of that novel is very high. "Ahab's savagery," he
writes, "not unlike that of a Hebrew prophet, has rejected the
warmly material pantheism of the Greeks; but Melville's breadth
has effected, not a fusion, but a unique counterpoint of both. . . .
This means that he had cut through the dead tissues of the culture of his day, and had rediscovered the primitive and enduring
nature of man. . . . it is significant of Melville's difference from
Emerson that he did not conceive of art as an ever higher and
more refined ascent of mind. He wanted nothing less than the
whole of life" (p. 466). But despite this praise of *Moby-Dick*'s
elemental quality, Matthiessen has insisted that the novel was
not really tragic, a conclusion that stems from his Christian conception of the tragic. He rates *Billy Budd*, on the other hand, as
"purer" and "more balanced" and thus has great insight into the
novella precisely because it fits his definition of the tragic. His
view of tragedy, then, helps him to understand much that is
closed off to other critics and helps him to provide a clear and
intelligible basis for judgment. But since ultimately the judgments
are based on the definition of tragedy, they become no more
"absolute" than does the definition itself, and they are just as
debatable.

One other issue here is especially relevant to the distinction
Matthiessen makes between *Billy Budd* and the rest of Melville's
possibly tragic works and to his view of tragedy in general.
George Abbott White, whose several provocative and important
essays concerning Matthiessen are among his various achievements in literature and psychology, has suggested that my notion

that Matthiessen's tragedy was "reduced" contravenes Matthiessen's experience in that "no matter how the rules are laid down, or argued, it is the constant *living out* of contradictory positions that is the hardest; the knowledge that someone might judge one's perceptions as 'reduced' tragedy, or the establishment of 'another standard,' or 'insufficiently dogmatic,' was Matty's own special trial, which even Eliot, at his suicide, pronounced 'inadequate.'"[28] What I perceive in White's comment is that Matthiessen's particular version of tragedy was less the consequence of thought-out ideology or critical theory than of personal need, so that he was able to draw personal comfort from the possibility that in *Billy Budd* Melville was able to come to some sort of catharsis of his own, a catharsis not unlike that which Matthiessen would have wished for, and which, had he been able to achieve it, would have kept him from suicide.

The suggestion is quite sound, of course, and no one is more qualified to make it than White, who has steeped himself deeply in Matthiessen's life. There is little doubt in my mind that in Matthiessen's case, or in that of any other thinker, a careful examination of a person's work will reveal a relationship between psychological need and intellectual convictions. Indeed, recently psychohistorians and Freudian and other psychoanalytic critics, who often argue unconvincingly in my view, have begun to reveal the psychological motivations behind acts of historic import, works of art, or critical constructs. In this connection, however, I agree with Lucien Goldmann who argues against transferring "problems with an individual subject to a collective social context —or vice versa. . . ." I do not wish to suggest by any means that there is not a good deal to be gained and a good deal to be learned about the American experience in the first half of this century by a careful biographic, even perhaps a psychoanalytic, study of Matthiessen, which would include an examination of the reasons for his need to develop the Christian view of tragedy I have attributed to him—but I would not wish to substitute such a study for an examination of the view itself or of its relationship to Matthiessen's critical methodology.

Every critic must approach the tragic with some sort of definition in mind. Psychological needs aside, that definition will ultimately rest not only on perceptions of the tragic but also upon his or her essential metaphysic. If Susan Sontag, whose definition of tragedy I have cited earlier, comes to a different conclusion about the nature of the form than Matthiessen does, it is because she has tried to leave behind any vestiges of a Judeo-Christian religious view. Matthiessen's every attempt at philosophy, on the other hand, is to meld his Christian views with his social concerns. That being the case, all critics, like Matthiessen, will find themselves defining the "purest" tragedies as those that accord with their own definitions of the tragic in the universe. Unless they are shallow or dishonest about their positions, we can learn from them and deepen our understanding of the tragic work of art. But we must, as with Matthiessen, achieve awareness of the sources of the critic's approach and thus understand its limitations. It is from this point of view, and with such an understanding in mind, that Matthiessen's use of tragedy as a critical tool in *American Renaissance* must be seen.

Allegory and Symbolism

I have already indicated the importance Matthiessen attached to allegory in my discussion of the organic theory, and I have quoted his approach to the connection between organic theory and the Puritan habit of seeing "remarkable providences" in the minutiae of daily experience. He develops these connections so as to make a distinction between Hawthorne and the other four writers he assesses in *American Renaissance*. But Matthiessen's distinctions between allegory and symbolism are greater than I have so far indicated. They are, in fact, important enough to provide the title for his 76-page chapter VII, "Allegory and Symbolism." The chapter falls, logically enough given the methodology of *American Renaissance*, in the middle of Book Two, which he calls "Hawthorne," for it is here that Matthiessen wishes to distinguish most clearly between Melville's mode of thought and that of the author of *Twice-Told Tales*. Although one critic, complaining of Matthiessen's tendency to "keep upon these divergent bridle paths too long," calls this section a "proleptic, if germane, account of Melville's symbolism,"[29] Matthiessen's logic is clear. Because he feels that allegory and symbolism are two opposing modes of thought that define a chief difference between Melville and Hawthorne and that explain two casts of mind important in mid-nineteenth-century America, he places this section where it will most clearly elucidate such differences. He writes:

> The differentiation between symbolism and allegory, be-tween Melville and Hawthorne at their most typical, is thus seen to be allied to Coleridge's fundamental distinction be-tween imagination and fancy. Using some of Coleridge's terms, it may be said that symbolism is esemplastic, since it shapes new wholes; whereas allegory deals with fixities and definites that it does not basically modify. As a result *Moby-Dick* is, in its main sweep, an example of the reconcilement of the general with the concrete, of the fusion of idea and image; whereas, even in *The Scarlet Letter*, the abstract, the idea, is often of greater interest than its concrete expression. [pp. 249–50]

Matthiessen makes the distinction here between the "esem-plastic," shaping capabilities of the symbol and the retelling capa-bilities of allegory. From that distinction Matthiessen derives the idea that Hawthorne, with his "Crucial Definition of Romance" (the title to section 3 of chapter VII), was to be contrasted with Whitman, who stood at the farthest remove from him, and with Melville, who "while trying to compose *Pierre*, felt that it was impossible to write 'without apparently throwing oneself help-lessly open' to experience. That suggests his more passionate relation to life than Hawthorne's" (p. 265).

Matthiessen never gives a definition of romance, which was the central mode of Hawthorne's work. What he does do, how-ever, in the main through an examination of Hawthorne's pref-aces, is to indicate that Hawthorne considered the romance a genre different from the novel, one in which the writer had "'a certain latitude, both as to its fashion and material.' . . . He might even, though he had best handle these ingredients sparingly, make some use of the strange and marvelous. This suggests Hawthorne's way of finding beauty in a moonlit room, beauty that could not exist 'without some strangeness in the proportion,' as the romantic movement had followed Bacon in affirming" (p. 267). Matthiessen amplifies this by citing Hawthorne's later declaration that he wished to affirm "various modes of truth."

The upshot of this is to be found in Matthiessen's conclusion in regard to *The Scarlet Letter*. "Hawthorne's imaginative energy," he writes, "seems to have been called out to the full here by the continual correspondences that his theme allowed him to make between external events and inner significances" (p. 276), a statement that brings us fairly close to the earlier distinction he had made between allegory and symbolism.

Melville's highest achievements, on the other hand, are contrasted with Hawthorne's by special reference to the famous forty-second chapter of *Moby-Dick*, "The Whiteness of the Whale." Here Matthiessen believes that "Melville's most effective symbols expand thus from indicated analogies into the closely wrought experience of whole chapters, and that such a quality as whiteness can hold different contents at different times, or indeed at the same time, should emphasize the futility of the game which was so popular a decade ago, of trying to 'spot' in a paragraph exactly what the white whale stands for" (p. 290). He goes on to clarify his distinction:

> A created symbol, in contrast with allegory, is dynamic; "its components, not to be equated with anything else, function in their own right." It is "a total communication," in which thought and feeling have become one.[30] . . . "The Whiteness of the Whale," Melville's show-piece for tastes that have been developed by metaphysical poetry, could stand beside "Governor Pyncheon"—the irony of which chapter heading is that the Judge has been robbed of that election by death— as a prolonged contrast of the differing operations of the Imagination and the Fancy. . . . For the nearest analogy to a chapter like this ["The Whiteness of the Whale"] it seems that . . . we must look forward rather than back, to the extensions of the symbolical novel, particularly those made by Joyce, and to Mann's use of snow in *The Magic Mountain*.
> [p. 291]

In further discussion, which contrasts and compares Hawthorne with James, Milton, and repeatedly with Melville, and which turns to others of Hawthorne's works, especially *The Marble Faun*, the differences that Matthiessen seeks to explicate finally become clear. What he is demonstrating is that allegory, in Hawthorne's hands, and symbol in Melville's, are means of understanding the fullness and the richness of life, but that the symbol, because it is in effect one with life and has a life of its own rather than a life deriving from another source, has greater richness and density and vitality than does the allegory. "In all of these [various scenes from the Hawthorne novels, including Dimmesdale's moment of recognition, Zenobia's denunciation of Hollingsworth and Miriam's and Donatello's union under Pope Julius's statue], Hawthorne's method of procedure would appear to be the same," Matthiessen writes.

> He started with a dominant moral idea, for which his picture, like Spenser's, was to be an illustration. He might advise himself, as in his notes for *The Ancestral Footstep*, that he should build "a very carefully and highly wrought scene"; but the fact would remain, at least to eyes as acute as James', that Hawthorne had gained picturesque arrangement but not dynamic composition, that he had hardly shown himself more concerned in his writing than when he had looked at pictures, with anything except the sentiment which the artist had wanted to express. [p. 301]

Such a distinction between the symbol and the allegory derives, above all, from a notion of the importance of the organic theory. Although Matthiessen does not make the connection, three key terms—organic art, symbol, and objective correlative—form a triad that defines the grounds of Matthiessen's approach. To illustrate this further, we may note one more example.

Matthiessen traces James's debt to Hawthorne and then notes the similarities between the two writers. He comments that "James, in a sense, started where Hawthorne left off. He seized first upon a dramatic image . . . and then carefully worked it into a climax of his action, or rather made it the concrete core of his range of feeling and thought. His sense of the inadequacy of Hawthorne's loosely finished sketches could again have furnished the stimulus for his reiterated imperative to himself, 'Dramatize, dramatize'" (p. 301). A little later, Matthiessen points the direction further forward toward his own time: "It was from James' example that Eliot and Pound . . . learned that 'poetry ought to be as well written as prose'; and by extending and tightening up such a note as this of James', Eliot could have arrived at his formulation of the 'objective correlative' " (p. 305).

What Robert E. Spiller has called Matthiessen's "two chief poles of reference"—Coleridge and Eliot—are thus clearly established.[31] His distinctions between allegory and symbol are derived from the larger theory of literary creation defined by these two men. Citing the passage quoted earlier from Matthiessen concerning the esemplastic nature of literature, Richard Ruland comments: "We have learned enough of Matthiessen by now to feel the weight of words like 'more human,' 'new wholes' and 'reconcilement of the general with the concrete.' The 'fusion' sought clearly relates to man's soul and body and to his relations with his society as much as to the mode of his artistic expression."[32] Ruland makes clear here the relationship between Matthiessen's theory of allegory and symbol, on the one hand, and his man-oriented Christianity connected to his socialism, on the other.

This matter requires further discussion, since it indicates, in part at least, the wholeness of Matthiessen's aesthetic. He sees Hawthorne's use of allegory as reflecting a view of man. He says of him that "what Melville and Eliot considered his [Hawthorne's] realism was the accurate reading of human nature, which he shared with Milton and Bunyan. Hawthorne's ability to relive in his imagination some of their dramatic conflicts between passion and reason, and to understand the validity of their traditional moral standards, gave him a principle, which, as Emerson said, is an eye to see with. It gave him what the artist most requires, the power not merely to record but likewise to interpret the significance of what he has observed" (p. 312). This assessment is similar to Matthiessen's previously discussed analysis of the influence on Hawthorne of Puritan and of eighteenth-century modes of thought and eventually to his notion of the tragic. Thus Matthiessen interprets "Young Goodman Brown" as essentially allegorical, although he is ample in his praise of the story [but he takes exception to Faith's ribbon, which, he considers, "short circuits the range of association" because it "obtrudes the labels of a confining allegory" (p. 284)]. The reason he considers it a successful allegory makes clearer the view of man he sees at work in this fiction. Here Matthiessen asserts that "Hawthorne has the kind of situation where his moral perception and imaginative resources are able to coalesce. . . . Hawthorne's main concern with this material is to use it to develop the theme that mere doubt of the existence of good . . . can become such a corrosive force as to eat out the life of the heart" (pp. 282–83). For Matthiessen, then, allegory works best when its purpose is to explicate the kind of duality—evil while good is still present—which he considers necessary for tragedy.

In contrast, and as evidence of the limitations Matthiessen sees inherent in the allegorical mode, he says of the use of whiteness in *Moby-Dick* that it clearly shows "the virtual impossibility of conveying the complex applications of Melville's symbols except in their own words," an impossibility that "is posed by the properties of the symbol itself" (p. 288). It is, in other words, Matthiessen's view that the clearest perception of the tragic dichotomy, on which he insists, can produce a "Young Goodman Brown," an allegory, but that an increasing awareness of human complexity, a complexity that *includes* such a dichotomy, leads to a symbol like the whiteness of the whale.

Another way of viewing this dichotomy is to see allegory as essentially able to *explain* the tragic, as in the case of "Young Goodman Brown" or even *The Scarlet Letter*, while the symbol *renders* the tragic for the reader's perception. Matthiessen contrasts Hawthorne's relationship to eighteenth-century writers with Melville's ties to the Metaphysicals and in turn the romantics. He argues that Hawthorne's is a more didactic, that is, explanatory art, while Melville's is a more fully rendered, that is, dramatic and esemplastic art. I suspect that it would be difficult for any theorist, and for that matter, for Matthiessen, to make a "genuine" tragedy of any sort out of Young Goodman Brown's disillusionment or even out of Hester's story or Dimmesdale's although both fictions are surely dramatic and exemplary. In denying the stature of tragedy to *Andromaque*, Lucien Goldmann provides a distinction that seems to me telling in this regard.

He quotes Racine's prefaces to both *Andromaque* and *Phèdre* as follows:

> tragic characters, that is to say "those whose misfortune con-stitutes the tragic catastrophe" are "neither wholly good nor wholly evil." It is a formula which did apply to many Greek tragedies, and which is still applicable to *Andromaque*. . . .
> From the point of view of Racinian tragedy, the expression "neither wholly good nor wholly evil" also applies to the majority of the inhabitants of this world; and it is this quali-tative distinction between tragic man and the man who lives in this world, a distinction peculiar to modern tragedy, which differentiates it from the tragedy of classical Greece. . . .

> What characterises tragedy and provides its real perspective is a primacy accorded to ethics, and to an ethical system which does not admit degrees of difference. People either have authentic awareness or else they lack it completely, in exactly the same way as Pascal's God is both present and absent, un-reachable and even unapproachable through any spirituality or any paths of gradualness or degree.[33]

With regard to Hester's and Dimmesdale's guilt, Goodman Brown's temptation and near-fall, Faith's ambiguous status, Haw-thorne's delicate awareness is always one of degree and rarely one of an absolute distinction between good and evil. But Mel-ville, despite the great character he creates in Ahab, leaves us in no doubt as to the absoluteness of his evil, just as Milton, despite the profound power of his mighty Satan, leaves us in no doubt as to Satan's evil and God's goodness. If we apply Goldmann's distinction here to the world views expressed respectively by Hawthorne and Melville, Matthiessen's position becomes clearer. Hawthorne's attachment to the explicating power of allegory derives from his effort to demonstrate the ambiguity of moral judgment. Melville's attachment to the esemplastic power of the symbol derives from the depth of his effort to demonstrate the absolute distinction—however complex it may be—of evil from good. Melville's most impressive character is not a mixture of good and evil—though complex, he is not ambiguous; Hawthorne's most impressive character is both good and evil—though complex, she is ambiguous. Melville's Ahab lives in the world of tragedy; Hawthorne's Hester lives in this world, that is, in *our* world.

It is essentially a theological view, then, not unlike that of Reinhold Niebuhr, that leads Matthiessen to conclude that although allegory can do much, even at its best it lacks the greatness of the well-wrought, true symbol. He closes his "Allegory and Symbolism" chapter with a "Coda" in which he deals with modern symbolism in such a way as to clarify his view even further:

> We thus come back, reinforced by many examples, to the basic distinctions with which we opened this long chapter; to the truth in Conrad's remark that a novel is very seldom fixed to one exclusive meaning, since "the nearer it approaches art, the more it acquires a symbolic character"; and to Lawrence's intuitive recognition that "symbols are organic units of consciousness with a life of their own, and you can never explain them away, because their value is dynamic, emotional, belonging to the sense-consciousness of the body and soul, and not simply mental. An allegorical image has a *meaning*. Mr. Facing-both-ways has a meaning. But I defy you to lay your finger on the full meaning of Janus, who is a symbol."
> [p. 315]

These ideas of Matthiessen's, while fresh in his time, were not particularly his alone, although their application to the particular works he discussed show them used to their fullest extent. Susanne K. Langer's *Philosophy in a New Key* appeared in 1942, just a few months after *American Renaissance*, and in that volume Matthiessen's important contemporary confirmed his ideas. The whole question of symbolism and allegory, especially under the impact of then recent fiction and poetry, was "in the air." Matthiessen himself cites C. S. Lewis's *The Allegory of Love* (p. 246, n. 3), first published in 1936, which discussed the same set of relationships from a somewhat different point of view.

Matthiessen's analysis of these two modes of expression gives him additional theoretical groundwork for other aspects of his discussion of the five writers of *American Renaissance*. This analysis, furthermore, is related closely to his ideas of organicism and the nature of tragedy. But as with other aspects of his work, it is the *use* Matthiessen makes of his distinction between symbol and allegory that is most striking. One may question the theory, but one is struck by the extent to which the use of the theory, regardless of its intrinsic merits, provides us with insights into the work of the writers Matthiessen is discussing. The theory here, as elsewhere, provides the groundwork that undergirds Matthiessen's critical sensitivity.

The Artist and Democracy

American Renaissance was published in 1941. Throughout its pages one can find that date's imprint in the work's indirect concern with the assault against democracy represented by growing fascism in Spain and Italy and in Nazi Germany. "Democracy" was in every way a crucial concept for Matthiessen. For him, the figures of his Renaissance are above all those who expressed the needs of an emerging democratic nation. He writes, in his introduction:

> Emerson, Hawthorne, Thoreau, Whitman and Melville all
> wrote literature for democracy in a double sense. They felt that
> it was incumbent upon their generation to give fulfilment to
> the potentialities freed by the Revolution, to provide a culture
> commensurate with America's political opportunity. Their
> tones were sometimes optimistic, sometimes blatantly, even
> dangerously expansive, sometimes disillusioned, even de-
> spairing, but what emerges from the total pattern of their
> achievement—if we will make the effort to repossess it—
> is literature for our democracy. [p. xv]

Just exactly what Matthiessen meant by democracy is a little difficult to ascertain. The evidence of his devotion to such an idea, in social and economic terms, in his devotion to a vision of man ennobled through an abundance of available opportunities, and in his personal and professional life, is everywhere. His devotion to socialism, although not to any doctrinaire Marxism and certainly not to communism in any parochial sense, is attested to by any number of those who knew him best.[34]

Henry Nash Smith points out that "it would not be appropriate to try to reconstruct Matthiessen's politics from *American Renaissance* because this subject is only incidental to the purpose of the book. Nowhere in it does he undertake a systematic statement of his own ideas. But his general position comes out repeatedly in the course of his exposition. The governing image or norm of value is 'man in his full revolutionary and democratic splendor as the base and measure of society'—a formulation in this instance derived from Greenough."[35] And that is where the problem lies, for Matthiessen does not really tell us what he means by "man in his full revolutionary and democratic splendor." To a large degree he has taken on the spirit of his generation. Such figures of left-wing culture as emerged from the 1920s and moved through the 1930s without becoming fully attached to one or another of the more organized, theory-based socialist movements, whether Communist or Trotskyist or social-democratic, seemed frequently to believe in a kind of amorphous, often hard to analyze, vision of "democratic man." They held to an a priori belief that the human being has great potential, that this potential is most likely to be realized when institutions of class and economic or political structures are not oppressive, and that the "value" of a society can, in large part, best be gauged by the degree to which men and women, and in particular "the common man," can achieve their potentialities.

Such a thumbnail description is intended neither to over-simplify nor to denigrate one of the most informing ideologies of our time. It might better be exemplified in the words of another "democratic" thinker, writing during the period in which Matthiessen was working on *American Renaissance*. "The foundation of democracy," wrote John Dewey, "is faith in the capacities of human nature; faith in human intelligence and in the power of pooled and cooperative experience. It is not belief that these things are complete but that if given a show they will grow and be able to generate progressively the knowledge and wisdom needed to guide collective action."[36] For Matthiessen, democracy would have included an economics that eliminated the private appropriation of capital and a belief in the mystique of the common man not so clearly perceived in Dewey's words, a belief that traces back to Rousseau and French romanticism, their American counterparts, and Matthiessen's own political experiences and actions.[37]

In describing the background for Book Two of the first volume of *Main Currents in American Thought*, Parrington provides a good description of what appears to have been for Matthiessen an important aspect of the "democratic splendor." Parrington writes of "these scattered and undistinguished colonials" to whom "French romantic theory was brought by a group of intellectuals in the later years of the [eighteenth] century" which seemed to provide "an authoritative sanction for the clarifying ideals of a republican order." Then he describes the theory as follows:

> Exploring the equalitarian premises of the doctrine of natural rights, it amplified the emerging democratic theory by substituting for the Puritan conception of human nature as vicious, the conception of human nature as potentially excellent and capable of indefinite development. It asserted that the present evils of society are the consequences of vicious institutions rather than of depraved human nature; and that as free men and equals it is the right and duty of citizens to re-create social and political institutions to the end that they shall further social justice, encouraging the good in men rather than perverting them to evil. Romantic theory went further and provided a new economics and a new sociology.[38]

These views dovetail neatly with Matthiessen's belief that, although human nature may turn to evil, there is always the possibility of good. In *From the Heart of Europe*, where Matthiessen makes some efforts to explicate his political views, we find the following illuminating passage on this subject:

> What makes Whitman the central figure in our literature affirming the democratic faith is that he does full justice, as no one else does, to all three elements of the classic French articulation of that faith. Liberty and equality can remain intellectual abstractions if they are not permeated with the warmth of

fraternity. . . . Whitman knew, through the heartiness of his temperament, as Emerson did not, that the deepest freedom does not come from isolation. It comes instead through taking part in the common life, mingling in its hopes and failures, and helping to reach a more adequate realization of its aims, not for one alone, but for the community. . . . And so, trying to clarify my own American politics in these notes . . . I re-affirm allegiance to the Whitman tradition. I am a socialist, though still without a party.[39]

For Matthiessen, then, notions of fraternity, of the dignity of men and women, and of man's democratic potential are supported not only by his literary researches but also by his Christianity and his socialism. His Christianity makes him assert the value of love,[40] which in social matters takes the form of "fraternity." His socialism makes him recognize the special value of working people and the dignity of common labor and reject the hegemony of the rich and the powerful. It makes him aware of and opposed to the deracination of life because of the unwitting division of labor. This awareness leads him, especially through Thoreau's unifying efforts in this regard, to sum up these phenomena of his time as the evils of capitalism.

He makes important critical use of these political and social ideas—they provide another "place on which to stand." His ideas about democracy give him, in the first place, a sensitivity to political and economic content, although he avoids, because of the limitations he places on his work, becoming a "cultural critic" after Parrington's or Hicks's mold. He sticks rather closely to his avowal to look primarily at the works of art and not at their political or intellectual background; yet he makes connections to that background where he thinks it will help to explain the work. He says of Thoreau, for example, that his contribution "to our social thought lies in his thoroughgoing criticism of the narrow materialism of his day" (p. 78).

For a more extended example, we can look at a most illuminating chapter, called "Hawthorne's Politics, with the Economic Structure of *The Seven Gables*" (pp. 316–37). In this excerpt from a long passage Matthiessen writes:

By pointing out that it was owing to her father's having married beneath his rank that Phoebe possessed such plebeian capabilities as being able to manage a kitchen or conduct a school, Hawthorne deliberately etched a contrast between the Pyncheon family and the rising democracy. This contrast is sustained even down to the inbred hens in the garden, who have a "rusty, withered aspect, and a gouty kind of movement," in consequence of too strict a watchfulness to maintain their purity of race. . . . The main theme that Hawthorne evolved from this history of the Pyncheons and the Maules was not the original curse upon the house, but the curse that the Pyncheons have continued to bring upon themselves. Clifford may phrase it wildly in his sense of release at the Judge's death: "What we call real estate—the solid ground to build a house on—is the broad foundation on which nearly all the guilt of this world rests. A man will commit almost any wrong,—he will heap up an immense pile of wickedness, as hard as granite, and which will weigh as heavily upon his soul, to eternal ages,—only to build a great gloomy, dark-chambered mansion, for himself to die in, and for his posterity to be miserable in." But this also corresponds to Hawthorne's view in his preface, a view from which the dominating forces in this country had just begun to diverge most widely with the opening of California: "the folly of tumbling down an avalanche of ill-gotten gold, or real estate, on the heads of an unfortunate posterity, thereby to maim and crush them, until the accumulated mass shall be scattered abroad in its original atoms." Hawthorne's objections to the incumbrance of property often ran close to Thoreau's. [pp. 325–26]

Here we can see examples of the use Matthiessen makes of his political views in analyzing the material before him and how these views make him sensitive to nuances and ideas that others, not so inclined, might not perceive. This example of Matthiessen's use of "social background" and ideas of democracy is aptly described by George Steiner in his examination of the group of critics he calls, following Michel Crouzet, the "para-Marxists." Steiner writes:

What do the para-Marxists (or we might call them, the "Engelians") share in common? The belief that literature is centrally conditioned by historical, social and economic forces; the conviction that ideological content and the articulate world-view of a writer are crucially engaged in the act of literary judgment; a suspicion of any aesthetic doctrine which places major stress on the irrational elements in poetic creation and on the demands of "pure form." Finally, they share a bias towards dialectical proceedings in argument. But however they may be committed to dialectical materialism, para-Marxists approach a work of art with respect for its integrity and for the vital center of its being.[41]

Although Matthiessen was certainly not committed to dialectical materialism—or to any other kind—he does seem to fit the rest of Steiner's description. His work exemplified in this régard what Steiner has also called one of the "resources" Marxism has contributed to literary criticism. The third of these resources is that "Marxism has sharpened the critic's sense of time and place. In so doing, it has carried forward ideas initiated by Sainte-Beuve and Taine. We now see the work of art as rooted in temporal and material circumstances. Beneath the complex structure of the lyric impulse lie specific historical and social foundations. The Marxist sensibility has contributed a sociological awareness to the best of modern criticism."[42]

The danger exists that such a special viewpoint will make the critic "force" the material into a mold that will satisfy his viewpoint. But this does not seem to me to be the case with Matthiessen. Although his notion of democracy constitutes a value not susceptible to proof—like all such essentially moral positions—he does not make it the chief criterion of his work in a way such as to distort the material he is reading. Nor does he, like Parrington, use it to remove important works from the canon of American literature because they fail to satisfy political criteria. Nor can one find analogs to Parrington's two-and-a-quarter-page chapter on Poe, in which the writer is dismissed with the cavalier "the problem of Poe, fascinating as it is, lies quite outside the main current of American thought, and it may be left with the psychologists and the belletrists with whom it belongs."[43] Matthiessen uses the sensibility his viewpoint gives him for the acquisition of fresh and meaningful insights into the motivations of his writers and the relations between them, but he does not use it, like Hicks, for example, in such an exclusive or doctrinaire fashion that it becomes a hindrance.

Matthiessen also connects tragedy and democracy in such a way that the one notion has a profound effect upon the other. He develops the thesis, for example, that Melville's conception of tragedy is stimulated by the overexpansion of individualism in the American mind and that hence his "fervent belief in democracy was the origin of his sense of tragic loss at the distortion or destruction of the unique value of a human being. . . . His continued assertion of the nobility, not of nobles but of man, was couched in religious terms from *Redburn* to *Billy Budd*. But the terms were equally democratic. . . . As Melville examined man's lot, he was impressed, no less than Hawthorne, by the terrifying consequences of an individual's separation from his fellow beings. . . . The one thing that could redeem 'the wolfish world,' the Ishmael of *Moby-Dick* found, was sympathy with another human being" (pp. 442–43).

Although Matthiessen offers a good deal of proof for this conception from both Hawthorne's and Melville's writing, it is really another a priori idea that he is expressing. One need not suffer the horror of loneliness or the danger of separation from one's fellows because one has a sense of "democratic" man, as Matthiessen would have it. Such a horror of loneliness can be found as easily in that unregenerate Tory, Samuel Johnson, as in that thoroughgoing democrat, Herman Melville. The problem here is not so much that Matthiessen is wrong as that he assigns as *the* cause for a writer's feelings only one among many possible causes. A person's psychological experience, the sense of alienation from God, perhaps failure as husband or wife, lover, father, or mother—all these might well cause the same feelings of separation from other human beings. We have some difficulty accepting Matthiessen's allegation for the source of the idea of tragedy in democracy only because both notions are not sufficiently clear, not sufficiently delineated. As suggestion, we find it fascinating—but only as one suggestion among other possible ones.

Matthiessen supports this particular argument in another way. In discussing Newton Arvin's biography of Hawthorne, he writes: "In recording the tragic implications for humane living of a whole phase of American development, the novelist has helped free us from our reckless individualism in pointing to the need for a new ethical and cultural community. By understanding him, the goals of our own society become more clear. Yet what Arvin has seemingly overlooked is that it was not primarily Hawthorne's social observation, but his initial religious conception of man's nature which gave coherence to his interpretation of life" (p. 343).

Matthiessen's point here is that Hawthorne understood not only the need for an expanding democracy in terms of the history of his country but that he also understood the democracy of tragedy. He realized that in the universality of suffering all men and women are indeed equal. This is a more challenging and tenable position than the assignment of the sources of tragedy to democracy, since it derives from the essentially Christian basis of the thought of Hawthorne and Melville and certainly of Emerson. Furthermore, it is precisely the kind of idea Matthiessen himself cherished, so that it provides another example of how the critic's "biases" can open him up to perceptions that might not be available to others. Such a notion also reinforces Goldmann's distinction between "this world" and the world of tragedy.

When, near the end of *American Renaissance*, Matthiessen cites a notebook entry of Emerson's that projects the possibility of treating Christ as "representative man," he brings together mos effectively his use of the ideas of Christianity and democracy:

Looking back at this book [*Representative Men*] a dozen years later, he [Emerson] said that he had sensed when writing it that Jesus was the "Representative Man" whom he ought to sketch, but that he had not felt equal to the task. What he might have tried to present is suggested by a few sentences in his journal several years before (1842): "The history of Christ is the best document of the power of Character which we have.

A youth who owed nothing to fortune and who was 'hanged at Tyburn,'—by the pure quality of his nature has shed this epic splendor around the facts of his death which has trans-figured every particular into a grand universal symbol for the eyes of all mankind ever since." That is similar to Melville's conception of democratic tragedy, and also to what Hawthorne had perceived in Sodoma's picture of Christ bound to a pillar—the union of suffering and majesty. [p. 634]

Matthiessen makes no real effort to clarify precisely what he means by democracy, and so it is not always easy to check his perceptions. But he does use the ideology, which seemed so nec-essary to his own sense of values, to give us rich, original in-sights into the works of his five writers. Moreover, though he has not clearly defined his terms for us, we have not been able to point to contradictory interpretations in his own work either, which indicates that there was a clearer idea in Matthiessen's mind than in his book, or at least that the ideas were a felt pres-ence in this thought. In any event, he does retain his avowed purpose of sticking to the works rather than dealing primarily with their background, which might have happened had he at-tempted any thoroughgoing definition of democracy.

I believe that the foregoing shows *American Renaissance* to be a critical work of tremendous usefulness. It is not flawless—and what work of such scope is? It does not seem to me overelaborate praise to say of it, as does Robert E. Spiller, that it is "perhaps the most profound work of literary criticism on historical principles by any modern American with the possible exception of Lowes' 'Road to Xanadu.' "[44] The work is especially profound in the ap-plication of Matthiessen's critical sensibility to the styles of his writers, in the application of the critical and philosophical posi-tions that he firmly holds to the work of his writers, in his perse-verance in doing what his preface says he intends to do, and finally in his use of materials from many literary periods and from many other disciplines to provide a larger context in which to see the works of the five writers and the connections between them. A further quality of *American Renaissance* is its implicit, passionate dedication to art as a human good, a dedication that speaks to us from every page. Matthiessen's style, the very sweep of his ideas, the breadth and depth of his knowledge—all have shaped a book that convinces us that Matthiessen wants us to understand the American renaissance as he saw it and to use his understanding as we move toward our own.

And yet there are problems with the book's overall impact. The most serious attack on the book came from Granville Hicks, whose goals were enough like Matthiessen's so that one could assume that he wished Matthiessen well. The point of examining Hicks's critique of Matthiessen is less to show the book's flaws than to show that its greatness refutes its most serious detractors. A close look at Hicks's criticism will, I believe, demonstrate in its refutation the outstanding qualities of *American Renaissance*.

Hicks's review begins with the following attack: "There is, I think, an essential lack of clarity, which can be traced to specific confusions and evasions. In particular, one has to ask whether Matthiessen has sufficiently analyzed 'the conceptions held by five of our major writers concerning the function and nature of literature,' and whether he has satisfactorily evaluated 'the adequacy of the different writers' conceptions of the relation of the individual to society, and of the nature of good and evil.'"[45]

Hicks cites several examples of what he means by his question. In one instance, dealing with Matthiessen's discussion of organic form, Hicks asks the question I have raised earlier: Must we conclude that organic form worked for these writers "because of, or in spite of, their philosophical premises"?[46] But Hicks takes the case much further than I have, and in that heightening of the objection—and its refutation—helps us to see the quality of Matthiessen's work. Hicks writes:

> Admittedly the finest writers of the past held views of the universe that most of us cannot share, and that does not diminish their greatness and their importance for us. But the act of appreciation consists precisely in taking what one can take, and criticism renders explicit the processes of the discerning reader. That is what the repossession of the past must be— a finding of what is alive for us. Emerson would have said that,

if we denied his three propositions, we destroyed his whole theory of art. I do not believe it. Does Matthiessen? I do not know, and that is the basis of my objection. There was a problem here, literary and philosophical, which he has evaded.[47]

Hicks overstates his case considerably. I do not agree with Hicks that we do not know what Matthiessen *does* believe. We do not require a stated credo to understand that Matthiessen does indeed think that Emerson's theory of art had a great deal to do with his own and with his contemporaries' artistic accomplishments and with their failures. He says so, quite explicitly.

We may wish to doubt Matthiessen's judgment on this score, because we may believe that other theories of art yield similar results, though certainly not the same results. But these are doubts of a different order. They imply not that Matthiessen evaded the problem but rather that he solved it in line with his own critical-historical perceptions and that he left some doubt about whether his were the only possible perceptions. That is, however, the lot of almost every critical viewpoint—as the history of critical thought amply demonstrates. Criticism is not a murder trial. One cannot really expect proof beyond a reasonable doubt. All we can ask is that a sound, believable case based on understandable premises be made—and, on the whole, Matthiessen is highly successful in this regard.

Such a defense of *American Renaissance*, however, leads to another of Hicks's charges, one more difficult to deal with and central to his caveat about the book:

In his treatment of the problem of evil, in his comments on time and eternity, and in his remarks on the transient and permanent in human nature, Matthiessen constantly seems to be availing himself of the support of religious attitudes. . . . Matthiessen, I think, should have told us, as Eliot has done, exactly where he stands, should have been as candid about his views on Christianity as he is about his views on democracy. It may be objected that his religion is a private matter, but after all, religious issues do figure on almost every page. The whole book is based on the proposition that what a writer believes about man, about society, and about the universe has a great deal to do with what he writes; and yet Mr. Matthiessen refuses to be explicit about his own beliefs. One gathers that he accepts some part of Christian doctrine, but what part, and in what sense, and for what reasons? . . . I can easily imagine Matthiessen's impatient dismissal of these questions. But, having rejected so much that logically belongs with Greenough's democratic ardor, and having accepted so much that logically belongs with Eliot's royalism, he ought not to be surprised if we find in his passion for democracy something of a paradox. He will say, I suppose, that he is interested in a synthesis, that democracy will function only if men's individual and collective hopes are curbed by a sense of man's inevitable limitations. I agree. But it will not do to destroy the hopes in order to check them—and for the moment their destruction seems all too possible. Furthermore, it is precisely his failure to achieve a synthesis that I am objecting to. Conceivably that synthesis can be accomplished on the basis of religious dogma, but only if men are willing to examine that dogma with the candor that Matthiessen so surprisingly lacks.[48]

Hicks's charge is crucial, for he accuses Matthiessen of precisely the lack of clear assumptions in regard to some basic principles that I have already attempted to document, although I have suggested that Matthiessen was as unclear about democracy as he was about religion. One can presume that such a lack of clarity may be the result of one of two possible factors. One is that Matthiessen lacked *candor*, that is, he failed to provide information he knew to be important. The other, however, is that he lacked *clarity*, that is, he failed to give a fully clear statement about a number of important assumptions because he was not able to do so. Although Hicks suggests that the former is true, the case seems entirely presumptive. Given what we have already seen of Matthiessen's limitations in carrying to their logical conclusions a number of his ideas, the much stronger case to be made is that he lacked clarity. He could not be any clearer than he was either about the relationship between literary and religious positions or about politics and literature, because he had not achieved sufficient clarity himself. No deliberate obfuscation is intended by Matthiessen, but the contradictions inherent in his various positions in relation to Christianity do make themselves felt.

Hicks's comments raise still another question. Must a critic state all major premises, must he be "explicit about his own beliefs"? Although one can readily understand that the Hicks who wrote this critique of *American Renaissance*—the Marxist Hicks of the militant, polemical 1930s—would insist on such explicitness, it is not necessarily true that Matthiessen, or any other critic, must agree to such a requirement. There is nothing self-evident about Hicks's view in this regard. One could argue as well that too much space spent on an explicit statement of the critic's position would do an injustice to the work being discussed and would place the critic rather than the work of art at the center of the critical discussion. The "Method and Scope" introduction to *American Renaissance* seems to demonstrate that this is Matthiessen's position, if not by direct statement, then by his repeated focus on the ideas of the writers he is discussing. "My aim has been to follow these books through their implications, to observe them as the culmination of their authors' talent, to assess them in relation to one another and to the drift of our literature since, and, so far as possible, to evaluate them in accordance with the enduring requirements for great art" (p. xi), and again, "[T]he phase of my subject in which I am most interested is its challenge to pass beyond such interrelations to basic formulations about the nature of literature" (p. xiii). The point to be noted here is that Matthiessen stated his own views almost completely through his subject and that he did not see the need in *American Renaissance* to provide the kind of credo Eliot supplied in the introduction to *For Lancelot Andrewes* or throughout in the later "Religion and Literature." When Matthiessen writes, then, that "works of art can be best perceived if we do not approach them only through the influences that shaped them, but if we also make use of what we inevitably bring from our own lives" (p. xiii), he means to bring from his own life his reading and his deep acquaintance with the great works of literature that have influenced him, as his examples—Shakespeare, Milton, Hopkins—seem to demonstrate. He apparently does not mean to bring his political and religious ideologies, at least not in any overtly stated form. One may certainly quarrel with such a position, as Hicks obviously does, but it is not true, as Hicks apparently assumes it is, that such a view is the only possible or the only logical one.

It seems, then, that although Hicks's accusation of a failure on Matthiessen's part to state positions clearly in regard to religion—and as I have suggested in regard to democracy—is justified, his assumption that such a failure derives from a lack of candor is not convincing and neither is his assumption that such candor must be part of every critical statement. Furthermore, Hicks draws a number of false conclusions from his valid premise concerning the consequences of the error of which he accuses Matthiessen. Hicks ends his review, it must be added, with a lavish tribute to *American Renaissance*'s great value, but his stated position that its value is seriously vitiated by a lack of clarity is overstated and subject to emendation.

One way of lessening the seriousness of Matthiessen's failure to state nonliterary premises clearly—and that is what is at issue here—is pragmatic. *American Renaissance* does provide for many new, rich perceptions concerning its subject, as Hicks agrees. This is so in part because Matthiessen has not limited himself to any credo. He lets his imagination and his critical sensibilities take him where they will. I do not mean by such a phrase to argue for a theory of literary spontaneity, but rather to point to the limitations that a preconceived set of sharply delineated principles may impose on a critical work—and no book is a better example of this weakness than Hicks's own *Great Tradition*. Because Matthiessen has not delineated himself too sharply, he can achieve insights that might otherwise be closed off to him.

Another way of saying this is that at any moment in American history a number of contradictory streams coexist. The critic who chooses only those that suit his preconceptions must, then, do injustice to some of the others. A case in point here is Parrington's contempt for the ''belletrists'' and their interest in Poe. Although such a limited critical view may well produce superb criticism of a certain kind, it cannot also acquire the broad sweep of Matthiessen's looser, more inclusive methodology. It is precisely because Matthiessen's ideas in themselves partake of a number of seemingly contradictory views—Greenough and Eliot, Christianity and tragedy, or Christianity and "revolutionary [that is, democratic] splendor," for example—that he is forced to try to bring together in some sort of synthesis the contradictions of his book. Matthiessen's lack of a stated credo does lead to certain difficulties but by that very token avoids others.

Hicks extends his charge even further when he says that "the five writers of the renaissance were searchers, and, in spite of some of their generalizations, discoverers. In so far as Matthiessen has helped to make their discoveries available to us, his book is a fine achievement, but in so far as he has failed to 'repossess' their discoveries, in terms of our knowledge and our convictions and our dilemma, he has failed the ultimate test of serious criticism."[49]

Hicks has here announced a function for criticism that is certainly of the highest sort. But I am troubled by any stance that judges a piece of criticism because it fails to do all the things criticism might do or which establishes a hierarchy of critical values and assigns top spot to one function only. Hicks is asking Matthiessen to attempt to do something such as Hicks himself attempted to do. But Matthiessen sees his function differently. For him, "repossession of the past" does not necessarily mean a comparison of the past with present views. Rather, his concern is to "repossess the past" in large part by understanding that past. A most illuminating footnote in this regard appears in the "Method and Scope" section of *American Renaissance*. Matthiessen is annotating the phrase "but what emerges from the total pattern of their [the five writers'] achievement—if we will make the effort to repossess it[5]—is literature for our democracy." Footnote 5 then reads:

> Santayana has said that the American mind does not oppose tradition, it forgets it. The kind of repossession that is essential had been described by André Malraux in an essay on "The Cultural Heritage" (1936): "Every civilization is like the Renaissance, and creates its own heritage out of everything in the

past that helps it to surpass itself. *A heritage is not transmitted; it must be conquered*; and moreover it is conquered slowly and unpredictably. We do not demand a civilization made to order any more than we demand masterpieces made to order. But let us demand of ourselves a full consciousness that the choice made by each of us out of the past—out of the boundless hopes of the men who came before us—is measured by our thirst for greatness and by our wills." [p. xv; italics are in the original, both in Malraux and in Matthiessen]

Matthiessen offers here a different approach to "repossessing the past" from the one Hicks indicates, an approach suggested by Malraux when the French novelist was in his most "left" phase. It has to do with understanding the past in its own terms much more than in reinterpreting it or selecting from it for narrow purposes those elements that are useful to the present. Although such a view of "repossessing the past" can lead to Matthiessen's awareness of the limitations of Emerson and Whitman, for example, it does not lead to a condemnation of their work or to a virtual exclusion of works—as in Hicks's and Parrington's books—that will not directly illuminate the present. The presumption here is that the past must be understood before it can be repossessed, and that is what Matthiessen has attempted to do.

To shed light on "our dilemma"—whatever that may be at any point in time—is certainly one of the most important tasks of the critic. But to let the past do so, we must first discern what the past was about. To extend the time frame from the American 1850s to an earlier period will, perhaps, clarify the point a little more. We may seek light for our own time by a study of the Greek tragedians. Indeed, we go to see their works on the stage for that reason. But if we begin our study with a primary intent to let them clarify what we already believe to be true in our time, it is likely that we will distort them to suit our purposes. It is such distortion that Matthiessen escapes by not defining his own credo too precisely, or, more important, too narrowly. He keeps a balance between "a place to stand" and "a platform." Whether this is intentional or not it is almost impossible to tell from the work itself.

It is interesting to note that Hicks's anxiety comes, in part, from his fear that men's "collective hopes" are endangered, that "for the moment their destruction seems all too possible." The hallmark of rising fascism and of the war in Europe, which the United States was to enter before the year was out, is upon these phrases. But Matthiessen's particular "repossession of the past" has continued to have meaning during the variety of historical situations that have come to pass since the publication of *American Renaissance*. Radicals of the quiescent 1950s found comfort and a model for possible sources of hope in his pages during years in which it seemed that whatever they had thought of the American Dream was to be smothered in the soft billows of Henry Luce's "American Century." Younger radicals of the 1960s, filled with anger and anguish by the war in Vietnam and the rising, often thwarted, hopes of black Americans, could turn to his pages for a meaningful corrective to their notion that ours is simply the history of capitalism at its most rapacious. George Abbott White, who is one such younger radical of the 1960s, indicates tellingly in this regard the contrast he sees between Matthiessen and the Progressive historians: "the Progressive historians . . . pointed to a great country that had somehow gone shamefully wrong," but "the ideology inherent in Matty's reading of our past could affirm 'still undiminished resources' and possibility, though with restraint and a deep sense of humility and limitation."[50] I suspect that such "uses" of the book will continue, each period's readers enabled by its depth and breadth to find something they particularly need in it—a kind of "repossession of the past" that one suspects would have pleased Matthiessen immensely.

Matthiessen makes clear that the writers of his renaissance were struggling with questions of democracy of all sorts, of isolation and of alienation, which occupy us so much. For the conservative historian who would point back to Emersonian self-reliance and Whitmanesque celebrations of America as the "truth" about the United States that young radicals seek to subvert, Matthiessen points out that the complexity of the minds of his writers saw some of the same flaws—economic aggrandizement, suppression of individuality—in their simpler, smaller, much less technological world. The fact in itself, it seems to me, overcomes

Hicks's criticism, at least to a large extent, and points toward the values of Matthiessen's methods. For had Matthiessen tied himself more closely to the ephemeral views he held in 1941, we might suspect that his book, like Hicks's, would seem terribly outdated and disingenuous now. Although one may charge Matthiessen with lack of completeness, one cannot, I think, consider him dated. He seems to speak clearly to each generation, as he did to his own, and that says a great deal about his work. Finally, it seems to me unwarranted to conclude that Matthiessen has failed to repossess the past in terms of "our knowledge, and our convictions and our dilemma," as Hicks charges. Matthiessen provides many connections to our present—if not to *the* dilemma, then to some of our smaller dilemmas. He provides far too many connections between his writers in 1850 and the writers of the twentieth century to be subject to such a charge; his connection-making skills are everywhere manifest. They can be seen in his discussion of the transcendental mode of thought and that of the impetus behind symbolist poetry in general and, in particular, in a poet like Yeats; his explication, in the "American Demigods" section of the book's final chapter, of how American heroes are created; his already-mentioned discussion of the relationship between tragedy and democracy—all these relate to Matthiessen's time, to our own time, and to any immediately foreseeable epoch. In this aspect of his work, in fact, we can see one of Matthiessen's greatest strengths.

Hicks raises a valid objection—perhaps the most important one—when he points to the incomplete articulation of many of Matthiessen's philosophical premises, but he drives it too far, toward an invalid conclusion, when he says that Matthiessen failed "the ultimate test of serious criticism" because he failed to repossess the "discoveries" of his five writers and their period. The depth of Matthiessen's knowledge, his passionate concern for such ideas as democracy, tragedy, Christianity, the organic principle, and others, and his sensitivity to both form and content in literature, save him from such a charge, leave him free to follow his critical sensibilities where they will take him, and help him, and us in turn, to perceive connections to which we might otherwise have remained blind.

Henry Nash Smith, in his especially cogent discussion of *American Renaissance*, sums it up well. He writes:

The tragic character of man's fate and the validity of democratic equalitarianism are truths which Matthiessen considers to have been apprehended and embodied in literature in this fashion. They seem to him at the same time to be the primary insights of the Christian tradition. He was not a system-builder and had no inclination to force such propositions to a logical conclusion. If he had, he would almost certainly have found himself involved in difficulties that have always beset the efforts of Christian thinkers to reconcile the belief in revelation as an accomplished fact with the continued possibility of fresh individual access to truth. What counts most in his probing of the American past is the concrete results to which his philosophic undertaking led him—the remarkable deepening of literary study consequent upon his determination to subject the writers he had examined to ultimate tests of their value, by relating them at once to the long cultural past of western Europe, to the tensions of American society in the mid-twentieth century, and to his urgent personal need for integration. It was a gigantic task, perhaps an impossible one. But his commitment to it was heroic, and it gave to his scholarship an intensity and dignity that are unique in our contemporary cultural life.[51]

5 ❧ Indiana Boy in the City

THERE is a sense in which Matthiessen's career ended with the same sort of work with which it began. In 1929 the burgeoning young scholar had produced the literary biography of a writer who provided a picture of American life that was nearly dead when she wrote about it. In 1949 and 1950 the man approaching his forty-eighth birthday, having received wide critical acclaim for his work on Eliot and James and especially for *American Renaissance* as well as the most ferocious condemnation for his *From the Heart of Europe*, worked on the critical biography of a writer who dealt with the contemporary world—with the city, its strength, its horror, its beauty, and above all its struggling, suffering people. In his last work the critic who divided his time between his home at Kittery Point and his apartment in Boston's Louisburg Square chose to study the writer of the city perhaps because that was the reality of his own time.

Matthiessen's *Theodore Dreiser*, a volume in the "American Men of Letters" series, was the work he was doing when he killed himself. According to the editor's note, he had "completed it before his death but had not revised it beyond the point of penciling many alterations and corrections in the manuscript, the last two chapters of which were in his own handwriting."[1] Some critics, and apparently many of his friends, expressed surprise at seeing Matthiessen turn to Dreiser with increasing interest in the last years of his life, and some tended to attribute that interest to political apologetics rather than to literary-critical concerns. "His tongue-tied consideration of the last years," writes Brom Weber,

> during which Dreiser chuckleheadedly joined the Communist Party, is more of an obdurately naive apologia than an evaluation. . . . throughout he lays great stress upon the historical importance of Dreiser's writing and life rather than upon their intrinsic values. Dreiser as historian, breaker of the gen-

teel tradition, chronicler of life among the lower classes, there is little else in Dreiser which Matthiessen can unreservedly praise. . . . Torn between his belief in the literary relevancy of social forces and the indubitable artistic inadequacy and intellectual shallowness stubbornly adhered to by America's outstanding social novelist, the composition of this study must have been a tortured affair for Matthiessen.[2]

But Matthiessen's interest in Dreiser had gone back a long way, "at least into the thirties," as Richard Ruland points out, "for although he appears only a few times in *American Renaissance*, the context on each occasion is a significant one."[3] Ruland might also have pointed out that in *Sarah Orne Jewett*, that is, as early as 1929, Matthiessen had mentioned Dreiser, but then as an example of a clumsy stylist. The interest was an abiding one, as we can see from Matthiessen's explanation of what must have been at least part of the impetus for writing a book on Dreiser. In discussing the choices he had made in 1947, while teaching a group of students from many European countries in a seminar on American civilization that he gave at Salzburg, Matthiessen says: "I had chosen James and Dreiser for the pivotal contrast of our modern literature. They are so totally different both in their methods and in the Americas they reveal that they bear out the complexity of our modern development and the impossibility of reducing it to any single generalization."[4] Alfred Kazin, who was a participant with Matthiessen as a teacher at the Salzburg seminar and who describes Matthiessen as its "star," comments that he focused on Dreiser because "for Matthiessen, Eliot represented Christianity, and Theodore Dreiser—a novelist about whom he wrote without conviction—American 'radicalism.'"[5] Kazin's "without conviction" is gratuitous, because Matthiessen's interest in Dreiser was visible and intense by 1947.

In *From the Heart of Europe*, Matthiessen discusses James and, in particular, the impact that reading *The Portrait of a Lady* in Europe had upon him, and then concludes his discussion of James and turns to Dreiser:

> In a world of breakdown such as he [James] never conceived, we can now find in his work, not an escape, but a renewed

sense of the dignity of the human spirit, however precarious this may be in our own overwhelming sense of imminent ruin.

The Europeans' experience caused some of them to discount Dreiser in a different way. His naturalism bothered them by being far clumsier than Zola's. Some . . . disapproved of his characters for their lack of moral reactions. Only a few . . . became absorbed in Dreiser's massive study of the gap in America between wealth and poverty, in his knowledge—in which Henry George was his forerunner—that America is the most terrifying country in which to be really poor.

But could any European quite respond to what still excited me so much in reading Dreiser: the great new domain he opened by bringing into our literature the city as it was felt to be by those struggling in it, particularly by the outsiders looking in, or rather up, at the world of financial power? The glamor of Chicago which Carrie felt is felt also by Dreiser, the immigrant's son from the wrong side of the tracks. And in no other author is there a more accurate recognition that in the fierce competitive jungle of the big city there are no equals, only those moving up or down.[6]

One certainly cannot deny that Matthiessen shows himself partial here to Dreiser's views in several ways or that he considers him a figure of historical importance. But one also cannot deny that Matthiessen is reflecting here his own movement through time with regard to his own concerns, which are reflected in his literary interests. I do not mean to imply that there was a planned survey of our literature in Matthiessen's mind from his first work about a writer of rural America to his last work about our first major entirely urban novelist. But it does seem to me that Matthiessen's efforts at understanding our literature begin with the rural past of the nation and eventually come closer to his own time as he seeks to repossess a useful past.

In *Sarah Orne Jewett* Matthiessen on the whole accepted that garden, suffused with the smell of roses, which characterizes Jewett's work. By his life's experiences, and by his study of Eliot and other poets, including Yeats and Poe and Wallace Stevens, he

learned something about tragedy, about the falseness of the sentimental that goes with Norman Rockwell country scenes, and
about those "headier passions," the lack of which he merely
noted in Sarah Orne Jewett's world. In his study of the five
figures of *American Renaissance* such knowledge, the product of
maturity and of experience as well as of reading, is applied to the
major figures of our predominantly rural 1850s. In the studies of
James and Eliot, and in the book on Dreiser, that knowledge is
applied to an America much like that of his own time, although
James's world, a world of men and women who know nothing of
the most grinding poverty and the most abject economic degra-
dation, is really rooted in an earlier, a more "genteel" time.
Dreiser's world is the world of men and women who must work
to live and who are profoundly involved in the crass and the new
that is part of the city—the tavern, streetcar strikes and streetcar
franchises, telephones and flophouse hotels. They live and suffer
and die in what is surely one of the most significant manifesta-
tions of Matthiessen's time and ours—the big city on the way to
megalopolis.

It seems to make sense to suggest that Matthiessen's interest in
Dreiser's world had been sharpened not only, as his detractors
would have it, by his increasingly radical posture but by his personal experiences, which sharpened his radical posture *and* his
interest in Dreiser. The 1930s had made him aware, in a number
of ways, of the lives of working people. His participation in the
trade union movement had brought him into contact with teachers
and professors wishing to organize and with the leaders of the
then still-new CIO unions of unskilled and semiskilled workers.
For many professionals and intellectuals of the period, their participation in the organization of the CIO was one of the major
events of their political experience, especially because it made
them feel allied with working people, an idea of great importance
to Matthiessen. During the period following World War II when
he was writing *Theodore Dreiser*, Matthiessen canvassed for votes
for Henry Wallace in Boston's working-class areas and met and
talked with workingmen and working women in Czechoslovakia.
In brief, he attempted further what had been a concern of his for
some time—to establish contact with those he considered vic-

timized by society. That his success in this effort was at best indifferent, in all probability is really beside the point. His interest in Dreiser's world of working people and business people and in that vast America outside the academy and outside the upper middle class of James's experience was sharpened by these efforts, I suspect.

All this explains adequately why Matthiessen would be interested in Dreiser, though many of his fellows in the profession thought his interest specious and even dishonest. What it does not explain is why the New Critical aspects of Matthiessen's convictions would permit him to deal so extensively with so peculiar a stylist as Dreiser. How can Dreiser become a subject for the critic who said in *American Renaissance* that "an artist's use of language is the most sensitive index to cultural history, since a man can articulate only what he is, and what he has been made by the society of which he is a willing or unwilling part"? It is this question that is at the heart of a comment about *Theodore Dreiser* such as the following: "It might be considered surprising that the student of Henry James and T. S. Eliot should have been drawn in his last work to consideration of a writer so far removed from the cultural and artistic traditions." Nor are we satisfied to read so simple a conclusion as that "this breadth of interest is the measure of Matthiessen's fullness as a man."[7]

One can hardly doubt that Matthiessen's interests were catholic. A bibliography of his work documents that fact. But a full-length book on Dreiser is another matter, and it leads to other questions. How does he handle the problem of Dreiser's style? Does he let his political and religious biases skew his judgment so that he overlooks Dreiser's crudities and flaws? Does he give us useful critical insights into Dreiser or does he become, rather, an apologist for an author with whose political beliefs his own have affinities?

Theodore Dreiser is thus a testing ground for Matthiessen's critical acumen and therefore these questions are central to this examination of Matthiessen's critical method. It is one thing to be objective—if such a condition is possible at all—about Emerson and Thoreau whose work represents the past, even though it is a past one may wish to recover. It is something else to be objective about a writer like Dreiser who speaks directly to the contemporary political issues of one's own day, and it is especially difficult to be objective if one is, as Matthiessen obviously was, deeply involved in current political controversy. If it was relatively easy to be sentimental about the past with Jewett, wasn't it easy to be overly partisan about the present with Dreiser? Matthiessen was himself under all kinds of political and personal pressures while writing his book about Dreiser. It is worth quoting a portion of Leo Marx's essay in the *Monthly Review* memorial issue here:

> The failure of Henry Wallace's third-party movement, which Matty had enthusiastically supported, was a hard blow. Then the critics of the Left joined those on the Right in attacking his journal of his 1947 trip abroad, *From the Heart of Europe*. The *Partisan Review* and *Life* treated him as a dupe of the Communists, while the *Masses* thought him a soft idealist. His sense of loneliness became more intense. He received threatening letters. All of these things strengthened his determination to speak out, as if he were mindful of Emerson's warning to the American Scholar not to defer to the popular cry. Cut off from many former friends, Matty was now actually more dependent than ever upon teaching as a means of communication, and it is to be noted that his death came toward the end of the academic year during which he had had no teaching duties. This was the year he devoted to his book on Dreiser.[8]

In *Theodore Dreiser*, then, we can see Matthiessen's literary theory and his sensibilities working under pressure. If he was able to retain his objectivity despite his subject, which he was studying under personal strain, it seems to me to speak well for the theory and the man. Conversely, if the theory falls apart under such conditions, or he permits his sensibilities to deteriorate, we would have to conclude that either the theory or its practitioner was seriously flawed.

Fortunately, we do not have to make the latter choice. Although I believe that *Theodore Dreiser* is a lesser work than any of Matthiessen's others except *Sarah Orne Jewett*, it seems to me nonetheless an extremely useful book. Its flaws, furthermore, are by and large the flaws of Matthiessen's other works and not the result of special pleading for a political viewpoint.

It is necessary to recall that because the book was not quite finished much that we find inadequate now might have been eliminated in the process of rewriting. On the other hand, the manuscript, with the exception of the Bibliographic Notes, is completely Matthiessen's, and not an editor's, and must therefore stand as part of his canon.

The reviews of the book were sharply divided. Many found *Theodore Dreiser* valuable, some even considered it excellent, but others certainly did not. One of the most seriously damaging reviews came from Richard Hofstadter, who wrote the following:

> Reviewing this book, the last and the weakest of a fine critic, is an unhappy task. I cannot but feel that the late F. O. Matthiessen was drawn to Dreiser more because he felt for him a vague political and religious affinity than because his native taste and literary interests were centrally or deeply engaged by Dreiser's writing. Although he saw, no doubt, that it is harder to say why Dreiser was at times a good novelist than it is to show that he was a poor writer, his effort at appreciation turns out, after all, to be a laborious one. The result is a summary view of Dreiser's life and work . . . which in most of its sequences conveys chiefly a sense of weary desperation. . . .
>
> No longer close to the center of interest even of those who appreciate him, Dreiser today is not an enviable subject for any critic. . . . He was, as Mr. Matthiessen says, an American primitive, a naive fabulist of genuine power, an observant reporter endowed with a revolutionary genius for candor and with a simple massive, almost maternal tenderness that is rare enough in any literature. But for more than forty years, in and out of his fiction, his mind persistently addressed itself to problems it had not the remotest competence to deal with. . . . Mr. Matthiessen . . . seems to have suffered from a compulsion to declass himself intellectually in order to find a meeting ground with Dreiser. The chapters that deal with Dreiser's incredible philosophy and equally incredible politics

take on an unhappy—and unsuccessfully—apologetic tone and even then fail to come to grips with the limited possibilities of their subject.

[Dreiser's] fumbling with metaphysics and social philosophy derives its interest . . . from its representative and even symptomatic character. Dreiser is the common man thinking. Just as his ornate and archaically allusive prose is the attempt of an Indiana boy to be "literary," so his ponderous love of generalization is the attempt of a citizen to be a philosopher.[9]

One is struck, in this commentary, not only by Hofstadter's criticism of Matthiessen but almost more by his disdain for Dreiser, and, uncharacteristically for Hofstadter, for the "common man," which says something about the lukewarm critical reception of Matthiessen's book. Dreiser was not "in" four decades ago, in the 1940s, when the James revival was at its height, when the New Criticism was most completely dominant, and when sufficient time had elapsed for the young men trained in the late 1930s to go off to war, come back, and establish themselves as scholars. Thus those working within the then-developing "consensus-oriented" framework of scholarship in American history, like Hofstadter, found their approach in regard to Dreiser and similarly rebellious figures dovetailing with that of the New Critics who seemed more and more to attend to "pure" artists, that is, artists whose social views were not a major issue. That new winds in both criticism and history came along more or less simultaneously in the 1970s, in the aftermath of the political events that destroyed the "consensus" that historians like Hofstadter thought central to the American experience, is no accident. In commenting on a recent volume concerning the aftermath of slavery, C. Vann Woodward writes of "neoclassical economists" and "a school of neo-Marxists," which he calls part of "the embattled schools of New History."[10] Critical thought has been much affected by structuralists and deconstructionists and other schools since Hofstadter—and Matthiessen—wrote, so that New Criticism is now one among many schools of critical thought, although no one can question the many contributions to criticism it has made. In any event, no such great divergence of critical opinion or historical opinion existed when *Theodore Dreiser* first appeared. "Consensus" historians and New Critics dominated their respective disciplines.

Furthermore, the hostility to Dreiser was certainly not unconnected with the growing forces of McCarthyism in American life. Any writer who was an avowed Communist—even so peculiar a Communist as Dreiser—or any writer who proved useful to the views of socially concerned criticism, especially on the left, was bound to find himself out of favor with many in the years of the beginnings of the cold war, the Hiss case, and the Smith Act prosecutions. If such a writer's commentator was also on the left, obloquy was almost inevitable. It is, it seems to me, to the credit of many of the reviewers of Matthiessen's book that they were not to be stampeded by such considerations into condemning the book out of hand. Nor do I wish, by some perverse McCarthyism of my own, to imply that every critic of Dreiser or of Matthiessen's book about him was motivated only by a desire to suppress the political left. But the atmosphere of conservatism, and sometimes of hysterical anticommunism, was present. Political judgments were being made. Thus, when Hofstadter asserts that Dreiser is "no longer close to the center of interest even of those who appreciate him," his judgment is at least as much historical and political as it is critical, as he makes clear later on, when he calls Dreiser a "folk figure" and then goes on to say:

He was the crucial actor in the emergence of a distinctly new strain in our literature at the turn of the century, when a relatively bookish culture, given to reflection and possessing a great deal of poise, was being challenged by a crass but enterprising kind of reportorial imagination whose primary condition was not books but experience—very often an overwhelming kind of experience too full of shock to be easily mastered. Dreiser still needs to be placed in historical context with other, less viable writers like Jack London and Frank Norris—almost all of them realists and naturalists, most of them undereducated men driven by a need to express themselves in large elemental terms and obsessed with ill-digested philosophical systems.[11]

But this is precisely the position Matthiessen will not accept, this relegating of Dreiser to the nonliterary limbo of sociological documentation. Dreiser is, Matthiessen suggests, an artist, and although as a critic he is profoundly aware of what Hofstadter calls Dreiser's "limitations," Matthiessen will not agree, here as elsewhere, that a writer can be used, to quote *American Renaissance*, "in a purpose of research" without considering him as an artist.

Matthiessen was not the only one who believed in Dreiser's art, nor was Dreiser the exclusive subject of a then-current and important debate, although Dreiser and James came to stand as symbols for the sides in the controversy. R. W. B. Lewis, in describing the terms of the debate, looks back on the period from the somewhat cooler vantage point of 1956 and places the issues as follows:

> The list I have recorded [a list of writers of fiction in order of their then current estimation, i.e., James, Faulkner, Hemingway, Fitzgerald, Dreiser, Crane, Wolfe, Anderson, Wharton, Cather, and Dos Passos] is deceptive, in any case. It conceals, for example, the fertile quarrel between those who articulately prefer the subtle moral and artistic qualities, the intricate psychological webbing of Henry James; and those who prefer the head-on assault on the raw American scene of Theodore Dreiser. . . . This is the one controversy within the field of fiction which can compare to the poetic debate between the admirers of Eliot and the enthusiasts of Whitman: and here again, it is a matter of the sophisticated, ironic, civilized, and quasi-European against the bald, rumbling, nakedly American, "liberal" and uncomplex. A quick view of this argument may be had by comparing Lionel Trilling's essay, which deprecates Dreiser and elevates James, in *The Liberal Imagination* (1950); and Alfred Kazin's introduction to *The Stature of Theodore Dreiser* (1955). . . . Kazin, not unexpectedly, wants to re-establish the native significance of Dreiser; and while the appeal of Dreiser's naturalistic humanism is strong and honest in him, Kazin's attitude towards James remains one of contrived courtesy. No less unexpectedly, it is F. O. Matthiessen

who has known how to deal fairly with both James and Dreiser, by detecting in both of them themes and obsessions and literary accomplishments at once traditionally American and perennial.[12]

The critical situation that faced Matthiessen, then, when he wrote his book about Dreiser, is analogous to those that faced him when he was writing his books on Eliot and James. I have described these books, at least partially, as polemics. The term is applicable to the Dreiser book as well. For it is clear that Matthiessen was prepared to engage in controversy once again, this time on behalf of another aspect of the critical view he had developed.

Lionel Trilling's charge against the supporters of Dreiser is a crucial point here, as Lewis points out. Trilling's essay, "Reality in America," the first in his collection *The Liberal Imagination*, was originally published in two parts. The first part, published in 1940 in *Partisan Review*, is a critical appraisal of Parrington's work, on behalf of "mind" and against what Trilling considers a mythical opposition, fostered by Parrington, between "mind" and "reality." The second part, more to my purpose here, was published in 1946 in the *Nation* and is primarily an attack on "liberal" criticism, more or less in the Parrington tradition, which seeks to glorify Dreiser but deprecates James. It deals with a review of *The Bulwark* written by Matthiessen for the *New York Times Book Review*, some years before *Theodore Dreiser* (another indication, by the way, of how long-standing an interest Matthiessen had in Dreiser). Trilling concludes his discussion of Hicks's reaction to Dreiser and then turns to Matthiessen's:

But Dreiser is to be accepted and forgiven [by Hicks] because his faults are the sad, lovable, honorable faults of reality itself, or of America itself—huge, inchoate, struggling toward expression, caught between the dream of raw power and the dream of morality.

"The liability in what Santayana called the genteel tradition was due to its being a product of mind apart from experience. Dreiser gave us the stuff of our common experience, not as it was hoped to be by any idealizing theorist, but as it actually was in its crudity." The author of this statement certainly cannot be accused of any lack of feeling for mind as Henry James represents it; nor can Mr. Matthiessen be thought of as a follower of Parrington—indeed, in the preface to *American Renaissance* he has framed one of the sharpest and most cogent criticisms of Parrington's method. Yet Mr. Matthiessen, writing in the *New York Times Book Review* about Dreiser's posthumous novel, *The Bulwark*, accepts the liberal cliché which opposes crude experience to mind and establishes Dreiser's value by implying that the mind which Dreiser's crude experience is presumed to confront and refute is the mind of gentility.

This implied amalgamation of mind with gentility is the rationale of the long indulgence of Dreiser, which is extended even to the style of his prose.[13]

Matthiessen's position is not quite what Trilling leads us to believe it is. He had already, in *American Renaissance*, pointed extensively to the difference between action and thought and between perception and actuality, especially in his discussions of Hawthorne and Emerson. It was not a problem he perceived in Dreiser alone.

Furthermore, he had effectively demonstrated in *American Renaissance*, as well as in *T. S. Eliot* and *Henry James*, that the work of the artist is a reflection of the world in which he lives insofar as the artist is able to find the objective correlative that best shows his emotional perception of and reaction to that world. In Eliot and James the sources and the method for finding the objective correlative are, to use Lewis's words, derived from the "sophisticated," the "ironic," and the "European." But in a writer like Whitman, as *American Renaissance* shows, as well as in Dreiser, there are other ways of depicting the artist's emotional state in his world, other sources for the objective correlative.

Matthiessen's most significant comment in this regard is his description of Dreiser as a "primitive." In placing the novelist in the tradition of American literature, Matthiessen writes:

He is a primary example of the frequent American need to begin all over again from scratch. His case would seem to be different from that of Whitman, who found the gap so wide between what he had to say and any usual poetic form that he could not possibly bridge it. But in Whitman's day American poetry had hardly any tradition behind it, whereas fiction had been accruing a considerable background since Hawthorne had felt the thinness of his resources. Yet Dreiser was representative of a far cruder America than Hawthorne's. He was only half-educated, and was scarcely a conscious artist at all when he set out to write *Sister Carrie*. In an authentic sense he was a primitive, not unlike the occasional American sign painter who has found that he possessed the dogged skills to create a portrait likeness, and then has bent all the force of a rugged character to realize this verity. [pp. 59–60]

One is reminded by such a statement of early American painting, of, for example, the portrait by an unknown artist from the last quarter of the seventeenth century, "Mrs. Freake and Her Baby Mary": wooden and flat, with forms reminiscent of pre-Renaissance Italian painting but lacking the conviction and élan of such work, it nevertheless evokes the woman and the period. One thinks also in this connection, of the apprentice work of the most important of our early eighteenth-century portraitists, John Singleton Copley. Matthiessen means by designating Dreiser a primitive precisely what Lewis means when he describes one side of the literary tradition as "bald, rumbling, nakedly American." Dreiser is not concerned with literary effects, but when he is we get his often-disastrous "fancy" language. He is, rather, like the Balzac whom he discovered in the Carnegie Library (p. 38), trying to present "solid slabs of continuous experience" (p. 60). Matthiessen gives us a brilliant analysis of Dreiser's portrayal of Hurstwood as an example of what he means. While granting Dreiser's essential failure in depicting Carrie because "he has tinged his conception of her with banality and sentimentality," he points to the description of Hurstwood's decline and eventual suicide as the place where "the central vitality of the novel, however Dreiser may have conceived it, lies" (p. 73).

Here Matthiessen is describing another way of finding an objective correlative by the artist. In commenting, for example, on Hurstwood's vacillation in stealing the money from the safe at Fitzgerald and Moy's, he writes: "This central image of insecurity

—and the full picture of Hurstwood's wavering back and forth is masterly—symbolizes the whole society that Dreiser evokes. It is a society in which there are no real equals, and no equilibrium, but only people moving *up* and *down*. The thoroughness with which he pursues this fact provides him with the successive links in his structure. . . . As always with Dreiser, only the massed details themselves rather than any summary of them can convey the solidity of their effect" (p. 75).

Matthiessen follows this example with a long and fascinating discussion—using all the techniques of his New Critical training and imagination—of Hurstwood's movement through the novel. He provides us with an important analysis of Dreiser's use of clothes as a primary symbol and of the few other symbolic devices of the novel, as follows:

> Dreiser's few basic and recurrent symbolic images serve to underscore this view. The symbol he makes most of—as we have already seen—is that of clothes, which Veblen was singling out at the same time, in *The Theory of the Leisure Class*, as giving a peculiarly representative expression of "pecuniary culture." Clothes in Dreiser are the chief means of display, of lifting a character above where he was, and by that fact above someone else. They lure—but really they separate.
>
> His use of other images is rudimentary; he hardly thinks of them as a resource; but for this very reason there is a particular significance in a cluster that helps to create the *movement* of life as he feels it. As Carrie steps out of the train in Chicago, she is—in the last phrase of the opening chapter—"a lone figure in a tossing thoughtless sea." Other water images heighten the sense of division. . . . More recurrent are the phrases which project Dreiser's feeling that people are swept by forces far beyond their control. "The little shop girl was getting into deep water. She was letting her few supports float away from her." . . . He uses this word ["drifting"] very often, perhaps more often than he realized, though not often enough to make the reader too conscious of it. . . . By the close [of Hurstwood's suicide scene] not only the crowds outside the flop-house are "of the class which simply floats and drifts,

every wave of people washing up one, as breakers do drift-
wood upon a stormy shore."

   Dreiser's other chief image of movement is, curiously
enough, one of slow calm within the ceaseless flux. . . . Here
Dreiser's repetition—there are more than a couple of dozen
instances—probably becomes too obtrusive. But his instinctive fondness for this image [of a person in a rocking chair] is
very revealing of the rhythm of experience he is projecting.
The back-and-forth sway of the chair can do nothing to arrest
the drift of events. Both movements are slow, but one is
inexorable. [pp. 83, 84, 85]

It is hardly valid, then, as the above shows, to accuse Matthiessen of having written a book concerned only with the sociological
aspects of Dreiser's work, for again and again (and the material
concerning *Sister Carrie* is merely one example) Matthiessen approaches Dreiser essentially as he approached James or Eliot or
Melville, through a careful examination of technique and of the
"use of language" as well as through the personal and social
realities from which that language sprang. Although Matthiessen
does not pretend that Dreiser's method is as complex, rich, or
subtle as that of more symbolically oriented authors, he does
show him as one who seeks for, and at times finds with felicity,
those symbols of his experience that help him to render for us the
quality of life as he perceives it. In other words, Dreiser too, at
times, finds his objective correlatives.

   Nor does he ever seek to gloss over his subject's glaring in-
adequacies. He concludes his discussion of *Sister Carrie* with an
overall view of Dreiser's achievement in the novel. He begins by
quoting Charles Walcutt's comparison between Dreiser and Zola:
"Where Zola's theory would 'put most emphasis—on the extrac-
tion of laws about human nature—Dreiser is most uncertain and
most sure that no certainty can be attained.'" Matthiessen then
continues:

   A novel resulting from such a reading of existence is, not
surprisingly, more impressive in its main sweep than in all its
details. The same thing is true of Dreiser's style. Emerson

found Whitman's language a strange "mixture of the *Bhagvat-Geeta* and the *New York Herald*." Dreiser's mixture was even stranger since his journalistic usages were not counterbalanced by any pure body of poetry or scripture. . . . If one began enumerating the fancy clichés that spatter his pages—"lightsome," "halcyon," "prancing pair of bays," "airy grace"—one might conclude that this writer could not possibly break through to freshness. But what bothered his first reviewers was the opposite tendency, the extent to which Dreiser introduced words from his own conversation: "flashy," "nobby," "truly swell saloon," "dress suit affair." . . . Charges of clumsiness have been repeated against him so often that they have obscured the many passages where, like the journeyman painter, he has a mastery of the plain style. When his mind was most absorbed with what he had to say, the flourishes of the feature-writer fell away, as did also the cumbersome, only half-accurate abstract terms ("affectional," "actualities"). Then he could write long passages where nothing is striking except the total effect. [pp. 85–86, 87]

This analysis is not very different from Matthiessen's careful examination of Hawthorne's language in *The House of the Seven Gables*. It is of the essence of Matthiessen's method to analyze the writer's language and then to put his own sensibility to work on it. His perceptions here are as questionable, or as convincing, as they were when he disparaged some of Whitman's language—although his is a sensibility finely trained to achieve rich perceptions. As he does with the poet, Matthiessen focuses on the sources of Dreiser's language in the novelist's personal experiences, in the language-milieu of the writer's period, and in the social reality of that period. The judgment he then makes is based on his perception of the freshness or the appropriateness of the use of such language. Matthiessen's interest is focused on his subject's ability to convey through language that subject's own feeling, and, by extension, the feelings engendered by the time in which the subject is writing. Ultimately he must make this judgment by comparison with the works of others writing during the same period, as he does when he contrasts Dreiser with Howells or Whitman with Longfellow. He does not, as Trilling charges, accept or forgive or oppose crude experience to more intellectual pursuits. Rather, he attempts to find that which is powerful in Dreiser and to understand it, both as a social artifact and as a product of the artist's imagination. Critics certainly can disagree about the relative aesthetic value of one or another line, or image, or stylistic device. But Matthiessen's perceptions are as good as Trilling's, although in both cases their sensibilities are affected by their biases. But such differences in sensibility cannot sustain a charge that Matthiessen "accepts the liberal cliché" or that he has shown "indulgence of Dreiser . . . even to the style of his prose."

Matthiessen applies the sort of analysis we have seen in his treatment of *Sister Carrie* to the bulk of Dreiser's major work. He finds *Jennie Gerhardt* rather successful. He is intrigued by, but sharply critical of, the not-quite-realized portrait of Cowperwood as he is developed in *The Financier*. He considers *The Genius* Dreiser's worst novel, because, despite some differences, it was too close to Dreiser's own life. Of that book he says: "He possessed none of the hard artistic control that such an act demands when the material is so completely the writer's memories. As a consequence *The Genius* does not have the full genuineness of his autobiographies, and is yet very formless as a *Bildungsroman*" (p. 160).

In a cogent, not entirely laudatory, review of *Theodore Dreiser*, John Berryman (whose own *Stephen Crane* came out almost at the same time, so that a number of other reviews yoke the two books together for comparison) sums up Matthiessen's positive contributions to an understanding of Dreiser's work as follows:

> Mr. Matthiessen is nearly always right. He attributes Dreiser's formidable descriptive power to a freshness of eye and obstinate memory fused with a deep sense of changingness [sic] which made it seem historically important to preserve appearance. He analyzes handsomely the debts to Balzac and Spencer, and the devices, such as they are, used by the novelist to organize his materials. . . . He denies genuine stature to Frank Cowperwood and does not conceal the progressive weakening through the financial trilogy. He notes

that Dreiser's naiveté above a certain social level is simply the price we pay for the marvelous keenness of longing represented in his characters for successive levels of luxury and achievement far above them, but still below most of his cultivated readers. Matthiessen is right above all in insisting on the word "rhythm" as a key to Dreiser's method.

It is well to have this position—which looks like a critical haven—stated by someone as scrupulous, as cautious as Matthiessen. . . . He describes Dreiser's style as . . . "the groping after words corresponding to a groping of the thought, but with both words and thought born along on the diapason of a deep emotion"—"of a deep grounding, at its best, in the rhythm of his emotions." This seems to me to be profound, the only way, indeed of accounting for the immense effects achieved by means so banal and shabby.[14]

But the New Critical treatment described by Berryman is only one aspect of Matthiessen's effort to deal with Dreiser, albeit the most generally acceptable one. In the two concluding chapters of his book, entitled "Dreiser's Politics" and "Dreiser's Philosophy," Matthiessen attempts to explicate the sources of Dreiser's thought and of his political actions, and in part thereby to deal with the last of his works, the posthumously issued *The Bulwark* (1946) and *The Stoic* (1947). Joseph Warren Beach, in an appreciative review, describes the two sections as follows:

But what must have drawn Matthiessen to this man more than anything else was his philosophy of life—not so much what it was as how he came by it, how he hammered it out from the stubborn realities that were his world. The key chapters are doubtless the last two. . . . Matthiessen's special interests most often led him to feature the effect on Dreiser of men like Henry George and Clarence Darrow, of Coxey's Army, Passaic and Harlan, and of the increasingly serious plight of the poor. . . . Matthiessen would naturally be interested in the process by which the unpolitical Dreiser was drawn towards Communism and the stubbornness with which he refused to be bound by any party line; and above all by the gradual passage from extreme individualism to his late recognition of the claims of the social community upon the individual.

In cosmic philosophy Matthiessen features Spencer, Jacques Loeb, and Woods Hole as significant for Dreiser. He was doubtless fascinated and saddened by Dreiser's materialism, and relieved to find him near the end moving towards recognition of Creative Force, even Creative Intelligence, in the universe. Matty could not himself do without the religious concept of sin; but he nowhere tries to read this into the pagan Dreiser. His account is fair, objective, and well-balanced. . . . It must have been some comfort, in [Matthiessen's] last year of desperate trouble, to present the picture of an Independent Radical in social theory, and in philosophy a mechanist who could not maintain that position to the end.[15]

Matthiessen's discussion of Dreiser's politics includes an interesting inquiry into the nature of his anti-Semitism, almost as if he were answering Trilling's earlier charge that "it is much to the point of his intellectual vulgarity that Dreiser's anti-semitism was not merely a social prejudice but an idea."[16] He traces its course in some detail, from Dreiser's first public statement on the matter in an essay in the *American Spectator* in 1933, through an interview with a group from the *New Masses*, to an Office of War Information broadcast to Germany in 1944 when he seems completely to have changed his position. Matthiessen never exonerates or excuses Dreiser. He does, however, want to show that "the gradual clarification of Dreiser's position affords another instance of his slow but impressive reeducation as a man moving from his sixties into his seventies" (p. 227). Although "clarification" does seem like too soft a word to use here, since it implies that he was somehow unclear and confused and needed only to learn a little something to overcome his anti-Semitism, the phrase does serve to help us understand that Dreiser changed profoundly in a number of ways in the decade before his death.

This change, or reeducation as Matthiessen would have it, is also central to Dreiser's joining the Communist party, a step that earned the novelist endless abuse, as one might expect, and one that Matthiessen never took, or, in the American context, seriously contemplated. In 1940 Dreiser had plunged more fully into politics than ever, arguing against involvement in the war in Europe in his book *America Is Worth Saving*, and thus echoing the position of the Communist party and of others on the left. Of course, we were in the war just a year after the book appeared. It is difficult not to sense Matthiessen's sympathy with the experience Dreiser must have had. Matthiessen had centered his hopes for democratic socialism on Czechoslovakia, and he said so in *From the Heart of Europe*. I have already discussed how his hopes were dashed even before the book was off the presses. He did not change his book, although, at least according to Ernest J. Simmons, who had helped to arrange his teaching stint in Czechoslovakia, he had the opportunity to do so.[17]

By 1944, now seventy-three years old, Dreiser was fully in support of the war—again echoing the Communist position. Matthiessen explains Dreiser's change in the following way:

This brings us back to the central issue that motivated Dreiser's politics. In the feverish period leading up to the war he often seemed only to be echoing the Communist position without adequate investigation of his own, often seemed very close to one of the worst danger points of our time— an unqualified acceptance of mass force for the good it can theoretically do. He moved away from this danger point as his meditations on the nature of equality deepened, as he realized that equality meant the equality of individuals co-operating to create the only effective freedom. He would no longer say that he was for either the individual or the mass. His belief continued to grow that a society which would do justice to both could be built only through socialism. . . . At the same time he recorded his radio broadcast to the German people . . . which . . . after urging the need of "economic justice" in the postwar world, concluded with a plea for a renewed effort toward establishing "the Brotherhood of Man."

Our problem in evaluating all such utterances is the same as has confronted us throughout Dreiser's writing—the extent to which his standard terms still give expression to a depth of personal feeling. . . . In the summer of 1945, as the war was drawing to its close, he was more and more responsive to the principles of co-operation which Wendell Willkie had enunciated in *One World*. He was deeply stirred also by the way in which European writers and artists—Picasso and Sean O'Casey among them—were affirming their adherence to international solidarity by the symbolic act of joining the Communist Party. [pp. 231–32]

It seems clear to me that Matthiessen was at least in part drawing on his own experience in these lines to explain Dreiser's actions. Although Matthiessen was far too certain about his own differences with Marxism and far too concerned about continuing evidence of the lack of democracy in the Soviet Union to join the Communist party himself—despite his "acceptance" of the Russian Revolution—still his phrases echo those in *From the Heart of Europe*, which announced that he would have joined the French Communist party had he been a Frenchman and the English Labour party had he been an Englishman. The explanations he offers for Dreiser's action also echo those that help to explain his own allegiance to the Progressive party in 1948.

If Matthiessen had rested on such an explanation, then Arthur Mizener's charge, in one of the angriest reviews of *Theodore Dreiser*, might have been justified. "It is not easy to know," said Mizener, "how to take people who talk about writers' 'affirming their adherence to international solidarity by the symbolic act of joining the Communist Party.' There is no need to pry into the political confusion of Matthiessen's own mind suggested by such remarks: he is dead, perhaps partly as a result of it. Still, as his main effort to explain the meaning of Dreiser's career, it leaves something to be desired."[18] But such a statement distorts Matthiessen's explanation of Dreiser's action and thus does his position an injustice. Furthermore, his "main effort" to explain Dreiser's career is made, if anywhere, in the subsequent chapter on Dreiser's philosophy. In fact, Matthiessen makes little effort to approve or disapprove of Dreiser's action. Based on his assumption that Dreiser is an artist of importance, he means to explain it in terms of an understanding of Dreiser's world view.

Matthiessen's methodology in attempting such understanding

is to search for explanations on the basis of the writer's biography and the influences that shaped that biography—Dreiser's personal experiences, his intellectual experiences, that is, his reading and thinking, and the "Zeitgeist" that prevails in his time. He finds Dreiser's most dramatic political act explicable, then, given the combination of the man's family and social background, which have gone to shape his temperament, the literary and intellectual influences he found acceptable to that temperament, and the social atmosphere of the period in which the temperament was being shaped and in which his political act took place. In this regard, Matthiessen's method as a biographer had matured greatly since he had written *Sarah Orne Jewett*, for he had come to understand the importance of the historical period in which his subject lived, something he had hardly considered in the portrait of Jewett so tinged with the sentimental. He had also learned to accept the biographer's responsibility to explain his subject's actions by comparing or contrasting them with the actions of others during that period. Thus, when Matthiessen yokes political stands by O'Casey and Picasso with those of Dreiser, he is showing that other artists, of only slightly similar background, moved in the same direction as did his subject. Mizener may not know "how to take" such acts and their explanations, but Matthiessen does. In part this is a result of his own sympathies, but far more important, it is the result of his perception and understanding of a trend of the times. He tries to understand Dreiser by trying to understand how men like him can react to social experiences, given their personal histories.

When he turns to Dreiser's philosophy, Matthiessen is at some pains to show that unlike Zola and the other naturalists, the novelist had no similar fixed body of ideas. He goes on to say: "Yet there is a wider and looser, but still authentic, sense in which he was a naturalist. From first to last he was driven to try to understand man's place in nature, to a far more profound degree than any of his American contemporaries in fiction; indeed, for a parallel we should have to go back to Melville's grapplings. This is what gave Dreiser's books their peculiar breadth: they are universal, not in their range of human experience, but in the sense that an only partly known universe presses upon and dominates his searching consciousness of what happens to all his characters" (p. 236).

Matthiessen traces the development of Dreiser's thought through *Hey-rub-a-dub-dub* by pointing to his source in Loeb's *The Mechanistic Conception of Life*, which appeared to Dreiser "the next natural step after Spencer and Darwin and Haeckel, and his own description of love in terms of 'chemisms' derive from this source" (pp. 236–37). Matthiessen continues:

> Yet Dreiser was never a consistent mechanist. Paul Elmer More, reviewing *Hey-rub-a-dub-dub* with the cool distaste of the new humanist, declared the distinguishing feature of these essays to be an "oscillation between a theory of evolution which sees no progress save the survival of the rapaciously strong and a humanitarian feeling of solidarity with the masses who are exploited in the process." This is a particularly interesting formulation in view of Dreiser's later development. At this point he had depicted his strongest hero, but not his weakest one. . . . We have already observed how the sense of life that we feel in Dreiser's novels is larger and deeper than are any of the patterns of thought that they advance. Eliseo Vivas has argued that the very inconsistency in Dreiser's mechanism was what allowed this largeness to break through. Mechanism holds that life has no transcendent meaning that we can discover; but Dreiser, though he thought he accepted this, could not accept it with equanimity. . . . He never really adhered to the pitiless implications of the Darwinian universe. As he admired the strong and sympathized with the weak, he became deeply involved with both. As he kept groping to find more significance in their lives than any his mind could discover, he dwelt on the mystery of the inexplicable as no rigorous mechanist would have done. [pp. 237–38]

Such a comment is a gloss upon the political aspects of Dreiser's thought. But more important is Matthiessen's attempt to explain what it was in Dreiser's thought and experience that was to lead, almost simultaneously, to so mystical a book as *The Bulwark* and to Dreiser's allegiance to the Communist party. He makes no effort to show a consistency in Dreiser that did not exist, or to justify him. Rather, he seeks to show how "Dreiser squared this increasingly mystical thought," and especially his new-found Eastern mysticism, "with his concurrently developing interest in radical politics":

> Once again the comparison with Whitman is the most suggestive. Both of them, as they grew older, felt their strongest impulse towards a grasp of the universe in its wholeness. Neither had the formal training that would have raised barriers of logic against the synthesis that they felt bound to make between discordant realms. Whitman, no less than Dreiser, was occupied with the new discoveries of science while equally determined to pass beyond the limitations of science. And as he dwelt upon cosmic wholeness, he also dwelt more and more upon the need of solidarity in society, and his political thought—again like Dreiser's—moved from individualism towards socialism. [pp. 239–40]

It is typical of Matthiessen that he then relates Dreiser to Thoreau, whom the novelist said he had found "most illuminative of the implications of scientific result." Again, such a passage helps to explicate Dreiser's turn to communism and makes clear that Mizener's charge is not valid. Dreiser's political act is explained by his philosophical development, which runs as a deeper current beneath the political behavior.

Matthiessen turns to an explication of *The Bulwark*, which he had reviewed[19] upon publication for the *New York Times Book Review*, as a sample, even a fictional emblem, of how Dreiser combined these varying currents:

> The central truth that he wanted to affirm through Solon was that living authority lies not in the harsh judging mind but in the purified and renewed affections of the heart.
> The book in which Dreiser tried to affirm these values has been judged variously. . . . [T]hat the values were real for Dreiser himself cannot be the line of defense against this charge [of "religious speciosity"], since in order to move a reader they must be embodied in the work itself. . . . *The Bulwark* is very bare, many of its pages are blocked out rather

than written, and it will hardly hold a place with *Sister Carrie* or *An American Tragedy*. But it is moving as an authentic if belated primitive, even farther away from the current modes of fiction than he himself had been at the beginning of his career. Like the self-taught painter, Dreiser had found an adequately functional form for what he had to express. Like Melville in the forty years from *Moby-Dick* and *Pierre* to *Billy Budd*, he had progressed from a bitter questioning of the universe to a more serene acceptance—and yet his deepest burden was still compassion over all that remained inscrutable. [pp. 248–49]

Such an analysis of Dreiser's last work leads to Matthiessen's final conclusions about his philosophy, conclusions that explain, as the earlier discussion of Dreiser's politics did not, how he could be drawn at once to Woolman and communism, to mysticism and William Z. Foster:

One might simply say that he was an old man, untroubled by inconsistencies that subsequent events would have made obvious. But this is not really the main point. For he had found—if more essentially in Woolman than in Marx—beliefs that he was convinced the world could no longer afford to ignore. In the month after the end of the Second World War he said: "Only the mass can get the world out of its present mess. Interdependence, a new understanding between peoples all over the world is needed! . . . "But," he went on, "when I speak of the mass I speak of the individuals of which the mass is made up. As soon as one begins to think of the other side as a mass or a crowd, the human link seems to go. We forget that crowds consist of individuals, of men and women, and children, who love and hate and suffer." It was there he took his stand, as he had throughout his fiction. The chief purpose of "Interdependence" was to urge the widest possible interchange between peoples in order to avert a recrudescence of that nationalism which he could now regard only as a virulent disease. The fact that the next years were to belie his hopes would not have shaken his conclusions. "To know and to understand is to love, not to hate." [p. 251]

We can understand the basis for Dreiser's seeming inconsistency then, or at least Matthiessen's explanation of it, as lying fundamentally in Dreiser's effort to grapple with the contradictions of life as he had experienced them—his acceptance of the world's harshness as against his sympathy with those who were the unwitting victims of that harshness.

It is difficult, in light of the total body of Matthiessen's work, and what I have said about his life, not to see affinities between his efforts and Dreiser's. Matthiessen was constantly attempting to bring his Christianity—for which his key word was "love"— into correspondence with his socialism, so he understood the dilemma faced by Dreiser in becoming both a Communist and a universe-accepting mystic at the same time. Just as he could think his way into the feeling-state that had brought Dreiser to join the Communist party by bringing to it his own political experience, so could he understand Dreiser's apparently contradictory positions because they were composed of a set of contradictions Matthiessen himself had attempted to balance for most of his life. It is typical of Matthiessen to find in Woolman and Thoreau the sources through which this was made possible for Dreiser.

Matthiessen's analysis is convincing in part because it derives from personal experience. Again, he makes no effort to defend Dreiser. "The only kind of coherence that one can find in such diverse and apparently contradictory pursuits," he says, "is in the unity of the personality behind them" (p. 240). If his choice of subject, then, was dictated by any personal predilection—as every choice by a biographer must be—this was not merely a matter of political predilection. To look only to Dreiser's politics for Matthiessen's inspiration indicates a critical blindness that may well have been dictated by the then-current state of political hysteria over communism. "The late F. O. Matthiessen's study 'Theodore Dreiser', was presumably a labor of political love, inspired more by sympathy with Dreiser's views about social injustice than by admiration of his art," writes H. J. Muller, for example.[20] But Matthiessen's work on Dreiser was more than a labor of political love. It was love for a novelist who moves us despite his clumsiness, who tried to solve some of the same problems that worried Matthiessen, including a balance between religion and sociopolitical concerns, who contributed through his fiction to an understanding of contemporary America, and who, in a most important sense, sought to attain a "usable present" by his effort to understand the new men and women created by a newly urbanized, industrialized America. No scholar need be ashamed of such a labor of love. Beach is much closer to the truth than Muller when he suggests that Matthiessen was attracted to his subject by Dreiser's "philosophy" and especially how he arrived at it.

Yet Muller is quite right when he says that *Theodore Dreiser* "certainly . . . does not rank with Matthiessen's best work." Although it is a substantial piece of work and one that does not diminish Matthiessen's stature, it lacks in important ways the brilliance of some of his other work. One aspect of this cannot really be documented. One simply feels less of an impulse to say of its insights, "how true, how right," and "why, I should have seen that all along" when reading *Theodore Dreiser* than when reading *American Renaissance*. That is a comment one cannot prove, but one that I think most readers of Matthiessen would share. But there are two major, easily identifiable flaws in *Theodore Dreiser*. The first will remind us of Matthiessen's other book-length literary biography, *Sarah Orne Jewett*.

Maxwell Geismar's review of *Theodore Dreiser* treats the book, not unexpectedly, with great appreciation. His pro-Dreiser bias, perhaps even an excessive one, which can be seen in a statement such as "this novelist [is] the best of all the modern Americans in my opinion," disposed him to review Matthiessen's work favorably. "F. O. Matthiessen was one of the rare and admirable scholars in the field of American letters," he writes. "It was typical of his interests that his last book should be a study of Theodore Dreiser. . . . To his credit Matthiessen does not share the prejudices of the New Criticism (which is by now old, established, and highly respectable) about Dreiser's work."[21]

It is then all the more interesting that Geismar, from his sometimes psychoanalytic perspective, finds a glaring fault in *Theodore Dreiser*: "Matthiessen's study has a curious flatness, and one has the impression that he never quite got to grips with Dreiser's true temperament: ruthless as well as sympathetic, fascinated by power, by brutality, by suffering, ambivalent in its approach to experience as well as tortured and destructive. The biographical material in this study is simplified, too, and barely mentions the sexuality—which Dreiser himself stressed—that was at the center of his beliefs, if not indeed the secret core of his work. Dreiser was a social revolutionary only toward the end of his life, but he was always, and primarily, a sexual revolutionary . . . which Matthiessen's study hardly seems to understand."[22] The same point was made somewhat less forcefully by Milton Rugoff, who avers that some readers may feel that Matthiessen's book "does not do as much justice to the sexual force in Dreiser's work as to the economic and social."[23]

Geismar's contention that sexuality was at the center of Dreiser's beliefs is an overstatement, but the point he raises is an important one. It indicates in *Theodore Dreiser* a problem we have already encountered in Matthiessen's earlier full-length literary biography, *Sarah Orne Jewett*. In both these works Matthiessen employs an approach described in a review of *Theodore Dreiser* by Leonard Eaton, who points out that Matthiessen adopted "a method much favored by literary biographers" as he "intersperses the narrative of Dreiser's life with critical evaluations of his work."[24] In using such a method, the biographer must seek to understand in the writer's life—in its emotional, social, and literary aspects—the sources from which his or her art spring. We have a right to expect from such works an effort to understand psychological sources as well as literary and sociological ones. Although Matthiessen does deal to some extent with the psychological life of both Jewett and Dreiser, he does very little with regard to the sexual aspects of their lives or their works, and thus he fails to deal with an issue that is important in both writers.

Any work concerning Dreiser, of course, cannot so completely escape sexual matters as can a work concerning the much more antiseptic Jewett. Certainly Matthiessen makes us aware of Dreiser's repeated sexual adventures. We are all the more startled, then, when all he can do with Dreiser's very strong attachment to his mother is the following:

> But over this span of the years his heart reverted happily to Warsaw, to an idyllic picture of its tall sycamores and fragrant

hayfields, its nearby lakes and woods. More than any other place this little town meant his mother to him, for here he "first came partially to understand her, to view her as a woman and to know how remarkable she was. . . . I really adored her." He was to think of her as "pagan" in her hearty earthiness. But he felt himself held strongest by "the silver tether of her affection, understanding, sweetness, sacrifice." These are the qualities that he would weave into his own favorite heroine, Jennie Gerhardt, just as Jennie's old father would be a largely forgiving likeness of his own father's sternness. [p. 16; the ellipses are Matthiessen's]

It requires no sophisticated knowledge of Freud's theories to see at least the possibility here of a source of much of Dreiser's feeling about sexuality, especially when Matthiessen notes so carefully Dreiser's constantly banal presentation of women in love. Matthiessen might have been expected to suggest a complex set of relationships arising out of so strong an attachment to one's mother when one's father was such a thoroughly harsh, repressive individual.

One is further troubled by Matthiessen's quoting, without any more comment than that it represented a "curious . . . affinity," of which Dreiser was to speak with "a greater intensity than of any of his previous friends," Dreiser's remarks about his friendship with the Ohio newspaper editor Arthur Henry. Dreiser described the relationship, according to Matthiessen, as "an enduring and yet stormy and disillusioning friendship. If he had been a girl I would have married him, of course. It would have been inevitable . . . Our dreams were practically identical, though we approached them from different angles. He was the sentimentalist in thought, the realist in action; I was the realist in thought and the sentimentalist in action . . . He had dreams of becoming a poet and novelist, I of becoming a playwright. Meanwhile we reveled in that wonderful possession, intellectual affection" (pp. 33–34; the ellipses are Matthiessen's).

I do not mean to imply that Matthiessen had to posit here any deeply underlying, sexually aberrant behavior. But he is obliged to comment more fully about such an important friendship, especially when it is described in such language. Perhaps all he needed to do was to clear up the matter by indicating that this was no more than one of those crushes that are not unusual among young men. But he certainly should not have left it without comment as he did.

As long as such problems arise strictly in connection with biographical material, they are not very significant. When, however, Matthiessen's lack of comment about psychosexual material prevents insights related to literary analysis, the matter becomes more serious. Thus Matthiessen says of Carrie Meeber: "His [Dreiser's] most serious inadequacy in presenting his heroine is not what Mrs. Doubleday thought—that Carrie is too unconventional—but that she is not unconventional enough. The only way we could sense what Dreiser calls her 'feeling mind' would be to see her deeply stirred, and this she never is. Her affairs with Drouet and Hurstwood are so slurred over, in instinctive accordance with what was then demanded of fiction, that they are robbed of any warmth. She is never a woman in love" (p. 73). To attribute such a failure to an "instinctive accordance" with the fictional mores of the period can work for one novel, perhaps, but not for all of the artist's output.

But Matthiessen reverts to the same theme. With regard to *The Genius* he writes:

> The worst banalities are in the language of love. . . . But any defense . . . will not cover what are probably the most tasteless passages in all of Dreiser, those in which Witla addresses Suzanne: "Oh, Flower Face! Oh, Silver Feet! Oh, Myrtle Bloom!"
>
> The chief thing we have to remind ourselves of in connection with *The "Genius"* is why it was an important book. . . . What had been present in all Dreiser's novels so far, but incidental to their main themes, engaged the center of his attention when he wrote *The "Genius"* in prolonged revolt against the doctrine of "one life, one love." He was determined to speak out, as he did again in his autobiographies, where he acknowledged sex as "the controlling and directing force that it is." . . . On the theme that life is "incurably varietistic and pluralistic in its tastes and emotions," he went on to say that he had

found it "almost affectionately unavoidable to hold three, four—even as many as five and six—women in regard—at one and the same time." This is the kind of behavior later sociological study has confirmed to be very frequent in our rootless society, but it was not being voiced publicly when Dreiser first said it. . . . He referred to himself again and again as "changeful" and "uncertain." Unlike Witla, who finally begot a child, Dreiser—on the testimony of those best able to say— would seem to have been sterile. His continually restless desire to know more and more women may have been a product of basic insecurity, of an almost desperate need to keep on proving himself.

As far as his work was concerned, he never managed to make a fully affecting expression of the passion that had consumed him. . . . Angela, though presented far too prolixly, is real in her disappointments and defects; but the others, and especially Suzanne . . . are abstract monsters of unreality. Dreiser seems to have paid the price for his promiscuity in a progressive blunting of his sensibility. His Berenice Flemings and Suzanne Dales are his worst failures, stereotyped "ideals" with no more living differentiation than they would have had in the cheapest magazines. [pp. 164, 164–66]

One is inclined to echo Matthiessen's own words. Here must be one of the most banal and lame explanations in all of Matthiessen's work for an artist's major defect. Matthiessen was certainly aware of other writers who, personally "promiscuous" or not, had avoided the creation of women characters who were "abstract monsters of unreality." Whether it be Lawrence's efforts to deal with women, or Hardy's comments concerning the "doctrine of one life, one love" in *Jude the Obscure*, or F. Scott Fitzgerald's Jordan or Hemingway's Brett Ashley, or Henry Miller's peculiar portrayals, Matthiessen certainly knew of many other male writers who had dealt with women, if not with more accuracy than Dreiser, at least with less of a penchant for making of them "stereotyped ideals." Had he been writing two decades later, he might have had recourse to the oft-expressed notion by those in the women's movement that very few male writers can

effectively and truthfully deal with women, because of the un-
equal relationship between the sexes. But Carolyn G. Heilbrun's
Toward a Recognition of Androgyny and other such works were not
available to him. I have already discussed Matthiessen's lack of
exploration of questions of sexual experience that flaw *Sarah Orne
Jewett* and attributed that lack at least in part to a reluctance to
deal with the issue deriving from Matthiessen's complicated feelings about his own homosexuality and to a kind of characteristic
fastidiousness. It is understandable that such feelings interfered
with his critical judgments when he was in his twenties, as he
was writing *Sarah Orne Jewett*. Such a lack is less excusable in a
man nearing his fiftieth year, though it must be remembered and
seems significant that Matthiessen's personal life had been devastated by Russell Cheney's death, which destroyed the most
fulfilling relationship he had ever known. The reasons that pre-
vented him from dealing with biographical questions of sexuality
in *Sarah Orne Jewett* continued to operate in *Theodore Dreiser*, I
think it reasonable to assume. Personal experience, then, which
helped Matthiessen give us such rich insights into Dreiser's political and philosophical thought, seems to have had the opposite effect in helping him to deal with the important matter of sexuality
in *Theodore Dreiser*.

But whatever the cause of his failure, it is clear that this is an
aspect of the critical arsenal of his day that Matthiessen did not
use. In this instance, Matthiessen need not have run the danger
so frequently associated with psychoanalytically oriented criticism, that is, of reducing the work of art to a sort of public session
on the couch to be understood only in terms of the most arcane of
Freudian symbols. But one would expect that Matthiessen, in
writing what is after all a biography, would have availed himself
of some of the awareness of unconscious motivation deriving
from the flourishing, though still uncertain, pursuits of the psychologists and psychiatrists, to escape as mundane an explanation
as the "blunting of sensibilities" resulting from "promiscuity." If
nothing else, there is a peculiarly late-Victorian, "genteel" flavor
to the very language Matthiessen employs here, which is unlike
the much more muscular prose he usually writes and which indicates that he is not sufficiently up to date in this regard.

This was not a problem in most of Matthiessen's work. He is not primarily responsible for such psychological probing when he is writing critical works about the methods of Eliot or of James. In these works, which are primarily critical rather than biographical, Matthiessen did not have to concern himself with psychological causes for the writer's work. But he is surely responsible for probing into psychology when he writes literary biographies, especially full-length studies like *Sarah Orne Jewett* and *Theodore Dreiser*. Every critic will be limited in some way by his own psychological state as well as by his method and his knowledge. It is important to understand such limitations in estimating the value of a critic's work. Had Matthiessen written more full-length literary biographies, this limitation would have been far more debilitating than it was.

More important, since we have found it to be so important a matter in all of Matthiessen's work, is his analysis of Dreiser as a writer of American tragedies. Matthiessen obviously reserves this question for his chapter on *An American Tragedy*.

Matthiessen is not entirely clear with regard to how highly he rates Dreiser's best-known novel, as is indicated by the uncertainty implied in John Berryman's parenthetical remark that "his [Dreiser's] masterpiece—I would agree *with what I take to have been Matthiessen's opinion*—is 'An American Tragedy.'"[25] In his conclusion to the chapter, Matthiessen cites high praise for the novel not only from H. L. Mencken, as one might have expected, but also from H. G. Wells and Arnold Bennett. He quotes Wells as writing that "it gets the large, harsh superficial truth that it has to tell with a force that no grammatical precision and no correctitude could attain." Then Matthiessen continues in his own voice:

> The word "superficial" is important to note, particularly as coming from a European. The shallowness of a Clyde prevents his history from ever reaching the transfiguration that Dostoevsky dwells upon in the closing pages of *Crime and Punishment*.
>
> But the thoroughness of Dreiser's treatment, the realization we have at the end that his mind has moved inexhaustibly, relentlessly over every relevant detail raises the book to the

stature that made Joseph Wood Krutch speak of it as "the great American novel of our generation." There were still many dissenting voices. Clyde's whole experience was too undifferentiated, too unilluminated to compel the attention of some readers already habituated to the masterpieces of the modern psychological novel. But for young men growing up in the 'twenties and 'thirties here was a basic account of the world to which they were exposed. [pp. 210–11]

This conclusion is not only somewhat equivocal[26] but it also fails to declare the novel as tragic or as particularly American. However, Matthiessen does deal with the book in these terms, although not as cogently or as comprehensively as one might have wished. At one point he speaks of "Clyde's final tragedy" (p. 193). When he first poses the question of the tragic element in the novel, he deals with it as though it were self-evident that the novel *is* a tragedy. Matthiessen assays the weaknesses of the novel, in particular Dreiser's inability to portray Sondra and her upper-class college friends effectively. He also assays its strengths, among them its brilliant evocation of the status Clyde seeks, as exemplified by the luxury hotel where he is employed. He praises the novel's careful planning, its effective framing, and its use of substantial symbolic devices. Finally, he turns to the heart of his critical considerations. "But the large questions still remain: wherein is this novel particularly American, and wherein is it a tragedy?" (p. 201). The question Matthiessen poses, it is worth noting, is not "is the novel a tragedy?" but "wherein is it one?," thus making an assumption that other critics have certainly not made, namely that the novel is, in fact, genuinely tragic.

The questions are central to an overall consideration of Matthiessen's critical method as well as to an assessment of his approach to Dreiser, for we have seen earlier that Matthiessen treated Hawthorne's and Melville's approaches to tragedy as peculiarly American, stemming from such of his perceptions as Ahab as an example of the "individual will *in extremis*." He makes the same effort here. He is readily able to show the peculiarly American nature of the novel's disaster, especially because Dreiser saw Clyde's experience as a result of "how . . . 'pride and show, and even waste, were flaunted in a new and still fairly virgin land—in the face of poverty and want not on the part of those who would not work, but the poverty and want of those who were all too eager to work, and almost on any terms.' In the light of such facts he had come to believe that the case of Clyde Griffiths was a typical result of the fierce competitive spirit. He now reaffirmed how not only typical but also approved by all the standard *mores* was Clyde's longing to rise" (pp. 201–2). Although this explanation demonstrates effectively how such a novel can derive most especially from the American milieu, it does not show why the nature of its *tragedy*—if such it is—is peculiarly American, as Matthiessen was able to do in the cases of *Moby-Dick* and *The Scarlet Letter*.

When he turns, then, to the second question, that is, the novel as tragedy, he makes a rather standard case for the idea that Clyde Griffiths is simply not a figure of sufficient consciousness, capability, or strength to become a tragic protagonist:

> There has hardly ever been a more unheroic hero than Clyde, and Dreiser did everything he could not to build him up. He is good-looking, to be sure . . . indeed, not unlike a minor movie hero. But Dreiser keeps repeating that he is essentially selfish, with no steadily deep feelings for others, and with no serious consideration for Roberta in her trouble. Dreiser tells us near the beginning that Clyde . . . revealed "a soul that was not destined to grow up." As he moves into the final debate with himself over what to do about Roberta, his weak and scattered mind is never able to face the real facts. He shows no trace of greater maturity at this time of crisis. [p. 203]

Matthiessen indicates that one possible response to so "unheroic" a hero, made plain in no uncertain terms by a character in the novel, is to "kill the God-damned bastard and be done with him." But this is not the response Dreiser wishes us to share, says Matthiessen, "and we do not, despite the immense problem he faced in creating any sympathy for such a pawn [as Clyde]" (p. 204). He compares Clyde with figures in earlier American novels—Donatello, Billy Budd, and Hyacinth Robinson—who have been driven to murder, and he points out that each of these cases is essentially a study of "innocence, and the weakness of a Hyacinth Robinson is not enough to interfere with our feeling for him" (p. 204).

Matthiessen's most important statement about the novel's tragic dimensions is the following:

> But Dreiser had gone farther even than Melville in his questioning of free will. In presenting Clyde he gave the most complete illustration of his belief that "the essential tragedy of life" is that man is "a waif and an interloper in Nature," which desires only "to work through him," and that he has "no power to make his own way." He can lead us to respond to Clyde's situation only to the extent that we follow the defense attorney's description of him as "a mental and moral coward" into the further statement: "Not that I am condemning you for anything that you cannot help. After all, you didn't make yourself, did you?" . . . One of Clyde's last fumbling reflections in the death house returns again to the essential point: "Would no one ever understand—or give him credit for his human—if all too human and perhaps wrong hungers—yet from which so many others—along with himself suffered?" Powys said of Dreiser: "No man I ever met is so sympathetic with weakness." A crucial element in our final estimate of this novel is how far he can enable us to participate in this compassion.

> He has deprived himself of many of the most powerful attributes of traditional tragedy. Rejecting the nineteenth-century myth of the free individual, which his experience had proved to him to be false, he has now gone to the opposite pole in portraying an individual without any purposive will. He has decided that a situation like Clyde's was far more widely typical of America than one like Cowperwood's. But if in a sense Cowperwood was above tragedy, Clyde is below it, since there can be no real drama without conflict. In *Pierre* Melville had made his most devastating critique of optimistic individualism. But caught by his own despair he had also

presented a young character so dominated by fate that we do not have the catharsis that can come only out of some mature struggle against doom. Dreiser is not despairing in *An American Tragedy*. He is writing with objective detachment. But as is the case in most of O'Neill's plays, he sees man so exclusively as the overwhelmed victim that we feel hardly any of the crisis of moral guilt that is also at the heart of the tragic experience. [pp. 204–6]

This statement indicates that Matthiessen's decision, finally, is that *An American Tragedy* is not a tragedy in any full sense of the word. It is important to note that Matthiessen's definition of tragedy in this instance is quite traditional and Aristotelian. He is not concerned here with the two-sided nature of the tragic, in which "good" can at least be perceived, although "evil" may prevail; nor does he switch the catharsis from audience to hero. Dreiser's novel is not a tragedy, Matthiessen tells us, because the novelist has not created a conscious tragic protagonist but rather a victim, and a victim at that who is not even fully aware of his victimization. That sort of definition usually describes a work that is pathetic rather than tragic.

But Matthiessen does not take that step. Like most readers, he is profoundly affected by Clyde's misery and by the pathos of his story, and he seeks an explanation for why the novel is as effective as it is. His answer is a peculiar one. After amplifying fully why Clyde fails as a tragic hero by comparing him with Hamlet and with Raskolnikov in his inability to achieve any self-recognition, even under the prodding of the Reverend Mr. McMillan's efforts, and after discussing the novel's epilogue, which shows that Clyde's mother and father have learned no more than their son from their experience, Matthiessen concludes: "We feel 'the vast scepticism and apathy of life' with greatly increased pressure. Dreiser has not shaped a tragedy in any of the traditional uses of the term, and yet he has written out of a profoundly tragic sense of man's fate. He has made us hear, with more and more cumulative power, the 'disastrous beating' of the Furies' wings" (p. 207).

Matthiessen then tries to define "tragic sense" for us by discussing Clarence Darrow's development. The lawyer began with an eighteenth-century natural-rights position, moved through an increasing awareness of the meaninglessness of the universe, and finally came to a concern with the "immense fallibility" inherent in providing justice. Then he concluded that no society in which wealth had oligarchic powers could ever be a just one. This in turn led Darrow—and Matthiessen considers him "the reader who saw this novel most nearly with Dreiser's own eyes"—to cast off "all traditional sanctions, and to regard any belief in a purposive universe as mere delusion" (pp. 208–9).

But although Matthiessen is able to explain Dreiser's ideas through the agency of Darrow's similar thought, he really evades a definition of the tragic sense. In terms of Matthiessen's own Christian-tragic definition as we have seen it in his earlier works, a tragic sense would require at least an understanding of the duality of good and evil of which Matthiessen made so much. It would require an awareness on the part of the author or the audience, if not the protagonist, of the pervasiveness of evil but of the possibility of grace. We get no hint of such a thought here. In more classical terms, which are the ones Matthiessen seems to be employing, the least a tragic sense would require is a notion of a capricious, uncertain universe, devoid of verities, and of human beings who struggle against the effects of such a universe. This definition will not fit the case of *An American Tragedy* either, for although Matthiessen deals with Clyde's incapacity for struggle, thus eliminating "tragedy" as the proper category, the "meaninglessness" of the universe does not provide for any profound awareness that the individual's fate must necessarily be tragic but rather avoids the question.

The heart of the problem is that in *An American Tragedy*, though not necessarily elsewhere, Dreiser does speak as a naturalist of the Emile Zola-Jack London stamp. Clyde is simply a victim, as are the seals in London's sea hunt or the horses in Zola's mine shaft, and nothing more. The universe in which he lives is indeed malevolent, but the malevolence is not inexplicable. Rather, it is quite patently caused by the power of greed and the insensitivity of power as well as by the impossible strivings of the weak for a modicum of power and a minimum of possession. When Matthiessen, then, speaks of a tragic sense in Dreiser, he fails to offer an acceptable definition, one that could make the reader accept Dreiser as a writer of tragedy who fails in the creation of a pro-tagonist who can carry the burden of the genre. Rather, we must discount Matthiessen's Christian version of tragedy as well as any more conventional definition and substitute for tragedy the naturalists' merely malevolent, evil universe.

The term "tragic sense" causes difficulty for all commentators. It is used usually for precisely the reason Matthiessen uses it in regard to Dreiser. A work of literature evokes in a reader a sense that he or she is confronting something akin to tragedy, though the reader is aware that the work is not, in any conventional sense, a tragedy. Nevertheless, the sense that there is something tragedy-like about the work must be explained. An example il-luminating the difficulty facing Matthiessen in regard to Dreiser can be found in Walter Kaufmann's book-length essay concerning tragedy. Citing George Steiner's *The Death of Tragedy*, Kaufmann writes:

> It has been said that it was "not between Euripides and Shakespeare that the Western mind turns away from the ancient tragic sense of life. It is after the 17th Century." What becomes of the ancient—or *any*—"tragic sense of life"? If the Greek tragic poets lacked it no less than Ibsen and the moderns, was it merely an Elizabethan phenomenon? And if some few of the so-called tragedies of the Greeks really were tragedies in the more exacting sense of that word, can poets without a tragic sense of life write great tragedies, if only occasionally? In that case, is there any close connection be-tween the tragic sense of life and tragedy, and are there any good reasons for saying that tragedy is dead?[27]

And yet, as Kaufmann makes clear, we do sense that there is something that is not tragedy, but somehow partakes of some aspects of the tragic—hence what Matthiessen posits in Dreiser's tale of an unheroic hero is the tragic sense.

Matthiessen is here coming to grips with the opposite side of the problem he faced as a Christian attempting to define tragedy. As a Christian, Matthiessen had to insist on the possibility of grace so that tragedy could fit within the framework of Christian thought. As a socialist, aware of the power of tragedy, he insists on the tragic sense because he wants to explicate the force of a work in which the fate of the protagonist is totally determined by the social structure. The source of the malevolence in Dreiser's world in *An American Tragedy* is ultimately the society of the luxury hotel and the baby-talking Sondra. Clyde's disaster results not from any struggle against these forces but from his inability to see through them and, in fact, from his totally uncritical acceptance of these values. Matthiessen understands perfectly well that these are not the materials of tragedy, yet he perceives in the novel the power to move him in the way that tragedy does—hence he claims a tragic sense for the novel.

In *American Renaissance* Matthiessen was able to provide a logical explanation for Christian tragedy by switching his comparison from the Greek to the Shakespearean mode. The resulting definition of tragedy was not one that could fit the classical paradigm, but nevertheless it was one that helped to explain Melville. The greatest flaw of *Theodore Dreiser*, I believe, lies in Matthiessen's failure to achieve a similarly useful explanation here. The "tragic sense," Kaufmann's comment indicates, is too inchoate a notion to account for the power of Dreiser's book. That Dreiser himself sets up a contradiction by calling his novel a tragedy is a problem, since he wrote *An American Tragedy* at the point in his life at which his vision of human life was perhaps most deterministic. But Matthiessen does not help very much to resolve the contradiction we feel between the power that is akin to tragedy in Dreiser and his deterministic universe.

Matthiessen fails no more and no less than any other critic. No one has been able to provide a widely accepted, solid definition of tragedy that will fit the writings of contemporary novelists and playwrights, although the effort is constantly being made. Other critics of Dreiser, however, have been more successful, it seems to me, in finding explanations for the novelist's power that do not get mired in the tragic sense and that expose the source of Dreiser's success more usefully. Eliseo Vivas, for example, points out a contradiction between Dreiser's avowed philosophy and his novels. Vivas writes:

But fortunately for his greatness as a novelist, his explicit intellectual vision of the world is not point by point congruent with his vision as a novelist. And the philosophy which he has given us in essays and intercalated in the form of editorial comments in the movement of his dramas is not always true to the record. For there is more to his own concrete dramatic picture of men and society than he finds room for in his mechanistic philosophy. And if we miss this more, we miss, I am afraid, what is truly significant in Dreiser. His mechanism is indeed inadequate, but his dramatic vision of the world within the range of its discriminations is fully ripe and mature. . . . Few contemporary novelists have built up characters as solid, as three dimensional, as fully bodied as has Dreiser. And the reason he has succeeded where others have failed is that in spite of his naive mechanism, few novelists respond to human beings as sensitively as he does.[28]

Vivas makes no effort to find a place within the concept of tragedy for Dreiser's power. Rather, he locates its source in something else, in a sense of sympathy for or admiration for or pity for all kinds of men and women. Alfred Kazin, who is much closer to Matthiessen's political viewpoint than Vivas, also finds Dreiser's power important, but he does not locate it in anything like the tragic sense. "Dreiser is a particular example of the kind of mysterious strength," Kazin writes, "the strength with which a writer assimilates his environment, then recoils from it in order to tell a story, that makes the novelist's art possible." He goes on:

Dreiser was able to wheel into motion that enormous apparatus for suggestion and illusion that makes us lose ourselves in his books as if each were a profound and tragic experience of our own. The novel, as D. H. Lawrence said, is "the book of life." For more than two hundred years now it has been the only literary form able to suggest the ponderousness, the pressure and force, of modern industrial society. More significantly, it has been the only form . . . that has been able to find objective symbols for that increasing alienation from himself which man has come to feel in a society that is insensitive

to the individual and a universe that is wholly indifferent
to him.

On both these issues Dreiser is immense. In the wholly
commercial society of the early twentieth century, Dreiser
caught the banality, the mechanical routine, the ignorance of
any larger hopes, precisely because he was able to recognize
the significance of his own experience.[29]

I do not propose here to discuss the validity of any particular
reading of Dreiser's power. I do want to suggest, however, that
others, whether close to Matthiessen's political and religious
views or not, were able to find explanations for Dreiser's merits
that did not require the use of the term "tragic sense" by locating
the source of those merits quite outside any consideration of
tragedy.

The reasons for Matthiessen's failure in this regard are difficult
to determine. I can suggest, however, based on the available
biographical materials and especially on the enormous fact of
Matthiessen's suicide, that he failed because he himself wanted
to continue to believe in his Christian version of tragedy as an
important, indeed a crucial, criterion in literary matters, but that
as his personal strength and conviction began to fail him, he
found it difficult to do so. Matthiessen failed to measure the work
of a writer he so much admired against notions concerning the
possible amelioration of the human condition offered by Christianity, socialism, and "tragedy" in the sense in which he used
the term. That failure can only be explained, I believe, by the
terrible anguish he suffered as he worked on *Theodore Dreiser*.

The Matthiessen of *American Renaissance*, or the author of the
article on Poe in the *Literary History of the United States*, would
have, I believe, dealt more cogently with the issue and would not
have been content to explain Dreiser's power in terms of the
tragic sense. The closest Matthiessen comes to any full explanation of Dreiser's relation to the tragic tradition in America is the
following paragraph, which concludes his discussion of Darrow
as Dreiser's most like-minded reader:

This close correspondence between the values of the two
men makes us more aware of how representative these values

are of their times, more aware too of why Dreiser held them. He viewed a society in which the equality whereon alone democratic justice might be based had been destroyed by the oligarchy of wealth. At this point he was not thinking in political terms; he entertained no ideas of how Clyde's world might be changed; he only contemplated it with somber resignation. Contemplating for ourselves the extreme to which both Darrow and Dreiser had gone in their scepticism, we are faced with the grave question of how long positive values can endure only as the aftershine of something that has been lost. Dreiser began to sense this as the 'twenties moved into the 'thirties, and he was caught up far more directly into political thinking than he had ever been before. [pp. 209–10]

This passage demonstrates, perhaps, that Matthiessen too had come to despair of the possibility of "seeing the good" in the American tradition and had come to conclude that tragedy, of the sort that had so stirred him in *Billy Budd*, was no longer to be created out of the American experience. For the critic who thought of tragedy as so crucial a criterion for literary greatness and who was so profoundly involved in the American experience, this must have been a terribly debilitating—indeed, a tragic— realization. It is, perhaps, in an effort to retain some part of the "aftershine" that he posits the tragic sense. His suicide indicates that the effort was not successful, as do the major limitations of *Theodore Dreiser*.

On balance, *Theodore Dreiser* is a sound literary biography. It fails in that it does not deal sufficiently with Dreiser's sexuality, because Matthiessen seems incapable of applying contemporary knowledge in this area or of overcoming his personal feelings. More important, it fails in its approach to tragedy in Dreiser, resorting to an inadequate definition of the not-quite-tragic rather than providing an illuminating specialized definition of tragedy as had been provided elsewhere, or seeking sources for Dreiser's power in other attributes and abilities. It is not a brilliant work, as is *American Renaissance*, or a pioneering one, as are *The Achievement of T. S. Eliot* or *Henry James*. When Robert Elias, an earlier biographer of Dreiser, and one of those who helped develop the bibliographic notes for Matthiessen's book, claims that the book "is possibly a turning point in the career of Theodore Dreiser's reputation in the United States,"[30] we cannot agree, and the continued critical controversy of three decades proves him wrong. But Matthiessen's last work is by no means a failure, and it is by no means deserving of the critical obloquy heaped upon it by some. If it is not what we might wish it to be, that is only because we have come to expect a great deal from its author. But it must be pointed out finally that Matthiessen's two weakest efforts— coming at the beginning and at the end of his career—are both literary biographies, a sign perhaps that his particular cast of mind was more at home in the analysis of literary texts and in the world of ideas than in the more intimate relations between ideas and their authors.

6 ❦ "Renewed Contact with That Soil": The Responsibilities of the Critic

F. O. MATTHIESSEN's greatest contribution to criticism was not the articulation of a critical method that one can readily associate with his name. Unlike many of his contemporaries—I. A. Richards, Kenneth Burke, or John Crowe Ransom, to cite only a few—he was not a system builder. And yet his name is well known, his work widely influential. As one looks at significant figures in literary criticism in the present, especially in American letters, one is amazed at the number of leading figures who were Matthiessen's students at Harvard.

Was Matthiessen then primarily a fine teacher who wrote some useful explications? Such influential teaching in itself would be a major contribution to our understanding of literature. It is my contention, however, that Matthiessen was much more than a teacher and textual explicator, that he attempted to achieve something far larger. He sought to combine in his criticism a view of life with respect for the work of art as work of art. He attempted to look at literature with the eyes of a man with an ideology without letting his ideology blunt or dominate his taste and, conversely, he attempted to look at literature as a man of taste without letting his taste vitiate his ideology.

That was no simple task. As I have attempted to show earlier, a major breach dividing the various critics of Matthiessen's time, and in somewhat different ways our own, is that between formalist critics, who see the work of art primarily as a formal, aesthetic structure, and content-oriented critics, who see the work of art primarily as cultural or historical artifact. Matthiessen was not alone in trying to bridge the gap between the two views. Kenneth Burke attempted to do so by combining a methodology provided by linguistics with those deriving from the works of Frazer, Marx, and Freud. Edmund Wilson certainly attempted the same task, as he moved from his early fascination with radical politics into increasingly literary concerns and, near the end of his career, back toward political and historical matters. There were others who wrestled with the same problem. Most recently, various structuralists and post-structuralists have made similar efforts, and may have changed, as in the instance of Derrida, the very nature of the question.

Matthiessen's approach was unique in a number of different ways. Almost all his major works deal with American literature, so that his effort at bridging the gap between form-oriented and content-oriented criticism is also part of his effort to recover the American past or to make available his own "present" in American literature. Furthermore, unlike Wilson or Burke or others, Matthiessen hammered most tenaciously at his literary last. Although profoundly interested in politics, theology, other arts and much else, there are few major excursions on his part into other fields, into philosophy or history or linguistics or psychology. He is, above all, a *literary* critic.

The quality that distinguished Matthiessen from the other critics of his day is the nature of the synthesis he developed out of the sources from which his thought derives and the use he made of that synthesis. The sources are apparent in all of his work and can be seen more specifically in his most important work of literary theory, delivered as the Hopwood Lecture at the University of Michigan in 1949 and entitled "The Responsibilities of the Critic." Most significant among these are his social concerns, meaning those ideas having to do with the left, socialist, or as Matthiessen would have it, "democratic" side of such concerns, his Christian viewpoint, his adherence to important aspects of the New Criticism, his conviction concerning the importance of tragedy, and his concern with the most meaningful attributes of the adjective "American." But within each of these categories Matthiessen developed his own position, a position that led in some way toward the fusion he sought.

Because of his extensive extraliterary political activities and ideas, his social concerns are perhaps the best known. In them he was influenced by Marxism, but he was certainly not a Marxist. This is somewhat confusing, because in his political life Matthiessen on the whole found himself most comfortable with various factions of the radical, usually Marxist, sometimes Communist, left. But he stated that he was no Marxist in political affairs, and his literary views were consistent with his political positions in this regard.

At the time Matthiessen was writing, Marxist criticism was not a particularly prepossessing matter, and especially so in the United States, as I have already pointed out. Fredric Jameson describes the situation accurately in the preface to his imposing *Marxism and Form*. He writes:

> When the American reader thinks of Marxist literary criticism, I imagine that it is still the atmosphere of the 1930's which comes to mind. The burning issues of those days—anti-Nazism, the Popular Front, the relationship between literature and the labor movement, the struggle between Stalin and Trotsky, between Marxism and anarchism—generated polemics which we may think back on with nostalgia but which no longer correspond to the conditions of the world today. The criticism practiced then was of a relatively untheoretical, essentially didactic nature, destined more for use in the night school than in the graduate seminar, if I may put it that way; and has been relegated to the status of an intellectual and historical curiosity, as which, in the form of an occasional stray reprint of an essay by Plekhanov or a passing reference to Christopher Caudwell, it is presently maintained.
>
> In recent years, however, a different kind of Marxist criticism has begun to make its presence felt upon the English-language horizon. This is what may be called—as opposed to the Soviet tradition—a relatively Hegelian kind of Marxism, which for the German countries may be traced back to the theoretical excitement of Lukács' *History and Class Consciousness* in 1923, along with the rediscovery of Marx's *Economic and Philosophical Manuscripts of 1844*; while in France it may be most conveniently dated from the Hegel revival there during the late thirties.[1]

Although one may take some issue with the hauteur of Jameson's "night school–graduate seminar" distinction, his description, published in 1971, does indicate the nature of the Marxist criticism available in the 1930s and 1940s. There were other, more profound trends developing even in the United States, but Matthiessen seems not to have been much aware of them. It is a little startling that he makes virtually no comment about non-Communist radical and perhaps Marxist criticism, in particular that of Philip Rahv, William Phillips, and especially Irving Howe of the *Partisan Review*. He has little if any comment to make about such an impressive British Marxist as George Thomson, whose *Aeschylus and Athens* was published in 1941, or about Harry Slochower, who lived and published in the United States, and whose *Three Ways of Modern Man* appeared in 1937. John Howard Lawson, another interesting figure, is apparently unknown to Matthiessen. It must be said, however, that although such critics as Thomson and Slochower were beginning to move toward a deepening Marxist literary thought, there were no significant counterparts to them in the study of American letters, which was, after all, Matthiessen's major concern. Of those of his contemporaries who might have had an effect on Matthiessen, Maynard Solomon has written:

> The United States literature on Marxism and the arts was scattered in periodical files and ephemeral pamphlets, and most of the work of the Marxist *litterateurs* of the 1930's—when it dealt with works of art at all—was of a highly polemical and usually negative nature. Such books as Granville Hicks' *Great Tradition* (1933) and V. F. Calverton's *Liberation of American Literature* (1932) had left a somewhat bitter taste by their destructive use of class analysis and their total neglect of the aesthetic dimension of art. The Marxists in the universities (representative figures are Newton Arvin, Milton W. Brown, Oliver Larkin, Edwin Berry Burgum, and William Charvat) were scholarly, intelligent and always democratic, but their work showed only a faint awareness of the implications of Marxist philosophy. The better-known left-wing literary essayists—Malcolm Cowley, Joseph Freeman, Michael Gold, and Isidor Schneider—were largely occupied with transitory cultural-political issues; their work rarely used Marxist categories. The more interesting figures of the 1930's were rela-

tively unfamiliar to the left audience: the brilliant work of Harry Alan Potamkin on film was so dense and idiosyncratic that it generated little influence; T. K. Whipple died before his later work on American literature could find an audience; Edmund Wilson—ever passing through stages—had already settled his accounts with Marxism and was moving on in his unending search for a viable past; Kenneth Burke had introjected Marxism so completely that it disappeared within his synthetic philosophy of symbolic form and action; Meyer Schapiro continued to insist on his Marxism but rarely exercised it in his stylistic analyses; "Obed Brooks" had reverted to his professorial identity and abandoned the questions of Marxism and literature of which he had written so knowingly; F. O. Matthiessen had composed a great monograph on American literature (*American Renaissance*) with a profound grasp of humanist dialectics, but was not ready, nor did he ever become ready, to fully accept Marxism.[2]

It is interesting to note, in line with my earlier discussion of Matthiessen's connection with Communist party-dominated politics, how "Communist party dominated" Solomon's list of Marxist critics is, although certainly not all of those he mentions fall in that category. But Matthiessen seems to have had only limited connections with most of them, and he seems hardly to have been much affected in his critical methodology by their work, which was, as Solomon rightly points out, generally fragmented and scattered. Furthermore, as the United States moved into World War II at the end of the 1930s, much political controversy, including its literary facets, was muted under the impetus of "united front against fascism" ideologies and, as the nation moved out of World War II and into the cold war, any sort of Marxist ideology came under severe attack, both from internal stresses and from red-baiting ones.

Matthiessen's relationship to Marxist critical thought in the United States, then, is at best a limited one. It is limited in part by his own critical stance, which rejected any oversimplified politicism and any critical posture that did not pay the most scrupulous attention to the work of literature as work of art. It is limited also by those American Marxist critics who were Matthiessen's contemporaries. If we adopt Solomon's term for a moment and think of Matthiessen's own work as having "a profound grasp of humanist dialectics," we have one useful way of seeing Matthiessen's relationship to American Marxist criticism.

Matthiessen seems hardly to have been aware of the shift to a more rigorous Marxist criticism in Europe of the kind Jameson notes. Although obviously aware of Sartre and other French thinkers allied with him, he seems to have had only a limited grasp of the nature of existentialist thought—perhaps because the Communist left was busy attacking it—and certainly seems to have drawn no close connections between existentialism and Marxism of the kind Sartre was to make clearer after Matthiessen's death. A thinker like Antonio Gramsci,[3] the Italian Communist party leader whose work foreshadows later divergencies from Communist orthodoxy in literary matters, and such figures as T. W. Adorno, Hans Mayer, Walter Benjamin, and Lucien Goldmann, all of whose work Matthiessen might have known and several of whom were refugees in the United States during World War II, seem to have quite escaped his attention. Of course, he was not alone in this unawareness. Very few Americans knew these figures until the late 1950s and more generally the 1960s, when Matthiessen was no longer alive.

It is perhaps a little more surprising that he seems to have known nothing of Georg Lukács at all,[4] or at least not enough to mention him, and that although he knew of Brecht as a playwright, he had little to say about him as a literary theorist. Peter Demetz says, commenting on the group of European Marxist critics for whom the names I have given are only exemplary, that "in the last century one spoke of foundation and superstructure. . . . in recent decades interpretations have emerged that are trying to place economics and the work of literature in a complicated and oblique relationship."[5] One suspects that Matthiessen would have been drawn more closely to the rigors of such Marxist analysis, had he been aware of it, than he could have been to earlier American Marxism, although it is as certain as anything can be in such a speculation that he never would have embraced Marxism sufficiently to abandon his position as a Christian.

Matthiessen spends considerable time in the Hopwood Lecture discussing his relationship to Marxist thought. "Emerson held," he writes, "that a principle is an eye to see with, and despite all the excesses and exaggerated claims of the Marxists of the 'thirties, I still believe that the principles of Marxism . . . can have an immense value in helping us to see and comprehend our literature." Matthiessen then goes on to detail why that was true, but he follows immediately with a counterstatement that indicates the limitations he finds in Marxist thought:

> Marx and Engels were . . . pioneers in grasping the fact that the industrial revolution had brought about—and would continue to bring about—revolutionary changes in the whole structure of society. By cutting through political assumptions to economic realities, they revolutionized the way in which thinking men regarded the modern state. By their rigorous insistence upon the economic foundations underlying any cultural superstructure, they drove, and still drive, home the fact that unless the problems rising from the economic inequalities in our modern industrialized society are better solved, we cannot continue to build democracy. Thus the principles of Marxism remain at the base of much of the best social and cultural thought of our century. . . .
>
> This is not to say that Marxism gives what I consider an adequate view of the nature of man, or that it or any other economic theory can provide a substitute for the critic's essential painstaking discipline in the interplay between form and content in concrete works of art. But a concern with economics can surely quicken and enlarge the questions that a critic asks about the content of any new work of art with which he is faced, about the fullness to which it measures and reveals the forces that have produced both it and its author.[6]

One is struck, in this quotation, by Matthiessen's identification of Marxism with a kind of oversimplified economism—even when he is praising its basic impulses—which the more sophisticated group of recent Marxist critics entirely rejects. If as sound a mind as Matthiessen's saw Marxism entirely as an economic theory and not as what Lukács has called a *Weltanschauung*, a way of viewing the world, it is little wonder that Matthiessen's attraction to it was limited. It becomes apparent that Matthiessen's indebtedness to Marxism is not much greater than Parrington's was, and it is in some sense even less.[7] Socially concerned critics acknowledge the importance of the historical, the sociological, and the economic background, but they do not find the source for a literary theory exclusively in that background.

It was Christopher Caudwell's Marxism, sophisticated and complex at least in comparison with that of most other Marxists in the English-speaking world, that attracted Matthiessen, particularly because he could see in it aspects of Marxism that influenced his own critical theory. The young English critic, whose intriguing work was written as an extension of theories already adumbrated by the Russian, George V. Plekhanov, defends an anthropological explanation for the origins of poetry and defends a highly class-oriented criticism. Unlike Calverton, however, Caudwell pays serious attention to poetry as such and to its forms. But again and again he rejects any categories for the understanding and interpretation of literature except those which he can incorporate under the heading of "historical materialism."[8] Matthiessen can understand and accept Caudwell's passionate defense of the relations between art and society and can, in fact, find equivalences between Caudwell's and Whitman's statements on art. But this does not make Matthiessen a Marxist. Rather, it is much more accurate to say, as does Peter Demetz in his work concerning Marxist criticism, that "as a leavening yeast, sociological concepts are to be found . . . in F. O. Matthiessen's masterly *American Renaissance*."[9]

Thus Matthiessen's social concerns, although certainly affected by his reading of Marx and Engels, derive from the same source that gave us Parrington or Beard, that is, the generally "liberal" tradition in America. Beard himself, in his introduction to the 1935 edition of his *An Economic Interpretation of the Constitution of the United States* discusses the origins of this tradition and its relations to Marxist thought:

As I point out in Chapter I of my *Economic Basis of Politics*, the germinal idea of class and group conflicts in history appeared in the writings of Aristotle, long before the Christian era, and was known to great writers on politics during the middle ages and modern times. It was expounded by James Madison, in Number X of the *Federalist*, written in defense of the Constitution of the United States, long before Karl Marx was born. Marx seized upon the idea, applied it with rigor, and based predictions upon it, but he did not originate it. Fathers of the American Constitution were well aware of the idea, operated on the hypothesis that it had at least considerable validity, and expressed it in numerous writings. . . . Yet at the time this volume was written, I was, in common with all students who professed even a modest competence in modern history, conversant with the theories and writings of Marx. Having read extensively among the writings of the Fathers of the Constitution of the United States and studied Aristotle, Machiavelli, Locke, and other political philosophers, I became all the more interested in Marx when I discovered in his works the ideas which had been cogently expressed by outstanding thinkers and statesmen in the preceding centuries.[10]

One may find Beard's statement a little too simplified to accept fully, and one may feel that he is here "explaining away" the Marxist influence somewhat. Nevertheless, his statement points clearly to the many other sources besides Marxist thought that can lead to an awareness of economics as a major factor in history. There is thus affirmed the existence of an intellectual tradition, not exclusively Marxist though certainly influenced by Marxism, which explains the sum total of a people's experience, including its literature and art, in large part on the basis of social and economic concerns.

This relationship between Marxism and the broadly liberal and socially aware tradition in literature is important, of course. George Steiner, discussing Lukács's work, has commented on it as follows:

> But as a whole—and this is true of much of Lukács' best work—the Marxist critic has operated with the tools of

nineteenth-century historicism. Where he has not been
mouthing party propaganda or merely dividing art into progressive and decadent in a parody of last judgment, he has
applied, with more or less talent and finesse, those criteria
of historical condition and cause already implicit in Herder,
Sainte-Beuve and Taine. In so far as it locates the artist and
his achievement in a material setting of economic and social
forces, in so far as it insists on the essentially socially and
historically determined character of artistic perception and
public response (an insistence vital also to the argument of
such historians as Panofsky and Gombrich), Marxism is part
of a larger *Historismus*.[11]

One might well argue with the applicability of Steiner's description to more recent Marxist criticism, but his comment makes
clear the intertwining of the generally liberal, socially aware, and
historically based tradition in literature and Marxism, and it helps
us to understand how Matthiessen's brand of non-Marxist, Christian radicalism relates to the Marxist tradition of the time in which
he wrote.

It is this tradition, more generalized than any rigorous Marxism, which can lead Matthiessen to speak of the writer of tragedy
as having to have "a coherent grasp of social forces, or, at least,
of man as a social being; otherwise he will possess no frame of
reference in which to make actual his dramatic conflicts. For the
hero of tragedy is never merely an individual, he is a man in action, in conflict with other individuals in a definite social order."[12]

The Marxist views with which Matthiessen was most directly
acquainted, then, were all, in one way or another, reductive or
simplified views of the literary product. They all assumed that
one can read literature from one vantage point—in particular,
from the vantage point of the artist as a product of social and class
experiences and alliances. Matthiessen, who certainly favored
the idea of a critical vantage point, insisted, however, that the
literary product comes from far more complex sources, and he
rejected any simplistic determinism, economic or otherwise, as
the exclusive explanation for artistic creation.

Nothing can demonstrate such a refusal more clearly than

some of the rules he cites for the selection of poetry in one of his last works, the introduction he wrote for *The Oxford Book of American Verse*, published in 1950:

> The second rule accepted here is to include nothing on merely historical grounds, and the third is similar, to include nothing that the anthologist does not really like, no matter what its reputation with others. These rules recognize that there are differing reasons for liking a canto from "The Hasty Pudding" and a canto from Ezra Pound. They grant that the pleasure of savoring and comparing different periods is one of the rewards of a lively interest in cultural history. They merely insist that it is not a sufficient reason to reprint Lowell's 'Commemoration Ode' for the Civil War dead solely because it once passed for poetry in Cambridge.[13]

This is another example of Matthiessen's refusal to accept any literary judgment not ultimately based on his taste, while at the same time insisting on the importance, indeed the "pleasure," of cultural history.

Connected intimately with Matthiessen's generally socially aware approach to literature is his abiding belief in the value of "democratic man." His definition of this concept, as I have indicated earlier, is not very clear, although it must be added that it is not an easy concept to make clear. But it is connected, on the one hand, with the notion that all men and women are leveled to equality by the inevitability of the tragic in their lives and, on the other, by the conviction that a concern for the social good has as its goal the equality of all persons before the law, in their social status, and in the coming to fruition of all their possibilities. The striving toward the democratic ideal meant for Matthiessen economic as well as political equality—hence his socialism. But it also meant a description of the human condition in that human beings are in fact equal before God, although that equality can be temporarily destroyed by the pull toward evil through which some people take advantage of others.

To live in a democratic society also meant for Matthiessen the possibility of a sense of community, the lack of which doomed the totally lonely person, the isolate without human comradeship, to a kind of dehumanized condition. That Matthiessen felt great personal need for such community provides an emotional basis for his ideology. The concepts of society or community, democracy, and Christianity are thus inextricably woven in Matthiessen's thought in such a way that they provide the foundation for his social concerns. It is this complex of ideas that gives such brilliance, for example, to Matthiessen's discussion in *American Renaissance* of Ahab as the solitary man who breaks his last connections with humanity when he throws his pipe overboard. It is this weaving together of ideas that makes him perceive in Henry James's last works the criticism of society that is so easily overlooked.

Fundamental to all of these notions, of course, is the Christianity to which Matthiessen was committed. He is, in no rigorous sense, a "Christian" critic, but he was certainly, in the most fundamental way, a Christian. I have already cited his rebuke to his materialist friends, in which he indicates his firm belief in God and in the submission of man to a superior will, and I have mentioned Giles Gunn's perceptive point that Christianity was a given in Matthiessen's thought. Matthiessen is a firm believer in the truth, on the one hand, of original sin and, on the other, of the possibility of grace, which is necessary to make life explicable and bearable.

But this is not a doctrinaire basis for Christian criticism. As liberal a Christian as Nathan Scott has defined the task of the Christian critic in a way that will make clear why Matthiessen cannot be included under such a label. "The great effort of the Christian critic in our day," Scott writes, "should have as its ultimate aim a reconciliation between the modern arts and the Church, between the creative imagination and the Christian faith."[14] Even if we define "church" as Scott would want us to, in as broad a way as possible, meaning by it no institution at all but rather the broadest fellowship of Christians, that would not be acceptable to that "communicant in the Protestant Episcopal Church,"[15] F. O. Matthiessen. For just as he refused to put his critical sensibilities into the exclusive service of his social insights, so he refused to make them servile to his Christianity. He insisted, rather, that the critic must go, first of all, where his critical perceptions lead him, although he was quite convinced that these perceptions were shaped at least in part by his philosophical, social, and theological views.

In commenting, in the Hopwood Lecture, on the awareness of violence in the American experience and on Faulkner as an example of that awareness, Matthiessen says that Faulkner provides us with an important truth and that, although Faulkner "may often overwrite and use some of the cheap devices of melodrama, . . . we should not allow these to deflect us from the truth of his record. If we prefer a more smiling version of ourselves, we are liable to the peculiarly American dilemma of passing from innocence to corruption without ever having grasped maturity. By which I mean the maturity that comes from the knowledge of good and evil."[16] We have come to recognize this language as intrinsically connected with Matthiessen's view of tragedy and with his Christian perception of the fundamental nature of man's postlapsarian state.

It is from such essentially theological concerns that Matthiessen's theory of tragedy evolves. If there is one doctrinaire aspect to his work, it stems from his firm conviction about the nature of tragedy and its importance in assaying the value of works of literature. Moreover, although his is a particular definition of tragedy, it is one that he uses with great skill. The whole matter of the nature of tragedy is so debatable, so dependent on the overall world view of the critic, that one can hardly consider Matthiessen any more doctrinaire than anyone else in this regard. It is enough that Matthiessen's definition was applied with a great deal of flexibility. His essentially theological concerns, both in regard to tragedy and in connection with other ideas, make it possible for Matthiessen to develop some understanding for the peculiarity of Dreiser's seeming inconsistencies. As a socially concerned critic, Matthiessen does not shed his Christianity; as a Christian, he retains his Marxist-influenced social concerns.

Pointing to the influence of Reinhold Niebuhr, Giles Gunn writes:

Matthiessen would have agreed with Niebuhr that man is created free and, in his freedom, good. But he would also have agreed with him that man is constantly tempted into a misuse of that freedom by refusing to acknowledge anything more important than the individual, by arrogating to himself powers which belong to God alone, and by turning his fellow human beings into the means for his own selfish ends. In this, as in other aspects of his theology, Matthiessen was eager to maintain a balanced view. By accepting the doctrine of original sin, he did not think of himself as confessing to a belief that life, but for those evanescent moments when it is infused with the light of heavenly grace, is irremediably fallen. His theology, like his theory of tragedy, was founded on the twofold assumption that there can be no evil unless there is also good, or good unless there is evil.[17]

The coming together here of social awareness, democracy, the idea of community or fellowship, all based on an essentially theological position, is fundamental to Matthiessen's total outlook. In the importance given to such conceptions Matthiessen's Christianity reveals itself in his criticism. His Christianity remained what he thought it ought to be in the piece of Yale juvenilia I have quoted earlier, "a ground to stand on," but it never became a device with which he shaped the landscape so as to feature only his piece of ground.

Interwoven with all of these philosophical premises was Matthiessen's devotion to the technique developed by the New Criticism. That technique is itself grounded in the philosophical approach to art that stems most immediately in Matthiessen's time from Eliot and Richards, and it takes the form of a primary concern with the text and with the work of art itself as a linguistic structure to be understood first of all on its own terms with as few exogenous considerations as possible. He makes his devotion to this idea clear once more in the Hopwood Lecture:

What resulted from the joint influence of Eliot and Richards was a criticism that aimed to give the closest possible attention to the text at hand, to both the structure and the texture of the language. . . . The effect of this new movement upon the study of literature in our universities has been by now considerable. Although opposed by both the old guards of philologists and literary historians, most of the critics I have mentioned now hold academic appointments. . . . their work has thereby become instrumental in the revolt against concentrating exclusively on the past, and against concentrating on literary history instead of literature. As a result both teachers and students are more capable of close analysis and lively appreciation than they were a generation ago.[18]

But here again Matthiessen, who will not let a literary theory become frozen in its development, is aware of the dangers inherent in any unyielding, limited position the critic might take. Therefore he immediately follows this statement, which describes the contributions of the New Criticism, with another, which points to the destructive tendencies in the theory:

But by now we have reached the stage where revolt has begotten its own set of conventions. . . . As we watch our own generation producing whole anthologies of criticism devoted to single contemporary authors and more and more detailed books of criticism, we should realize that we have come to the unnatural point where textual analysis seems to be an end in itself. . . . the little magazines seem now to be giving rise to the conventions and vocabulary of a new scholasticism and to be not always distinguishable from the philological journals which they abhor. The names of the authors may be modern, but the smell is old. The trouble is that the terms of the new criticism, its devices and strategies and semantic exercises, can become as pedantic as any other set of terms if they are not handled as the means to fresh discoveries but as counters in a stale game. In too many recent articles literature seems to be regarded merely as a puzzle to be solved.[19]

Here as in his Christianity or in his social concerns, Matthiessen has found an approach to literature he considers useful, but he has discovered its limitations through his own experience in practice. He has learned, as time passed, to move from his announced concern in *American Renaissance* for "the foreground," the work of art itself, to an awareness that such a trend has gone too far. The significant words in the passage quoted above are, it seems to me, "scholasticism" and "pedantic," for what Matthiessen defended in the 1930s as a necessary corrective to Parringtonian and Marxist concentration upon intellectual and social history, he attacked at the end of the 1940s—and near the end of his life—as having engendered its own degeneration.

He was not, by any means, alone in this view. Howard Mumford Jones deals with the matter more than fifteen years later in his "Postscript, 1965," to *The Theory of American Literature*. He writes:

> It is not captious, I trust, to observe that the New Critics and their disciples, in reducing historical and biographical scholarship to an irrelevant act so far as literary interpretation is principally concerned, have nevertheless been silently compelled to employ the results of historical scholarship every time they consider a text. . . . If the New Critics have insisted upon slow and careful reading, they seem to have been unaware that not everything has to be read slowly and carefully. . . . The New Critics have made reading more difficult in an age when the mere reading habit has had to compete with visuality—television in particular. Their appeal is to a closed, highbrow audience. In this of course they resemble most literary specialists. Probably in any modern culture there will always be highbrows, middlebrows and lowbrows, but it seems fair to say that the general tendency of the New Criticism is to deepen the gulf between an elite group of highbrows who "go in" for literature and the vast population of middlebrows (Arnold's Philistines?) who buy paperbacks on impulse, keep up with the best sellers, subscribe to a book club, and get their reading matter from a lending library. In thus sharpening the distinction between two disparate groups of readers they not merely fail to furnish the general reader with any notion of the importance of literary history, they also tend to confine the elite to a highly specialized, and overstrained mode of interpretation.[20]

Jones's comment indicates how widespread was the concern discussed in Matthiessen's statement about the New Criticism. The comment also points to another aspect of Matthiessen's thought, worth mentioning because it dovetails so effectively with his social views. He became more and more aware, apparently, in the late 1940s, even before television had become as important as it is now, of the gulf developing in American life between what he called, using F. R. Leavis's phrase, " 'mass civilization' and 'minority culture' ":

> But to recognize that phenomenon in our democracy should only be to combat it.
>
> There is potentially a much greater audience in America for the art of literature than the blurb-writers, who often pass for reviewers in the Sunday supplements, would seem to suspect. The effectiveness of the critics in the little magazines in having by now prepared a wider public for, say, Joyce or Kafka or Eliot, amply testifies to that. But the dilemma for the serious critic in our dangerously split society is that, feeling isolated, he will become serious in the wrong sense, aloof and finally taking an inverted superiority in his isolation. At that point criticism becomes a kind of closed garden.
>
> My views are based on the conviction that the land beyond the garden's walls is more fertile, and that the responsibilities of the critic lie in making renewed contact with that soil.[21]

This comment brings together effectively those of Matthiessen's views I have explored so far. His concern with the substance of sociopolitical life and cultural history, his Christianity, and his espousal of New Critical methodologies lead him, in his efforts to combine them into effective critical principles, into a disavowal of the elitism of which the later Eliot has become a symbol. Thus Matthiessen's Christianity reinforces his sense of democracy, and his concern for a democratic culture makes him sharply aware of the growing scholasticism of New Critical methodology.

The way in which these conceptions manifest themselves in Matthiessen's work as a critic is in his continuing interest in the recovery of a useful American past and in the understanding of a useful American present. It is part and parcel of the American tradition, at least as Matthiessen and many of his contemporaries understood it, to focus on the problems of democracy; no other national tradition, they felt, is as profoundly steeped either in the avowal of democracy or in contradictions that occur when that avowal is not carried out in practice. This concern, so evident in the subject matter of the body of his total work, he expresses again in the Hopwood Lecture, by presenting another—the last— of the "awarenesses" he considered necessary for criticism:

> Mention of Caudwell's name has brought me to the last of the awarenesses that I would urge upon the critic: that of the wide gap which still exists between America and Europe. Henry James discovered long ago his leading theme in the contrast between American innocence and European experience. . . . that theme is still peculiarly urgent when we are faced with the difference between a Europe which has undergone fascism and destructive war at first hand and an America which has come out of the war richer and more powerful than ever before. . . . Allen Tate has described the kind of false superiority that can be engendered by such special isolation:
>
> > The American people fully armed
> > With assurance policies, righteous and harmed,
> > Battle the world of which they're not at all.
>
> How do Americans become part of that greater world? Not by pretending to be something they are not, nor by being either proud or ashamed of their vast special fortune. . . . The ironic lines of Tate's "Sonnet at Christmas" suggest a more mature way of meeting experience. None of us can escape what we are, but by recognizing our limitations, and comprehending them, we can transcend them by the span of that knowledge.
>
> Here is the area where breadth of concern becomes most rewarding for the critic. By perceiving what his country is and is not in comparison with other countries, he can help con-

tribute, in this time of fierce national tensions, to the international understanding without which civilization will not
survive. He will also find that he has come to know his own
country better.

The art of a country always becomes richer by being open to
stimulus from the outside, and criticism can find a particularly
fertile field in observing the results of that interchange.[22]

In urging this particular awareness, Matthiessen is again reflecting the needs of his day, for at least one aspect of the failure
to develop an American theory of literature has to do with the
failure to acknowledge sufficiently the distinctions between European and American experiences. This has been a failing of the
American left in politics as well as in the arts. Howard Mumford
Jones attempts to explain, in his "Postscript, 1965," what has
happened to the development of a theory of American literature
under the impact of the New Criticism, "image making," and
other, newer theories:

But has any perdurable theory of American literature been
shaped by the conjunction of these and other theories? On
the whole, the answer is no. The concept that a representative
republic should per se create a unique republican culture has
virtually vanished from the twentieth century. Modernists are
not concerned about the American qualities of American literature; they are concerned about the plight of Western man.
Books, formal or informal, on political theory continue to
celebrate the superiority of a representative democracy over
other forms of government but . . . it would be difficult to
assemble a library from 1948 to the present time which, so to
say, worried at the question of nationalism in literature. . . .
The *Times Literary Supplement* not long ago devoted a whole
issue to the American-ness of American literature. Most
American readers, I think, read the issue with interest but
without national curiosity or resentment. The thesis can at
least be defended that the qualities of present American
writing are the qualities of writing generally in the Western

world. A country that produces *Tropic of Cancer* and *Candy* as a kind of equivalent of the fiction of Céline would seem to have given up pretending to a special moral or aesthetic or intellectual virtue of its own.[23]

Matthiessen's comments concerning a critical awareness of the distinctions between European and American traditions, and the light these traditions shed on one another, might well be considered an answer to the problem Jones poses. Matthiessen's concern is primarily for American literature, but he sees American literature, especially in the aftermath of World War II, as a product not only of the American experience but of that experience plus the influence of European literature, which was, in turn, often influenced by American literature. Such interrelationships Matthiessen would most readily perceive by a line that runs from Poe to Baudelaire to Eliot living in England and back to the United States in, perhaps, a Wallace Stevens. That this kind of awareness comes to Matthiessen from his literary knowledge as well as his political concerns about world destruction is clear.

His application of that notion as well as of others I have been discussing, is best exemplified in his brief analysis of Wallace Stevens's "Sad Strains of a Gay Waltz," a poem that he quotes in full in the Hopwood Lecture. Here is an example of how complex Matthiessen feels the task of the critic to be, how profoundly he thinks the critic must search the work of art, and how he is to use his sensibilities, if he is to perceive the work in its totality both as creation in language and as social artifact:

Stevens' kind of symbolist poetry never makes the explicit approach. So far as he has any political or social views, they would appear to be conservative. Yet in "Sad Strains of a Gay Waltz," . . . he gave to the then young radical like myself a sudden clarification of the clouded time in which we are living. It is this kind of "momentary stay against confusion," as Robert Frost has said, that a poem is designed to give, and that becomes one of the measures of its authenticity.

In listening to almost any poem by Stevens, the first thing that strikes you is his past-masterly command of rhetoric, a reminder that, unlike the poets of the imagist movement, he is

still rooted in the older tradition that leads from Bridges back
to Milton. In this poem his rhetoric is formed into three-line
unrhymed stanzas of a basically iambic pentameter pattern,
but with many irregular line lengths which quicken but do not
break that pattern. The conflict that constitutes his theme is
between an age that is dying and a hazardous potential new
birth. He adumbrates this by offsetting a character whom he
calls Hoon, a lover of solitude like Thoreau, against the rising
masses of men in a still formless society. But his controlling
symbols are more oblique, they are "waltzes" and "shadows."
Music that has become played out seems to its listeners to be
"empty of shadows," and by a very effective repetition of
the phrase "Too many waltzes have ended," Stevens sets up
his counterpoise for a new, more dynamic music that will
again be full of shadows.[24]

Matthiessen brings to bear here on Stevens's poem many of
the critical attitudes I have discussed. He sees the poem as part of
a usable present, that is, as a means to elucidate the current state
of American life; as part of the European literary tradition, especially the tradition of English poetry; as the poet's own response
to his world; and as an effort of the poet as virtuoso of language.
Here, in only a few paragraphs, is an example of the synthesis of
methods Matthiessen sought for and achieved.

I have indicated some of Matthiessen's limitations in other sections of this study. He did not give us watertight theories of
tragedy, or of symbol, or of allegory. He was not entirely clear in
his theory of "democratic man." He was nearly as blind as were
most of his contemporaries to the failure of American criticism to
consider the racial and ethnic energies that have taken on such
great importance more recently in American letters. He assumed,
perhaps too readily, that his taste was the only possible "good"
taste. But, despite these limitations, the sum of the whole of his
work is a good deal more than its parts. Although one may question the detailed workings of some aspects of the theoretical
bases of Matthiessen's critical position, his critical theories correct
and complement one another in such a way as to make a remarkably unified critical structure. Building that structure out of

varied, seemingly incompatible elements, Matthiessen formed a
unity of those elements and avoided a disparate eclecticism with
awareness and skill.

His method as a critic shows him applying all the facets of his
mind and the force of his passions to the work before him: first,
he read the poem or the novel in such a way as to understand its
language in as much of its variety as possible; second, he brought
to bear upon that text all that he knew and understood of the
world about him, including its history and its morals, its literature and art and music, its politics and its religion; finally, he
made judgments, based indeed on his own intellectual and emotional response to the work, but judgments broadened by an
awareness of his fallibility and limitations, by a kind of humility
that is crucial and can perhaps best be attributed to a tragic sense,
an awareness of error in all things.

Matthiessen expresses the sweep of this task, and his conception of it, in the Hopwood Lecture when he says:

> In proposing an ever widening range of interests for the
> ideal critic, I have moved from his central responsibility to the
> text before him out to an awareness of some of the world-wide
> struggles of our age. We must come back where we started, to
> the critic's primary function. He must judge the work of art as
> work of art. But knowing form and content to be inseparable,
> he will recognize his duty to both. Judgment of art is un-
> avoidably both an aesthetic and a social act, and the critic's
> sense of social responsibility gives him a deeper thirst for
> meaning.
>
> This is not a narrow question of the wrong right or right
> left politics.[25]

At the end of his lecture, Matthiessen discusses Hamlet's response to one of Fortinbras's captains, and then he closes with a
peroration that gives clear voice to his view of the critic's function.
He writes:

> As John Gielgud speaks these lines, we feel what Shake-
> speare meant his audience to feel, the necessity for Hamlet's
> revenge. But we also bring to the passage our own sense of

vast insecurity, our need of being engaged in the public issues of our menaced time, and yet the need of making sure that the seeming issues are the true issues, that we are not betrayed into engagements that are merely ''th' imposthume of much wealth and peace.''

There is a basic distinction between bringing everything in your life to what you read and reading into a play of the past issues that are not there. All I am suggesting is the extent to which our awareness of ourselves as social beings is summoned by the greatest art. That is the root of my reason for believing that the good critic becomes fully equipped for his task by as wide a range of interest as he can master. . . . the critic should freely grant that the artist writes as he must. But for his own work the critic has to be both involved in his age and detached from it. This double quality of experiencing our own time to the full and yet being able to weigh it in relation to other times is what the critic must strive for, if he is to be able to discern and demand the works of art that we need most. The most mature function of the critic lies finally in that demand.[26]

This conclusion to what amounts to a critical creed points to the nature of the cause Matthiessen defended. He believed passionately in the value of literature. He believed equally passionately in the need to change, improve, and heighten the quality of modern life in America, emotionally and physically and certainly politically. He searched for means by which the literature produced by our writers could enhance the quality of life by helping us to understand how we live and by letting us perceive aspects of our lives we had not perceived before.

The passage quoted here also exemplifies two other aspects of Matthiessen's methodology that require comment. The first of these is the obvious and deep passion with which he approached his task as critic. There is nothing in his writing of the cold-blooded reserve stereotypic of the professor. He is, in the fullest sense of the term, an engaged critic, engaged with the belief that art is important and its understanding vital. He is engaged in the sense in which the term has been recently used, that is, he is convinced that it is the function of the intellectual to work at setting right the things that are wrong in this world, to make it one's task to humanize experience. Of course, Matthiessen was part of a generation of humanistic and humanitarian critics who shared such concerns. None, however, was more uncompromisingly engaged, more deeply committed to his humanism than was Matthiessen. John Rackliffe writes of him: "He himself wanted to be alert and 'aware' (one of his favorite words), missing nothing, evading nothing, permitting himself no retreats and no ambiguous compromises, allowing no blurred edges."[27] This wholeness of passion, it seems to me, is central to the man and apparent in his work.

The other aspect of Matthiessen's methodology apparent here and elsewhere is what one is inclined to call the dialectical quality of his mind. That is, although Matthiessen has strong opinions, he is never, or hardly ever, opinionated. He can see complexity, and he expresses that complexity by never permitting an idea to be driven too far toward fanaticism or foolishness. If, in his book about T. S. Eliot, Matthiessen's early polemic is partly in behalf of the New Criticism, he attempts to revise his views, in his last book about Dreiser, by asserting the importance of vision to balance the "scholasticism" with which the New Criticism has become associated. Although he believes in "bringing everything in your life to what you read," he quickly warns against any oversimplification or vulgarization of that idea—it does not mean "reading into a play of the past issues that are not there." It is perhaps in this sense that Maynard Solomon's description of *American Renaissance* as a book that displays "a profound grasp of humanist dialectics" is most applicable. It points to the ability of Matthiessen's mind to hold two contrary views in balance and to find, in the Hegelian sense, a "unity of opposites" in them. It points as well to the zeal with which he pursued the study of literature both for its own "autotelic" sake and for the sake of its power to change a world he found intolerable.

It is perhaps these two aspects of Matthiessen's critical endeavor that continue to be attractive and interesting to younger scholars and writers like Giles Gunn and George Abbott White. The latter, who was deeply involved in the political activities of the 1960s and early 1970s, and who now holds increasingly important positions in psychology as well as in literature, writes of Matthiessen:

> Matty's ideology, forged from religious and labor experiences across America and Europe, case-hardened in the painful fire necessary to give it expression and made supple by the encounter with the real world . . . , made resilient yet enriched, opened, by cooperative criticism given in friendship . . . , was not the ideology of a man who had not died to the world— who did not know its terrors and its joys. As he rejected the retrenched cynicism of the Academy so he rejected the blithe reformers *outside*, ignorant of the possible and the day-to-day limitations about ordinary people.
>
> It was an ideology of many tasks. *American Renaissance* was, in a most radiant way, one of those tasks, fulfilling a massive responsibility to what many saw as one community. But Matty lived in many worlds—and one world—and had many responsibilities—and one responsibility. There are those who disdained the implications of his ideology in other spheres, or worse, denied that the organic principle he so strenuously acknowledged and embraced had *any* validity, even for him. For them, his ideology was a "mistake," his manifold actions those of a "dilettante." The facts speak otherwise.[28]

White's emphasis on the complexity and the variety of Matthiessen's work as well as on the ardor of his dedication to his ideology indicate why Matthiessen the person continues to attract the attention of his students, his former colleagues, and younger people like White and Gunn, who could only have known him by reputation. Matthiessen's great effort, after all, was to enlarge our experience of literature, to enlarge our passionate understanding of it, and to enlarge our understanding of the human condition because of it.

What Matthiessen sought to do he came as close to achieving as one might. But the kind of criticism he hoped for as the norm of the craft has not yet fully flourished, and it certainly did not flourish in his own lifetime. The scholasticism he warned against at the end of his career is still very strong in our schools. The breadth of social view he urged upon us has been the exception rather than the rule. If there has been some progress in this direction, there has also been a sharp counterattack. The evils in the social structure about him, which led him to such profound distress about the possibilities in American life, are still present. Moreover, although we cannot doubt that Matthiessen would have rejoiced at the revival of political radicalism in the 1960s and the early 1970s, a revival that seemed so unlikely from the vantage point of the quiescent, witch-hunting year of his death, he would certainly have been distressed that the political radicalism of the young seemed often to bring with it the very literary and intellectual narrowness he excoriated in his own time and that the radicalism seemed so short-lived.

The fusion he sought has only rarely been achieved. In the study of American literature—Matthiessen's particular concern—strides have been made that are sometimes more apparent than real and that imply only a change in subject matter, not in methodology. Although Richard Ruland is certainly right when he says in his discerning book that the study of American literature, in part through the efforts of Matthiessen, has now achieved an academic status ". . . signaled by proliferating departments of American literature and autonomous American Studies programs,"[29] this does not necessarily indicate that the sort of fusion Matthiessen desired has been achieved. One wishes that one could as easily agree with Ruland's apparent conviction, in the same passage, that we have found our way to a less doctrinaire, broader criticism, dominated neither by the New Critics in their various guises nor by Parringtonian thought nor by other, newer scholasticisms. Although new names appear on the title pages of critical books and articles, it seems to me that we have still a long way to go before we can separate most critics, as Matthiessen would have wished, from a reliance on any particular kinds of scholasticisms. If nothing else, the distinction between mass civilization and minority culture continues to be a problem that faces us daily, as every teacher confronting a new freshman class realizes anew.

Richard Ruland's final assessment of Matthiessen's contribution helps to summarize important aspects of what I have attempted in detail to show is the case. For Ruland, Matthiessen is the crucial figure in bridging the gap, as he puts it in the title to his last chapter, "From *AL* to *AQ*." He writes that Matthiessen

> realized that "what makes the art of the past still so full of undiscovered wealth is that each age inevitably turns to the past for what it most wants, and thereby tends to remake the past in its own image." But . . . he never lost his sense of historical time or failed to insist on accuracy. . . . Matthiessen's own Christian Socialism and his own pained awareness of how badly his time cried for guidance never led him to falsify the past. . . .
>
> Matthiessen's own pursuit of aesthetic values led him to concentrate on what he deemed masterworks and to study them with the most subtle tools Eliot and New Criticism made available. . . . And yet, once deeply inside the work under examination, he was always led outward again by his conviction that art is intimately related to life and that aesthetic criticism must ultimately become social and cultural criticism. . . .
>
> I do not mean to suggest . . . that Matthiessen successfully fused all the components he found necessary to fruitful literary criticisms. . . . Most students of Matthiessen have noticed the disparate premises which, if carried through logically, would surely not mesh. . . . Furthermore, despite his insistence on close technical analysis as a requisite preliminary to cultural inquiry, Matthiessen himself seems more to sample the method than to pursue it comprehensively. . . .
>
> His foremost insight was his pragmatic approach to critical methodology. Matthiessen was more methodologically aware than any critic of his time. . . . Matthiessen wrote as a New Critic, as a Marxist, as a New Humanist, as a Freudian; he used and has inspired further investigation of biographical material and the implications of American myth, romance and symbolism. When he turned to European analogues, ancient and modern, to our British literary heritage, to economics, anthropology, painting, and architecture, he may not always have achieved the illuminating complexity he sought, but

he always eluded imprisonment in a single critical point of
view and he never sacrificed art to consistency.[30]

I do not agree with Ruland on a number of points: I find that
Matthiessen used Freudianism in only the most superficial fashion; I do not believe, in most instances, that his application of
New Critical methodology is incomplete; and I do not think he
wrote "as a Marxist." But fundamentally, Ruland assesses what
he calls Matthiessen's major contribution justly.

This, then, is Matthiessen's achievement—not a fully developed critical method, not a theory of literature, but a group of
exemplary works, the greatest virtue of which lie in their remarkable insights, in their profound appreciation of literature as a
humanizing force, in their ability to "make connections," and
in their freedom from most restraining intellectual or emotional
a priori patterns.

One of Matthiessen's nonliterary works, obviously a love-
offering, is a book of reproductions of the work of Russell Cheney,
with a running text by Matthiessen. The last plate in that book
has seemed to me a kind of gloss upon Matthiessen's own career.
It shows a Zapata-like figure, alone on horseback, in a desolate,
cactus-dominated desert landscape. It is called "The Lost Cause,"
and what impresses me about it is the dignity of the man who has
fought hard and has lost a fight in which he believes. His loneliness and courage is compelling as he rides through the desper-
ately arid landscape of defeat. Matthiessen seems to me to have
been such a figure, perhaps less aware than he might have been,
as such figures often are, of how much of the fight he really won.
He lived a life that was often difficult. As a radical socialist, as a
homosexual, as a Christian, as an intellectual, and as a man who
felt that he was without community in the larger sense, he had a
career aptly described by John Rackliffe as "energetic and often
lonely."[31] Thus Matthiessen rode in his landscape with courage
but saw it become increasingly desolate, until he could no longer
live in it and ended his life. One wishes, in vain, that he could
have lived at least his three score and ten, so that he might have
seen his labors bear fruit in the works of his friends and students,
in the great respect accorded his own work, in the articulation

of ideas of democratic socialism by significant portions of the American left. He would hardly have been entirely happy with the last two decades of his life—but as a man who understood profoundly the inevitability of the tragic, he would not have expected happiness.

He taught us much, this Harvard don, this believer in his own brand of Christian socialism, this defender of the tragic, advocate of democratic man, this scholar. What he taught cannot be fully documented, but must, before anything else, be sensed through a reading of his work. He said it best, perhaps, in the Hopwood Lecture: "The extension of our sense of living by compelling us to contemplate a broader world is the chief gift that literature holds out to us."[32] His work has immensely aided that contemplation and has helped us to perceive that broader world. He can teach us, if we are willing to learn, to understand a little more fully one of his favorite quotations from Shakespeare, Edgar's "Ripeness is all."

Notes

Author's Note: For the convenience of the reader I have used page numbers for Matthiessen's essays and reviews from *The Responsibilities of the Critic: Essays and Reviews by F. O. Matthiessen*, edited by John Rackliffe (1952). The original titles, dates, and places of publication are cited in the bibliography of this book.

Chapter 1

1. Richard Ruland, *The Rediscovery of American Literature*, pp. ix–x.

2. I am indebted to much printed material for the information in this biographical sketch and have acknowledged such materials in notes where appropriate. But I am also indebted to conversations with many people who knew Matthiessen for information that I could not conveniently acknowledge by means of notes. I have listed their names in my acknowledgments. There I have also acknowledged my gratitude for assistance received from several libraries that house material related to Matthiessen's work.

3. Louis Hyde, ed., *Rat & the Devil*, p. 125. This letter from Matthiessen is dated 8 April 1925.

4. F. O. Matthiessen, *From the Heart of Europe*, p. 71.

5. Hyde, *Rat & the Devil*, p. 47.

6. Paul M. Sweezy, "A Biographical Sketch," p. ix, in Paul M. Sweezy and Leo Huberman, eds. *F. O. Matthiessen, 1902–1950* (hereafter cited in the text as *FOM*).

7. Richard M. Dorson, *The Birth of American Studies*, pp. 5, 7.

8. I am grateful to Eugene Current-García, professor emeritus of Auburn University and editor emeritus of the *Southern Humanities Review*, for permission to quote from this letter to him.

9. Kenneth S. Lynn, "Teaching: F. O. Matthiessen," p. 91.

10. I am particularly grateful to Henry Reifesnyder of Indiana State University, and once again to Eugene Current-García, for giving me the opportunity to examine some of their classroom notes from Matthiessen's courses.

11. Hyde, *Rat & the Devil*, pp. 235–61 and passim.

12. Ibid., p. 260.

13. May Sarton, *Faithful Are the Wounds*.

14. Giles B. Gunn, *F. O. Matthiessen*, p. xxii.

15. This letter from Irving Howe is in the Matthiessen Collection

housed in the Beinecke Rare Book and Manuscript Library at Yale University. Professor Howe has graciously granted permission for my quotation here.

16. Matthiessen, *From the Heart of Europe*, pp. 82–83.

17. Ibid., pp. 48, 49–50.

18. H. Montgomery Hyde, *Stalin*, p. 557.

19. Howard K. Smith, *The State of Europe*, p. 121.

20. F. O. Matthiessen, *Theodore Dreiser*, pp. 232–33.

21. Hyde, *Rat & the Devil*, p. 361.

22. Ibid., p. 3. Ellipses are in the original.

23. W. H. Auden, "Criticism in a Mass Society," p. 112.

24. F. O. Matthiessen, ed., Introduction to *The Oxford Book of American Verse*, p. xxxiii.

25. John Dewey, *Art as Experience*, pp. 106–7. Italics are in the original.

26. A. C. Bradley, *Oxford Lectures in Poetry*, p. 8.

27. See, e.g., in regard to Babbitt, F. O. Matthiessen, "Irving Babbitt," pp. 161–65, and *From the Heart of Europe*, p. 74. In regard to Sherman see F. O. Matthiessen, "Sherman and Huneker," pp. 154–59.

28. See, e.g., F. O. Matthiessen, "Axel's Castle," pp. 159–61.

29. William Van O'Connor, "Modern Literary Criticism," p. 224.

30. Alfred Kazin, *New York Jew*, pp. 43–44.

31. Leslie A. Fiedler, "American Literature," pp. 162–63.

32. William Van O'Connor, *An Age of Criticism, 1900–1950*, pp. 167 and passim.

33. Vernon L. Parrington, *Main Currents in American Thought*, 1:iii.

34. John Crowe Ransom, "Criticism as Pure Speculation," pp. 82–83, n. 23. It is Ransom who identifies Marxist views as being represented "in some degree and shade by Mr. Wilson, and possibly Mr. Auden" (p. 81).

35. John H. Raleigh, "Revolt and Revaluation in Criticism, 1900–1930," pp. 194–98.

36. C. Hugh Holman, "The Defense of Art," p. 201.

37. See the table of contents in O'Connor, *An Age of Criticism, 1900–1950*.

38. Fiedler, "American Literature," p. 159.

39. F. O. Matthiessen, "Poetry," p. 1354.

40. Fiedler, "American Literature," p. 169.

41. Matthiessen, *From the Heart of Europe*, p. 82.

Chapter 2

1. See, e.g., Margaret Farrand Thorp, *Sarah Orne Jewett*, pp. 46–48.

2. Ibid., p. 12.

3. F. O. Matthiessen, *Sarah Orne Jewett*, p. 31.

4. Ibid., pp. 19–21.

5. F. O. Matthiessen, "New Standards in American Criticism, 1929," pp. 181–82.

6. Howard Mumford Jones, *The Theory of American Literature*, pp. 141–42.

7. Matthiessen, *Sarah Orne Jewett*, p. 135.

8. Ibid., p. 101.

9. F. O. Matthiessen, *Translation*, pp. 321–22.

10. Matthiessen, *Sarah Orne Jewett*, pp. 145–46.

11. O'Connor, "Modern Literary Criticism," p. 223.

12. Bernard Bowron, "The Making of an American Scholar," pp. 47–48.

13. Ibid., p. 49.

14. Ibid., pp. 49–50.

15. Paul M. Sweezy, "A Biographical Sketch," p. x.

16. F. O. Matthiessen, *Russell Cheney, 1881–1945*, p. 63. See also Hyde, *Rat & the Devil*, p. 144.

17. Matthiessen, *Sarah Orne Jewett*, pp. 144–45.

18. Jones, *American Literature*, p. 148.

19. *Verses by Sarah Orne Jewett* (1916). I found this volume in the Rare Book Room of the New York Public Library, where it is kept as an example of fine printing.

20. Richard Cary, *Sarah Orne Jewett*, p. 33.

21. See especially in this regard George Abbott White, " 'Have I Any Right in a Community That Would So Utterly Disapprove of Me If It Knew the Facts?' " pp. 58–62.

22. Cary, *Sarah Orne Jewett*, pp. 25–26.

23. Thorp, *Sarah Orne Jewett*, pp. 15–16.

24. An important essay in this regard is Carroll Smith-Rosenberg, "The Female World of Love and Ritual," pp. 1–29. Smith-Rosenberg's discussion of female friendships in the nineteenth century presents a significant approach to a consideration of Jewett's life and her friendship with Annie Fields. The absence in Jewett's life, however, of any possible adult heterosexual relationship makes her case rather different from most of those documented by Smith-Rosenberg. Nevertheless, Smith-Rosenberg's "alternative approach to female friendships—one which would view them within a cultural and social setting rather than from an exclusively psychosexual perspective" (p. 2) would certainly have to be considered in the kind of study of Jewett I am suggesting. I wish to thank my colleague, Judith K. Gardiner of the Department of English and the Women's Studies Program at the University of Illinois at Chicago Circle, for bringing this article to my attention.

25. F. O. Matthiessen, "Nathaniel Hawthorne," pp. 210–11.

26. F. O. Matthiessen, "Credo, 1922," p. 252.

27. Matthiessen, *Sarah Orne Jewett*, p. 149.

28. F. O. Matthiessen, "Phelps Putnam, 1894–1948," p. 257.

29. Bowron, "American Scholar," p. 50.

30. Gunn, *F. O. Matthiessen*, p. 41.

Chapter 3

1. F. O. Matthiessen, *The Achievement of T. S. Eliot*, facing p. vii. The first edition of this work (Boston: Houghton Mifflin; London: Oxford University Press, 1935), was augmented in the second edition (New York and London: Oxford University Press, 1947) with chapters on the plays and with "Four Quartets," but it is otherwise only slightly changed from the first edition. The third edition contains an additional chapter by C. L. Barber, dated 1958 and entitled "The Power of Development . . . in a Different World," a title Barber takes from quotes from Yeats and Eliot. The new chapter deals essentially with Eliot's later plays, i.e., from *The Cocktail Party* forward, and to a lesser extent with the criticism collected in *On Poetry and Poets* and in *Notes towards a Definition of Culture*. There is also a "Preface to the Third Edition (1958)" that deals as much with Matthiessen as with Eliot.

The stylistic changes between the two editions that Matthiessen oversaw himself are slight. An example from the opening lines of Chapter 1 of each edition will indicate their nature:

First edition: "In his latest book of criticism, 'After Strange Gods: A Primer of Modern Heresy', T. S. Eliot states that . . ."

Second and third editions: "In *After Strange Gods: A Primer of Modern Heresy*, T. S. Eliot stated that . . ."

I have here used the third edition throughout.

2. In the first printing of the 1935 edition Matthiessen uses the phrase "My one aim" at the outset of his preface. In all subsequent printings and editions, all of which include "Preface to the First Edition (1935)," the phrase has been changed to "My double aim." I take the change to indicate the increasing emphasis Matthiessen placed on the second clause of the sentence, i.e., "to emphasize certain of the fundamental elements in the nature of poetry which are in danger of being obscured by the increasing tendency to treat poetry as a social document and to forget that it is an art." This seems to me an indication of the increasing importance he attached to this concept, a matter I deal with more fully in my text.

3. Matthiessen, *Achievement of T. S. Eliot*, pp. vii–viii.

4. Matthiessen's effort to enlist in the Marines was thwarted because he was half an inch too short for Marine Corps standards.

5. F. O. Matthiessen, *Henry James*, pp. ix–xi. Oxford University Press reprinted the 1944 edition in 1963, and it is the 1963 edition that I have used throughout.

6. Matthiessen, *From the Heart of Europe*, pp. 76–79.

7. Ronald S. Crane, *The Languages of Criticism and the Structure of Poetry*, p. 99.

8. F. O. Matthiessen, *"The Great Tradition,"* p. 192.

9. Ibid., pp. 192–93.

10. Ibid., p. 197.

11. F. O. Matthiessen, "Henry James' Portrait of the Artist," p. 11.

12. T. S. Eliot, "The Function of Criticism," pp. 13, 19.

13. T. S. Eliot, *Notes towards a Definition of Culture*, p. 17.

14. F. O. Matthiessen, "The Flowering of New England," p. 207.

15. Ibid.

16. Ibid., pp. 202, 203.

17. F. O. Matthiessen, "Van Wyck Brooks," p. 234.

18. Ibid., p. 238.

19. Matthiessen, *From the Heart of Europe*, p. 74.

20. Matthiessen, *Achievement of T. S. Eliot*, p. 4.

21. Ibid., p. 23, n. 1.

22. Matthiessen, "Henry James' Portrait," p. 7. My italics added.

23. F. O. Matthiessen, "Sarah Orne Jewett," in Rackliffe, p. 66.

24. Matthiessen, *Achievement of T. S. Eliot*, pp. 20–21.

25. Matthiessen, *Henry James*, pp. 79–80.

26. Matthiessen, *Achievement of T. S. Eliot*, p. 106.

27. Ibid., p. 107.

28. Matthiessen, *From the Heart of Europe*, p. 82.

29. F. O. Matthiessen, *American Renaissance*, pp. 179–80.

30. Lucien Goldmann, *The Hidden God*, p. 42.

31. Ibid., p. 44.

32. Susan Sontag, "The Death of Tragedy," pp. 136–37.

33. Arthur Miller, "Tragedy and the Common Man," pp. 146–47.

34. The following passage in Gunn's book occurs shortly after Gunn expresses his disagreement with my position on this matter in an earlier version of this chapter. Gunn asserts that I accuse Matthiessen of "moral lapse" and that I believe that "the chief sources of Matthiessen's view of life and letters—Christianity, socialism, and tragedy—were inherently incompatible." On the latter count, Gunn is right about my position, though I argue throughout my work that Matthiessen managed a remarkable synthesis, given the inherent difficulties in reconciling his views. I do not think that I accuse Matthiessen of any "moral lapse," in any sense in which I understand the term "moral." The lapse, if any, in Matthiessen's vision results from the difficulty of reconciling such intellectually disparate, indeed even at times, contradictory positions. The problem is shared by many Christians and Jews who, though acting from the highest moral motives, are adherents in some form of the oxymoron implicit in the notion of the "social gospel." This disagreement

in no way detracts from my great admiration for Giles Gunn's outstanding and pioneering book.

35. Gunn, *F. O. Matthiessen*, pp. 191–92.

36. Goldmann, *Hidden God*, pp. 50–51.

37. Albert Camus, "The Myth of Sisyphus," p. 89.

38. Goldmann, *Hidden God*, p. 48.

39. Ibid., p. 42.

40. André Schwarz-Bart, *The Last of the Just*.

41. Goldmann, *Hidden God*, pp. 54–55.

42. Reinhold Niebuhr, "Christianity and Tragedy," pp. 155–56, 165–66.

43. Matthiessen, *Achievement of T. S. Eliot*, pp. 125–27, n. 6. Italics are in
the original. The elisions in these passages are examples of Matthiessen's
point, in connection with Eliot, Joyce, Lawrence, Tolstoy, Milton, and
other writers.

44. Ruland, *American Literature*, pp. 227–28.

45. Matthiessen, *Achievement of T. S. Eliot*, p. 56.

46. Ibid., pp. 60–61.

47. T. S. Eliot, "The Waste Land," in *The Complete Poems and Plays,
1900–1950*, p. 40, ll. 102–6.

48. Matthiessen, *Achievement of T. S. Eliot*, pp. 57–58. Italics are in the
original. It is worth noting that Matthiessen's—and Eliot's—rejection of
"pouring out personal emotion" is quite similar to Irving Babbitt's main
objections to romanticism in general, in *Rousseau and Romanticism*.

49. Matthiessen, *Achievement of T. S. Eliot*, p. 60.

50. Ibid., p. 70.

51. Matthiessen, *Henry James*, p. 72.

52. C. S. Lewis, *The Allegory of Love*, p. 44.

53. Northrop Frye, *Anatomy of Criticism*, p. 71.

54. Matthiessen, *Henry James*, p. xiv.

55. Ibid., pp. 86–87.

56. Ibid., p. 90.

57. Ibid., p. 93.

58. Ibid., pp. 101–2.

59. Ruland, *American Literature*, p. 230.

60. Eliseo Vivas, "What Is a Poem?," p. 111.

61. Matthiessen, *American Renaissance*, p. xv.

62. Matthiessen, *Henry James*, p. 94.

63. Matthiessen, *From the Heart of Europe*, p. 81.

64. F. O. Matthiessen, "The Responsibilities of the Critic," p. 18.

65. George Abbott White, "Ideology and Literature: *American Renaissance* and F. O. Matthiessen" p. 493. The special issue of *TriQuarterly*,
in which this article appeared, was sub-titled *Literature in Revolution*.
It lists White as "guest co-editor" and is important in the body of
commentary about Matthiessen.

66. There are three letters from T. S. Eliot to Matthiessen in the files

of the Houghton Library at Harvard University. Valerie Eliot has been kind enough to write me that she has, in addition, "found carbons of another eight in my files, two for 1934, two for 1935, two for 1943, and one for 1949 and 1950." She also mentions a letter, dated 8 August 1934, from Matthiessen to Eliot. I am most grateful to Ms. Eliot for her kindness. The letters from Eliot at the Houghton, all dated 1949, indicate that they are responses to letters from Matthiessen. Although I have not myself seen it, I have been told that there is other correspondence between the two men which has come to light.

67. Stephen Spender, *T. S. Eliot*, p. 2.

Chapter 4

1. Matthiessen, *American Renaissance* (hereafter cited by page numbers in the text).

2. George S. Hellman, "They Are the Mountains in Our Range of Letters," p. 4.

3. Stanley T. Williams, "In the Age of Emerson and Whitman," p. 201.

4. My private conversations with colleagues and friends who profess an interest in American letters and in Matthiessen have convinced me that *American Renaissance* is known more widely than thoroughly. A little probing will reveal, even with many fine scholars, that they have read "several sections" of the book or that they "never quite got around to finishing it." Fewer than one would expect have read the work from cover to cover, though many have used portions of the work for purposes of teaching or scholarship. I suspect that this is a result of the work's sheer length—some 678 pages plus a 13-page introduction—and of the complexity of its structure.

5. "Although I greatly admire Parrington's elucidation of our liberal tradition, I think the understanding of our literature has been retarded by the tendency of some of his followers to regard all criticism as 'belletristic trifling'" (Matthiessen, *American Renaissance*, p. ix).

6. See, in this regard, Don Cameron Allen, Foreword to *Essays in the History of Ideas*, p. vii.

7. Merle Curti, *The Growth of American Thought*, p. x and passim. Curti's book is dedicated as follows: "To the Memory of Frederick Jackson Turner."

8. Bernard Smith, "An American Renaissance," pp. 627–28.

9. Geoffrey Hartman, "Structuralism," p. 140, n. 3.

10. Lucien Goldmann, "Structure," p. 108; italics in Goldmann.

11. Robert E. Spiller, *The Cycle of American Literature*, p. 91.

12. John Crowe Ransom, "Criticism as Pure Speculation," p. 91.

13. See, e.g., Morris W. Croll, "The Baroque Style in Prose."

14. See, e.g., Leslie A. Fiedler, "American Literature," pp. 179–80.

15. Benedetto Croce, *Aesthetics*, p. 119. Italics are in the original.

16. Nathaniel Hawthorne, *The Scarlet Letter*, p. 261.

17. Harry Levin, Introduction to *The Scarlet Letter*, p. xvii.

18. Theodore Spencer, *Shakespeare and the Nature of Man*, p. 1. Spencer's book grew out of "a series of lectures which the Lowell Institute of Boston asked me to deliver in the spring of 1942." Thus the book's materials were first presented a year after the publication of *American Renaissance*.

19. F. O. Matthiessen, "Theodore Spencer, 1902–49," p. 279. This was jointly written with I. A. Richards, Kenneth B. Murdock, Harry Levin, J. H. Finlen, Jr., and Walter Jackson Bate, who emended an original draft by Matthiessen.

20. W. H. Auden, "The Christian Tragic Hero," pp. 40–41. This was originally published in the *New York Times Book Review*, 16 December 1945.

21. Hawthorne, *The Scarlet Letter*, p. 260.

22. See, e.g., George Abbott White, "Ideology and Literature," p. 496. I have also been told that Matthiessen was influenced by Olson by one of the anonymous readers whom I thank in my acknowledgments and whose name ethics forbid me from mentioning, even when I suspect I know it. That reader also directed me again to Lewis Mumford, whose influence in this regard certainly requires mention.

23. Charles Olson, "Lear and Moby-Dick," p. 169. My colleague, the poet Michael Anania, was helpful in locating a copy of this essay, for which my thanks.

24. Ibid., pp. 188–89.

25. Lewis Mumford, *Herman Melville*, p. 361. See also Mumford's *The Golden Day*, esp. chap. 3, sec. 8, "Night."

26. Herman Melville, *Moby-Dick*, p. 535.

27. James E. Miller, Jr., *A Reader's Guide to Herman Melville*, p. 228.

28. George Abbott White, "Ideology and Literature," p. 486.

29. Williams, "Emerson and Whitman," p. 201.

30. Matthiessen's footnote to this passage reads in part: "The quotations are from Robert Penn Warren's definition of myth in an essay on John Crowe Ransom. . . . My own discussion of the extension of symbols into myths is reserved for the final chapter of this volume" (*American Renaissance*, p. 291). That Matthiessen uses a definition of myth as raw material for his definition of symbol is further indication of his own "esemplastic" view.

31. Robert E. Spiller, "Emerson and Co.," p. 6.

32. Ruland, *American Literature*, p. 244.

33. Goldmann, *Hidden God*, pp. 319–20.

34. See, in this regard, the material in chapter 1 of this book and especially Paul M. Sweezy, "Labor and Political Activities," in Sweezy and Huberman, *F. O. Matthiessen, 1902–1950*.

35. Henry Nash Smith, "American Renaissance," p. 57.

36. John Dewey, "Democracy," p. 335. I have chosen this passage because it first appeared in *School and Society* in 1937, that is, at a time when Matthiessen was deeply involved in writing *American Renaissance*.

37. See especially Matthiessen, *From the Heart of Europe*, pp. 73, 154, 162; John Rackliffe, "Notes for a Character Study," in Sweezy and Huberman, *F. O. Matthiessen, 1902–1950*, pp. 76–92.

38. Vernon L. Parrington, *Main Currents in American Thought*, 1:iv–v.

39. Matthiessen, *From the Heart of Europe*, p. 90.

40. See especially the essay by J. H. Summers, in "Statements by Friends and Associates," in Sweezy and Huberman, *F. O. Matthiessen, 1902–1950*, pp. 141–44.

41. George Steiner, "Marxism and the Literary Critic," p. 310.

42. Ibid., p. 322.

43. Parrington, *Main Currents in American Thought*, 2:58.

44. Spiller, "Emerson and Co.," p. 6.

45. Granville Hicks, Review of *American Renaissance*, p. 559.

46. Ibid., pp. 559–60.

47. Ibid., p. 560.

48. Ibid., pp. 561, 562, 565.

49. Ibid., p. 565.

50. White, "Ideology and Literature," p. 475.

51. Henry Nash Smith, "American Renaissance," p. 60.

Chapter 5

1. F. O. Matthiessen, *Theodore Dreiser*, p. 2 (hereafter cited by page numbers in the text).

2. Brom Weber, "Two American Men of Letters," p. 333.

3. Ruland, *American Literature*, p. 266.

4. Matthiessen, *From the Heart of Europe*, p. 44.

5. Kazin, *New York Jew*, p. 169.

6. Matthiessen, *From the Heart of Europe*, p. 46.

7. "Current Books" (review of *Theodore Dreiser*), p. 148.

8. Leo Marx, "The Teacher," pp. 42–43.

9. Richard Hofstadter, "Native Sons of our Literature," p. 398.

10. C. Vann Woodward, "Not So Freed Men," p. 8.

11. Hofstadter, "Native Sons," p. 398.

12. R. W. B. Lewis, "Contemporary American Literature," pp. 215–16.

13. Lionel Trilling, *The Liberal Imagination*, pp. 14–15.

14. John Berryman, "Through Dreiser's Imagination the Tides of Real Life Billowed," p. 7.

15. Joseph Warren Beach, "Five Makers of American Fiction," pp. 747–48.

16. Trilling, *Liberal Imagination*, p. 18.

17. See Ernest J. Simmons, "Statements by Friends and Associates," in Sweezy and Huberman, *F. O. Matthiessen, 1902–1950*, p. 37.

18. Arthur Mizener, "Dreiser and Anderson," p. 720.

19. F. O. Matthiessen, "God, Mammon and Mr. Dreiser," pp. 1, 2, 44. A number of phrases and concepts in this review are used in *Theodore Dreiser*.

20. Herbert J. Muller, "Anderson and Dreiser," p. 462.

21. Maxwell Geismar, "Social and Sexual Revolutionary," p. 15.

22. Ibid., p. 16.

23. Milton Rugoff, "A Novelist's Pilgrimage," p. 12.

24. Leonard K. Eaton, Review of *Theodore Dreiser*, p. 301.

25. Berryman, "Dreiser's Imagination," p. 7; my italics added.

26. Berryman and, elsewhere, Robert Elias notwithstanding, I think that Matthiessen, although certainly aware that *American Tragedy* was Dreiser's most important book, really preferred *Jennie Gerhardt* and perhaps *The Financier*, and he had a special fondness for *Sister Carrie*. I am led to such an opinion by the following examples:

About *Jennie Gerhardt*: "Dreiser often seems to posit his characters rather than to develop them, but *Jennie Gerhardt* contains his most fully realized group. Father Gerhardt is one of his minor masterpieces" (*TD*, 114–15).

About *The Financier*: "In fine, when Dreiser told reporters that his aim was to portray his financier 'unidealized and uncursed,' he had in mind his most completely developed conception of a protagonist—one who could fuse, more effectively than anything else he had written so far, what Balzac and Spencer had helped teach him" (*TD*, 131).

About *Sister Carrie*: "He is at his rare best in conveying the first understated rift between Hurstwood and Carrie, with everything keyed down to the neutral phrases that passed between them over the supper table. Or in conveying the brutal blankness of Hurstwood's separation from his partner Shaughnessy, or the pitiful blankness of the scene where Hurstwood begs from Carrie. Or in the entire chapter dealing with the streetcar strike, or in the one on the 'curious shifts' of the poor" (*TD*, 87).

Matthiessen might well suppress such preferences, believing that they were capricious and not worthy of mention. Although conclusive evidence for such unstated feelings is obviously hard to find, one can nevertheless speculate that they are based not only on aspects of Dreiser's style but also on Matthiessen's predilection for strong protagonists who, unlike Clyde Griffiths, can provide the basis for tragedy-like situations.

27. Walter Kaufmann, *Tragedy and Philosophy*, p. 211.

28. Eliseo Vivas, "Dreiser, an Inconsistent Mechanist," pp. 11–12.

29. Alfred Kazin, "Dreiser," p. 88. This essay originally appeared as an introduction to the Laurel Press's Dreiser series in 1959.

30. Robert H. Elias, Review of *Theodore Dreiser*, p. 505.

Chapter 6

1. Fredric Jameson, *Marxism and Form*, p. ix.

2. Maynard Solomon, *Marxism and Art*, pp. 274–75. This is Solomon's introduction to portions of work by the critic Sidney Finkelstein, whose *Art and Society* was widely discussed in communist circles. Finkelstein's connections were clearly with the *New Masses* of the post-World War II era, and it seems unlikely that Matthiessen had not at least heard of the work.

3. See, e.g., Antonio Gramsci, *The Modern Prince and Other Writings*, pt. 2, pp. 55–132.

4. Thirteen pages of *From the Heart of Europe* are devoted to a brief trip Matthiessen took to Budapest in late November 1947. Although he mentions many other Hungarian teachers and intellectuals he met, he does not mention Lukács, rather surprisingly, since Lukács was the leading literary figure in Hungary during the period from 1944 to 1948, when he clashed once again with official Stalinism. Lukács has been described during this period as "the Pope of the communist theory of literature" and as dominating cultural life in Hungary (Ehrhard Bahr and Ruth G. Kunzer, *Georg Lukács*, pp. 84–85).

5. Peter Demetz, *Marx, Engels, and the Poets*, p. 236.

6. Matthiessen, "The Responsibilities of the Critic," p. 11.

7. See Howard Mumford Jones, *The Theory of American Literature*, p. 143. Jones says of Parrington in this regard: " 'I was a good deal of a Marxian,' Parrington wrote in 1928, though he came to doubt the sufficiency of the Marxian formula."

8. Christopher Caudwell [Christopher St. John Sprigg], *Illusion and Reality*, p. 12.

9. Demetz, *Marx, Engels, and the Poets*, p. 230.

10. Charles A. Beard, Introduction to the 1935 edition of *An Economic Interpretation of the Constitution of the United States*, pp. xii–xiii.

11. George Steiner, "An Aesthetic Manifesto," p. 341.

12. Matthiessen, *American Renaissance*, p. 179.

13. F. O. Matthiessen, Introduction to *The Oxford Book of American Verse*, p. ix.

14. Nathan A. Scott, Jr., "The Modern Experiment in Criticism," p. 167.

15. C. L. Barber, Preface to the third edition of *The Achievement of T. S. Eliot*, p. xiii.

16. Matthiessen, "Responsibilities of the Critic," pp. 13–14.

17. Giles B. Gunn, "The American Scholar at Work," pp. 149–50. Professor Gunn will forgive my use of language from the precursor to his book, since I have not found the exact counterpart to this statement in his much-revised work but find this statement apt for my purposes.

18. Matthiessen, "Responsibilities of the Critic," pp. 4–5.

19. Ibid., p. 5.
20. Jones, *American Literature*, pp. 201–2.
21. Matthiessen, "Responsibilities of the Critic," pp. 5–6.
22. Ibid., pp. 12–13.
23. Jones, *American Literature*, pp. 205–6.
24. Matthiessen, "Responsibilities of the Critic," pp. 15–16.
25. Ibid., p. 14.
26. Ibid., p. 18.
27. Rackliffe, "Notes for a Character Study," p. 76.
28. George Abbott White, "Ideology and Literature," pp. 495–96.
29. Ruland, *American Literature*, p. 286.
30. Ibid., pp. 282–85.
31. John Rackliffe, Foreword to *The Responsibilities of the Critic*, p. xii.
32. Matthiessen, "Responsibilities of the Critic," p. 17.

Bibliography

Allen, Don Cameron. Foreword to *Essays in the History of Ideas* by
    Arthur O. Lovejoy, pp. vii–ix. Baltimore: Johns Hopkins University
    Press, 1948.

Auden, W. H. "The Christian Tragic Hero." In *Moderns on Tragedy*, edited
    by Lionel Abel, pp. 40–44. Greenwich, Conn.: Fawcett, 1967.

―――. "Criticism in a Mass Society." In *The Intent of the Critic*, edited by
    Donald A. Stauffer, pp. 104–22. 1941. Reprint. New York: Bantam,
    1966.

Babbitt, Irving. *Rousseau and Romanticism*. Cambridge, Mass.: Harvard
    University Press, 1919.

Bahr, Ehrhard, and Kunzer, Ruth Goldschmidt. *Georg Lukács*. New York:
    Frederic Ungar, 1972.

Barber, C. L. Preface to the third edition of *The Achievement of T. S. Eliot*
    by F. O. Matthiessen, pp. xi–xiv. 3d ed. New York: Oxford University
    Press, 1958.

Beach, Joseph Warren. "Five Makers of American Fiction" (review of
    Theodore Dreiser by F. O. Matthiessen). *Yale Review* 40 (June 1951):
    744–51.

Beard, Charles A. Introduction to the 1935 edition of *An Economic Inter-
    pretation of the Constitution of the United States* by Charles A. Beard,
    pp. v–xvii. New York: Macmillan, 1956.

Berryman, John. "Through Dreiser's Imagination the Tides of Real Life
    Billowed" (review of *Theodore Dreiser* by F. O. Matthiessen). *New York
    Times Book Review*, 4 March 1951, pp. 3, 29.

Bowron, Bernard. "The Making of an American Scholar." In *F. O.
    Matthiessen, 1902–1950: A Collective Portrait*, edited by Paul M. Sweezy
    and Leo Huberman, pp. 44–54. New York: Henry Schuman, 1950.

Bradley, A. C. *Oxford Lectures in Poetry*. Bloomington: Indiana University
    Press, 1909.

Camus, Albert. "The Myth of Sisyphus." In *The Myth of Sisyphus and
    Other Essays* by Albert Camus, pp. 88–91. New York: Alfred A.
    Knopf, Vintage Books, 1951.

Cary, Richard. *Sarah Orne Jewett*. New Haven, Conn.: Twayne Publishers,
    1962.

Caudwell, Christopher [Christopher St. John Sprigg]. *Illusion and Reality:
    A Study of the Sources of Poetry*. New York: Dodd, Mead and Co., 1947.

Crane, Ronald S. *The Languages of Criticism and the Structure of Poetry*.
    Toronto: University of Toronto Press, 1952.

Croce, Benedetto. *Aesthetic as Science of Expression and General Linguistic*.
Translated by Douglas Ainslie. New York: Noonday Press, 1958.

Croll, Morris W. "The Baroque Style in Prose." In *Studies in English
Philology: A Miscellany in Honor of Frederick Klaber*, edited by Kemp
Malone and M. B. Ruud, pp. 427–56. Minneapolis: University of
Minnesota Press, 1929.

"Current Books" (review of *Theodore Dreiser* by F. O. Matthiessen).
Nineteenth-Century Fiction 6 (September 1951): 147–52.

Curti, Merle. *The Growth of American Thought*. New York: Harper and
Brothers, 1943.

Demetz, Peter. *Marx, Engels, and the Poets: Origins of Marxist Literary
Criticism*. Translated by Jeffrey L. Sammons. Chicago: University of
Chicago Press, 1967.

Dewey, John. *Art as Experience*. New York: Capricorn Books, 1934.
_____. "Democracy." In *Readings in Philosophy*, edited by J. H. Randall,
J. Buchler, and E. V. Shirk, pp. 334–39. New York: Barnes and Noble,
1946.

Dorson, Richard M. *The Birth of American Studies: Inaugural Address
Delivered at the Opening of the American Studies Center, Warsaw Uni-
versity, Warsaw, Poland, October 5, 1976*. Bloomington: Indiana
University Press, 1976.

Eaton, Leonard K. Review of *Theodore Dreiser* by F. O. Matthiessen.
Western Humanities Review 5 (Summer 1951): 301.

Elias, Robert H. Review of *Theodore Dreiser* by F. O. Matthiessen.
American Literature 23 (January 1952): 505.

Eliot, T. S. *The Complete Poems and Plays of T. S. Eliot, 1900–1950*. New
York: Harcourt Brace Jovanovich, Inc., 1952.
_____. "The Function of Criticism." In *Selected Essays of T. S. Eliot*,
pp. 12–22. New ed. New York: Harcourt, Brace and Co., 1964.
_____. *Notes towards a Definition of Culture*. New York: Harcourt, Brace
and Co., 1949.

Fiedler, Leslie A. "American Literature." In *Contemporary Literary Scholarship*, edited by Lewis Leary, pp. 157–85. New York: Appleton-
Century-Crofts, 1958.

Finkelstein, Sidney. *Art and Society*. New York: International Publishers,
1947.

Frye, Northrop. *Anatomy of Criticism*. New York: Atheneum, 1966.

Geismar, Maxwell. "Social and Sexual Revolutionary" (review of *Theodore
Dreiser* by F. O. Matthiessen). *Saturday Review of Literature*, 17 March
1951, pp. 15–16.

Goldmann, Lucien. *The Hidden God*. Translated by Philip Thody. London:
Routledge, and Kegan Paul. New York: Humanities Press, 1964.
_____. "Structure: Human Reality and Methodological Concept." In
*The Structuralist Controversy: The Languages of Criticism and the Sciences
of Man*, edited by Richard Macksey and Eugenio Donato, pp. 98–110.

Baltimore: Johns Hopkins University Press, 1972.

Gramsci, Antonio. *The Modern Prince and Other Writings*. Translated by Louis Marks. New York: International Publishers, 1957.

Gunn, Giles B. "The American Scholar at Work: The Critical Achievement of F. O. Matthiessen." Ph.D. dissertation, University of Chicago, 1967.

_____. *F. O. Matthiessen: The Critical Achievement*. Seattle: University of Washington Press, 1975.

Hartman, Geoffrey. "Structuralism: The Anglo-American Adventure." In *Structuralism*, edited by Jacques Ehrman, pp. 147–58. Garden City, N.Y.: Doubleday & Co., Anchor Books, 1970.

Hawthorne, Nathaniel. *The Scarlet Letter*. Cambridge, Mass.: Riverside Press, 1960.

Heilbrun, Carolyn G. *Toward a Recognition of Androgyny*. New York: Alfred A. Knopf, 1973.

Hellman, George S. "They Are the Mountains in Our Range of Letters" (review of *American Renaissance* by F. O. Matthiessen). *New York Times Book Review*, 15 June 1941, p. 4.

Hicks, Granville. Review of *American Renaissance* by F. O. Matthiessen. *New England Quarterly* 14 (September 1941): 556–66.

Hofstadter, Richard. "Native Sons of Our Literature" (review of *Theodore Dreiser* by F. O. Matthiessen). *Nation*, 28 April 1951, p. 398.

Hyde, H. Montgomery. *Stalin: The History of a Dictator*. London: Rupert Hart-Davis, 1971.

Holman, C. Hugh. "The Defense of Art." In *The Development of American Literary Criticism*, edited by Floyd Stovall, pp. 199–245. Chapel Hill: University of North Carolina Press, 1955.

Hyde, Louis, ed. *Rat & the Devil: Journal Letters of F. O. Matthiessen and Russell Cheney*. Hamden, Conn.: Archon Books, 1978.

Jameson, Fredric. *Marxism and Form: Twentieth-Century Dialectical Theories of Literature*. Princeton, N.J.: Princeton University Press, 1971.

Jewett, Sarah Orne. *Verses by Sarah Orne Jewett*. Boston: Printed for her friends, D. B. Updike, The Merrymount Press, 1916.

Jones, Howard Mumford. *The Theory of American Literature*. 1948. Reprint. Ithaca, N.Y.: Cornell University Press, 1956.

Kaufmann, Walter. *Tragedy and Philosophy*. Garden City, N.Y.: Doubleday & Co., Anchor Books, 1969.

Kazin, Alfred. "Dreiser: The Esthetic of Realism." In *Contemporaries* by Alfred Kazin, pp. 87–99. Boston: Little, Brown and Co., 1962.

_____. *New York Jew*. New York: Alfred A. Knopf, 1978.

Levin, Harry. Introduction to *The Scarlet Letter* by Nathaniel Hawthorne, pp. vii–xxi. Cambridge, Mass.: Riverside Press, 1960.

Lewis, C. S. *The Allegory of Love: A Study of Medieval Tradition*. New York: Oxford University Press, 1958.

Lewis, R. W. B. "Contemporary American Literature." In *Contemporary*

Literary Scholarship, edited by Lewis Leary, pp. 201–18. New York: Appleton-Century-Crofts, 1958.

Lynn, Kenneth S. "Teaching: F. O. Matthiessen." *American Scholar* 46 (Winter 1976–77): 86–93.

Marx, Leo. "The Teacher." In *F. O. Matthiessen, 1902–1950: A Collective Portrait*, edited by Paul M. Sweezy and Leo Huberman, pp. 37–43. New York: Henry Schuman, 1950.

Matthiessen, F. O. *The Achievement of T. S. Eliot: An Essay on the Nature of Poetry*. 1935. 3d ed. New York: Oxford University Press, 1958.

———. *American Renaissance: Art and Expression in the Age of Emerson and Whitman*. New York: Oxford University Press, 1941.

———. "Axel's Castle." In *The Responsibilities of the Critic: Essays and Reviews by F. O. Matthiessen*, edited by John Rackliffe, pp. 159–61. New York: Oxford University Press, 1952. First published as "A Critic of Importance." *Yale Review* 20 (1931): 855–56.

———. "Credo, 1922." In *The Responsibilities of the Critic: Essays and Reviews by F. O. Matthiessen*, edited by John Rackliffe, pp. 251–54. New York: Oxford University Press, 1952. First published in *Yale Literary Magazine*, 1922.

———. "The Flowering of New England." In *The Responsibilities of the Critic: Essays and Reviews by F. O. Matthiessen*, edited by John Rackliffe, pp. 199–208. New York: Oxford University Press, 1952. First published in *New England Quarterly* 9 (1936): 701–9.

———. *From the Heart of Europe*. New York: Oxford University Press, 1948.

———. "God, Mammon and Mr. Dreiser" (review of Theodore Dreiser's *The Bulwark*). *New York Times Book Review*, 24 March 1946, pp. 1, 2, 44.

———. "The Great Tradition: A Counterstatement." In *The Responsibilities of the Critic: Essays and Reviews by F. O. Matthiessen*, edited by John Rackliffe, pp. 189–99. New York: Oxford University Press, 1952. First published in *New England Quarterly* 7 (1934): 223–34.

———. *Henry James: The Major Phase*. 1944. Reprint. New York and London: Oxford University Press, 1963.

———. "Henry James' Portrait of the Artist." In *Stories of Writers and Artists by Henry James*, edited by F. O. Matthiessen, pp. 1–17. New York: New Directions, 1944.

———. "Irving Babbitt." In *The Responsibilities of the Critic: Essays and Reviews by F. O. Matthiessen*, edited by John Rackliffe, pp. 161–65. New York: Oxford University Press, 1952. First published as reviews of *Irving Babbitt: Man and Teacher*, edited by F. Manchester and O. Shepard, and *Spanish Characters and Other Essays* by Irving Babbitt. *New England Quarterly* 15 (1942): 142–46.

———. "Nathaniel Hawthorne." In *The Responsibilities of the Critic: Essays and Reviews by F. O. Matthiessen*, edited by John Rackliffe, pp. 210–11. New York: Oxford University Press, 1952. First published as "The

Isolation of Hawthorne." *New Republic*, 29 January 1931, pp. 281–82.

———. "New Standards in American Criticism, 1929." In *The Responsibilities of the Critic: Essays and Reviews by F. O. Matthiessen*, edited by John Rackliffe, pp. 181–83. New York: Oxford University Press, 1952. First published in *Yale Review* 18 (1929): 603–4.

———. "Phelps Putnam, 1894–1948." In *The Responsibilities of the Critic: Essays and Reviews by F. O. Matthiessen*, edited by John Rackliffe, pp. 256–76. New York: Oxford University Press, 1952. First published in *Kenyon Review* 11 (1949): 61–82.

———. "Poetry." In *The Literary History of the United States*, edited by Robert E. Spiller, Willard Thorp, Thomas H. Johnson, Henry Seidel Canby, and Richard M. Ludwig, pp. 1335–57. 3 vols. New York: Macmillan Co., 1948.

———. "The Responsibilities of the Critic." In *The Responsibilities of the Critic: Essays and Reviews by F. O. Matthiessen*, edited by John Rackliffe, pp. 3–18. New York: Oxford University Press, 1952. First published in *Michigan Alumnus Quarterly* [The Hopwood Lecture, 1949] 55 (1949): 283–92.

———. *Russell Cheney, 1881–1945: A Record of His Work*. New York: Oxford University Press, 1947.

———. *Sarah Orne Jewett*. Cambridge, Mass.: Harvard University Press, 1929.

———. "Sarah Orne Jewett." In *Dictionary of American Biography*, pp. 70–72. New York: Charles Scribner's Sons, 1935.

———. "Sarah Orne Jewett." In *Responsibilities of the Critic: Essays and Reviews by F. O. Matthiessen*, edited by John Rackliffe, pp. 64–66. New York: Oxford University Press, 1952. First published as "New England Stories" in *American Writers on American Literature*, edited by John Macy, pp. 99–113. New York: Liveright, 1931.

———. "Sherman and Huneker." In *The Responsibilities of the Critic: Essays and Reviews by F. O. Matthiessen*, edited by John Rackliffe, pp. 154–59. New York: Oxford University Press, 1952. First published in *New Republic*, 18 December 1929, pp. 113–15.

———. *Theodore Dreiser*. American Men of Letters Series. New York: Delta Books, 1951.

———. "Theodore Spencer, 1902–1949." In *The Responsibilities of the Critic: Essays and Reviews by F. O. Matthiessen*, edited by John Rackliffe, pp. 277–82. New York: Oxford University Press, 1952. First published with I. A. Richards, Kenneth B. Murdock, J. H. Finley, Jr., Harry Levin, and Walter Jackson Bate, *Harvard University Gazette*, 44 (1949): 141–42.

———. *Translation: An Elizabethan Art*. 1931. Reprint. New York: Octagon Press, 1965.

———. "Van Wyck Brooks." In *The Responsibilities of the Critic: Essays and Reviews by F. O. Matthiessen*, edited by John Rackliffe, pp. 233–38.

New York: Oxford University Press, 1952. First published as "Pilgrimage to the Distant Past," *New York Times Book Review*, 1 October 1944, pp. 1, 20.

————, ed. Introduction to *The Oxford Book of American Verse*, pp. ix–xxxiii. New York: Oxford University Press, 1950.

Melville, Herman. *Moby-Dick*. New York: Rinehart and Winston, 1964.

Miller, Arthur. "Tragedy and the Common Man." In *Death of a Salesman: Text and Criticism* by Arthur Miller, edited by Gerald Weales, pp. 143–47. New York: Viking Press, 1967. First published in *New York Times*, 27 February 1949, sec. 2, pp. 1, 3.

Miller, James E., Jr. *A Reader's Guide to Herman Melville*. New York: Farrar, Straus and Cudahy, Noonday Press, 1962.

Mizener, Arthur. "Dreiser and Anderson" (review of *Theodore Dreiser* by F. O. Matthiessen). *Partisan Review* 18 (November–December 1951): 718–21.

Muller, Herbert J. "Anderson and Dreiser" (review of *Theodore Dreiser* by F. O. Matthiessen). *Virginia Quarterly Review* 17 (Summer 1951): 460–64.

Mumford, Lewis. *The Golden Day*. 1926. Reprint. Boston: Beacon Press, 1957.

————. *Herman Melville*. New York: Harcourt, Brace and Co., 1929.

Niebuhr, Reinhold. *Beyond Tragedy: Essays on the Christian Interpretation of History*. New York: Charles Scribner's Sons, 1937.

O'Connor, William Van. *An Age of Criticism, 1900–1950*. Chicago: Henry Regnery, 1952.

————. "Modern Literary Criticism." In *Contemporary Literary Scholarship*, edited by Lewis Leary, pp. 221–57. New York: Appleton-Century-Crofts, 1958.

Olson, Charles. *Call Me Ishmael: A Study of Melville*. New York: Reynal and Hitchcock, 1947.

————. "Lear and Moby-Dick." *Twice a Year* 1 (1938): 165–89.

Parrington, Vernon L. *Main Currents in American Thought*. 3 vols. New York: Harcourt, Brace and Co., 1927.

Rackliffe, John. "Notes for a Character Study." In *F. O. Matthiessen, 1902–1950: A Collective Portrait*, edited by Paul M. Sweezy and Leo Huberman, pp. 76–92. New York: Henry Schuman, 1950.

————, ed. *The Responsibilities of the Critic: Essays and Reviews by F. O. Matthiessen*. New York: Oxford University Press, 1952.

Raleigh, John H. "Revolt and Revaluation in Criticism, 1900–1930." In *The Development of American Literary Criticism*, edited by Floyd Stovall, pp. 159–98. Chapel Hill: University of North Carolina Press, 1955.

Ransom, John Crowe. "Criticism as Pure Speculation." In *The Intent of the Critic*, edited by Donald A. Stauffer, pp. 73–103. 1941. Reprint. New York: Bantam, 1966.

Rugoff, Milton. "A Novelist's Pilgrimage" (review of *Theodore Dreiser* by F. O. Matthiessen). *New York Herald Tribune Book Review*, 4 March 1951, p. 2.

Ruland, Richard. *The Rediscovery of American Literature: Premises of Critical Taste, 1900–1940*. Cambridge, Mass.: Harvard University Press, 1967.

Sarton, May. *Faithful Are the Wounds*. New York: Rinehart, 1955.

Schwarz-Bart, André. *The Last of the Just*. Translated by S. Becker. New York: Atheneum, 1960.

Scott, Nathan A., Jr. "The Modern Experiment in Criticism: A Theological Appraisal." In *The New Orpheus: Essays toward a Christian Poetic*, edited by Nathan A. Scott, Jr., pp. 141–71. New York: Sheed and Ward, 1964.

Simmons, Ernest J. "Statements by Friends and Associates." In *F. O. Matthiessen, 1902–1950: A Collective Portrait*, edited by Paul M. Sweezy and Leo Huberman, pp. 135–37. New York: Henry Schuman, 1950.

Smith, Bernard. "An American Renaissance" (review of *American Renaissance* by F. O. Matthiessen). *Virginia Quarterly Review* 17 (Autumn 1941): 625–28.

Smith, Henry Nash. "American Renaissance." In *F. O. Matthiessen, 1902–1950: A Collective Portrait*, edited by Paul M. Sweezy and Leo Huberman, pp. 55–60. New York: Henry Schuman, 1950.

Smith, Howard K. *The State of Europe*. New York: Alfred A. Knopf, 1949.

Smith-Rosenberg, Carroll. "The Female World of Love and Ritual: Relations between Women in Nineteenth-Century America." *Signs: Journal of Women in Culture and Society* 1 (Autumn 1975): 1–29.

Solomon, Maynard. *Marxism and Art: Essays Classical and Contemporary*. New York: Alfred A. Knopf, 1973.

Sontag, Susan. "The Death of Tragedy." In *Against Interpretation* by Susan Sontag, pp. 132–39. New York: Delta, 1968.

Spencer, Theodore. *Shakespeare and the Nature of Man*. 1942. Reprint. New York: Macmillan, 1961.

Spender, Stephen. *T. S. Eliot*. Hammondsworth and Middlesex and New York: Penguin, 1975.

Spiller, Robert E. *The Cycle of American Literature*. New York: Mentor, 1961.
_____. "Emerson and Co." (review of *American Renaissance* by F. O. Matthiessen). *Saturday Review of Literature*, 4 June 1941, p. 6.

Steiner, George. "An Aesthetic Manifesto." In *Language and Silence: Essays on Language, Literature, and the Inhuman* by George Steiner, pp. 340–47. New York: Atheneum, 1972.
_____. "Marxism and the Literary Critic." In *Language and Silence: Essays on Language, Literature, and the Inhuman* by George Steiner, pp. 305–25. New York: Atheneum, 1972.

Summers, J. H. "Statements by Friends and Associates." In *F. O. Matthiessen, 1902–1950: A Collective Portrait*, edited by Paul M. Sweezy and Leo Huberman, pp. 135–37. New York: Henry Schuman, 1950.

Sweezy, Paul M. "A Biographical Sketch." In *F. O. Matthiessen, 1902–1950: A Collective Portrait*, edited by Paul M. Sweezy and Leo Huberman, pp. ix–xii. New York: Henry Schuman, 1950.

————. "Labor and Political Activities." In *F. O. Matthiessen, 1902–1950: A Collective Portrait*, edited by Paul M. Sweezy and Leo Huberman, pp. 61–75. New York: Henry Schuman, 1950.

Sweezy, Paul M., and Huberman, Leo, eds. *F. O. Matthiessen, 1902–1950: A Collective Portrait*. New York: Henry Schuman, 1950. The contents of this volume, except the biographical sketch, first appeared as the October 1950 issue of *Monthly Review*.

Thorp, Margaret Farrand. *Sarah Orne Jewett*. Pamphlets on American Writers, no. 61. Minneapolis: University of Minnesota Press, 1966.

Trilling, Lionel. *The Liberal Imagination: Essays on Literature and Society*. New York: Viking Press, 1950.

Vivas, Eliseo. "Dreiser, an Inconsistent Mechanist." In *Creation and Discovery: Essays in Criticism and Aesthetics* by Eliseo Vivas, pp. 3–19. Chicago: Henry Regnery, 1955.

————. "What Is a Poem?" In *Creation and Discovery: Essays in Criticism and Aesthetics* by Eliseo Vivas, pp. 111–41. Chicago: Henry Regnery, 1955.

Weber, Brom. "Two American Men of Letters" (review of *Theodore Dreiser* by F. O. Matthiessen). *Western Review* 16 (Summer 1952): 329–34.

White, George Abbott. " 'Have I Any Right in a Community That Would So Utterly Disapprove of Me If It Knew the Facts?' " (review of *Rat & the Devil: Journal Letters of F. O. Matthiessen and Russell Cheney*, edited by Louis Hyde). *Harvard Magazine* 81 (September–October 1978): 58–62.

————. "Ideology and Literature: *American Renaissance* and F. O. Matthiessen." *Triquarterly* 23/24 (Winter 1972): 430–500.

Williams, Stanley T. "In the Age of Emerson and Whitman" (review of *American Renaissance* by F. O. Matthiessen). *Yale Review* 31 (September 1941): 200–202.

Woodward, C. Vann. "Not So Freed Men" (review of *Been in the Storm So Long: The Aftermath of Slavery* by L. F. Litwak). *New York Review of Books*, 16 August 1979, pp. 8–9.

Index